Reading

The field of reading is a compelling one, characterised by many debates and discussions. It is also amenable to investigations through a range of theories and research studies. In this book, eight leading authorities provide a 'state-of-the-art' overview of reading, using perspectives that have informed their work. There are overviews from linguistic, psychological, sociological and literary viewpoints, as well as more hybrid ones from investigations of digital literacy and multi-modality. This book celebrates what has already been achieved by bridging research, scholarship and practice; it also suggests what still needs to be done to bring the positive rewards from reading to greater numbers of young people. It also recognises that the benefits of reading extend beyond the personal. Accomplished reading skills empower people to meet the challenges of everyday life: making decisions, solving problems and dealing with unexpected events.

The need to refresh and renew our knowledge of reading has gained further impetus in the 'information age'. New technologies for information and communication continually appear: manifestations of 'fake news', disinformation and conspiracy theories spread rapidly across the globe. This book underlines the importance of not only reading but also the fact that reading between and beyond the lines is more important than ever, in print and across multiple media platforms.

The chapters in this book were originally published as a special issue of *Education 3–13: International Journal of Primary, Elementary and Early Years Education*.

Roger Beard is Emeritus Professor of Primary Education at the UCL Institute of Education. He has published over a hundred articles and books and undertaken research reviews for the UK, Brazilian and European parliaments. In 2019, Roger was elected to the Literacy Research Association's Hall of Fame in the United States.

Reading

Multiple Perspectives

Edited by
Roger Beard

Routledge
Taylor & Francis Group
LONDON AND NEW YORK

First published 2023
by Routledge
4 Park Square, Milton Park, Abingdon, Oxon, OX14 4RN

and by Routledge
605 Third Avenue, New York, NY 10158

Routledge is an imprint of the Taylor & Francis Group, an informa business

British Library Cataloguing-in-Publication Data
A catalogue record for this book is available from the British Library

ISBN13: 978-1-032-07754-3 (hbk)
ISBN13: 978-1-032-07755-0 (pbk)
ISBN13: 978-1-003-20864-8 (ebk)

DOI: 10.4324/9781003208648

Typeset in Myriad Pro
by codeMantra

Publisher's Note
The publisher accepts responsibility for any inconsistencies that may have arisen during the conversion of this book from journal articles to book chapters, namely the inclusion of journal terminology.

Contents

Citation Information

The chapters in this book were originally published in *Education 3–13: International Journal of Primary, Elementary and Early Years Education*, volume 49, issue 1 (2021). When citing this material, please use the original page numbering for each article, as follows:

Introduction
Reading – a personal and professional view
Roger Beard
Education 3-13, volume 49, issue 1 (2021) pp. 1–9

Chapter 1
The linguistic base of initial reading and spelling in English: a tutorial review
Greg Brooks
Education 3-13, volume 49, issue 1 (2021) pp. 10–28

Chapter 2
How psychology helps us to understand word reading
Rhona Stainthorp
Education 3-13, volume 49, issue 1 (2021) pp. 29–40

Chapter 3
Literacies and social practice: sociological perspectives on reading research
Gemma Moss
Education 3-13, volume 49, issue 1 (2021) pp. 41–51

Chapter 4
Perspectives on dealing with reading difficulties
Sinéad Harmey
Education 3-13, volume 49, issue 1 (2021) pp. 52–62

Chapter 5
Reading children's literature
Victoria de Rijke
Education 3-13, volume 49, issue 1 (2021) pp. 63–78

Chapter 6
The reader, the text, the poem: the influence and challenge of Louise Rosenblatt
Anthony Wilson
Education 3-13, volume 49, issue 1 (2021) pp. 79–95

Chapter 7
Reading with technology: the new normal
Guy Merchant
Education 3-13, volume 49, issue 1 (2021) pp. 96–106

Chapter 8
Exploring reading in social semiotics: theory and methods
Jeff Bezemer and Kate Cowan
Education 3-13, volume 49, issue 1 (2021) pp. 107–118

Notes on Contributors

Roger Beard, UCL Institute of Education, London, UK.

Jeff Bezemer, UCL Institute of Education, London, UK.

Greg Brooks, School of Education, University of Sheffield, UK.

Kate Cowan, UCL Institute of Education, London, UK.

Sinéad Harmey, UCL Institute of Education, London, UK.

Guy Merchant, Sheffield Institute of Education, Sheffield Hallam University, UK.

Gemma Moss, Department of Learning and Leadership, UCL Institute of Education, London, UK.

Victoria de Rijke, Middlesex University, London, UK.

Rhona Stainthorp, Institute of Education, University of Reading, UK.

Anthony Wilson, Graduate School of Education, University of Exeter, UK.

INTRODUCTION

Reading – a personal and professional view

Introduction

Education 3-13 is an international journal of primary, elementary and early years education that has developed enormously over recent years. It is considered by its publishers to be one of their most successful journals, with 200,000 full text downloads a year. It recently gained ISI status as an 'emerging source'.

Since it was founded in 1973, the focus of the journal has been on generic issues in early years, primary and elementary education. I became an early subscriber because the journal struck an impressive balance between theory, research and practice. I was teaching in a primary school at that time and I recall several articles that made a big impact on my professional thinking.

One issue in 1975 had a particular impact: it included an insightful and prophetic editorial by Colin Richards, a topical article by Joan Tough on oracy and leading-edge articles on teaching spelling by Margaret Peters and on reading development by John Merritt. This language and literacy content may have reflected the interest created by the work of a Committee of Inquiry whose report was published in the same year (DES 1975). In the subsequent years, *Education 3-13* has covered a plethora of topics, although there has been relatively little coverage of reading, which has been tackled by other, more topic-specific journals.

A special issue on reading, a very special skill

The invitation to be guest editor of a Special Issue on Reading prompted me to reflect on the role and significance of reading and to revisit some landmark publications that have influenced my own thinking. A brief discussion of these publications may be of interest to readers of the journal who are relatively new to the field of reading. The discussion may also help provide some helpful background for the articles in this Special Issue.

Other, more profound, background has been provided by researchers who celebrate the deeper significance of literacy for humankind. Stephen Pinker (1994, 15) reminds us that, in the apparently straightforward act of reading, we are engaging in one of the wonders of the natural world. For we all belong to a species with a remarkable ability to shape events in each other's brains, with exquisite precision … Just by making … marks on a page or screen, we can reliably cause precise new combinations of ideas to arise in each other's minds.

Reading may also promote cognitive growth in particular ways. David Olson (2016) has recently gone as far as to suggest that serious human thought, including thinking about thinking, depends primarily not on spoken language but almost entirely on the existence of written language and engagement with it.

These celebratory words sparked further thoughts on the rewards that reading can bring. As an only child who grew up in a remote location in rural Cornwall, and who read avidly from an early age, I am struck by the poignancy of the following words of the children's novelist Naomi Lewis (1967). She is recalling a childhood memory of taking books, as well as food, on a picnic:

> I have read many books since that day … but I have never stopped marvelling at the magical power they can hold … Every book holds an invitation, making its reader a welcomed and honoured guest, free from all harm in the wildest and strangest places in the world: in bygone or future time …

The benefits of reading

Of course, the benefits of reading extend way beyond the personal. There are profound economic and social implications, as the Secretary-General of the Organization for Economic Co-operation and Development (OECD) has observed:

> Skills empower people to meet the challenges of everyday life, related to making decisions; solving problems; dealing with unexpected events ...
>
> Beyond better outcomes for the individual, skills also provide the vital glue for resilient communities and well-functioning societies, by strengthening inclusiveness, tolerance, trust, ethics, responsibility, environmental awareness, collaboration and effective democratic processes. (Gurría 2014)

Recognising the significance and power of reading has several implications for educational provision and practice: for maintaining a clear picture of what, and how much, children read; for ensuring that children have a sound grasp of key reading skills; for taking stock of new forms of literacy, including digital and multi-modal ones.

How much do children read?

The late twentieth and early twenty-first century saw a burgeoning of interest in children's literature, underpinned by scholarly publications, academic appointments and specialised courses. There have been several books on children's literature that have broken new ground in their coverage of leading-edge topics (e.g. Rudd 2010) and on children's poetry (e.g. Styles 1998).

However, survey research has indicated that this interest has not always been accompanied by positive findings on children's leisure reading. In the latest of a series of surveys undertaken by the *National Literacy Trust* (Clark and Teravainen-Goff 2020), 56,906 children and young people were asked a number of questions about reading, including their enjoyment of it, how often they read in their free time, the type of formats they read and what they thought about reading. The findings were somewhat concerning for teachers and parents, in that levels of reading enjoyment and participation have continued to decline; daily reading levels were the lowest recorded in the surveys, with just under 26% of children saying they read daily in their free time in 2019.

Unfortunately, there have not been similar surveys of children's poetry reading. The nearest to a national survey was a school inspections report over ten years ago that commented on the limitations of teachers' subject knowledge and their lack of confidence in poetry teaching (Ofsted 2007). In the light of the limited knowledge of current practices in poetry teaching, it is important to note that a recent publication from the Centre for Literacy in Primary Education (CLPE) could offer the means of a much-needed boost to effective practices. In 2017, the CLPE was funded by the Arts Council for a project on the 'The Power of Poetry', in which five poets worked alongside twenty teachers to investigate how to make the most of poetry teaching in primary schools. The resulting recommendations are now available online (CLPE, 2018). These include providing poetry friendly classrooms, enthusing children and celebrating the value of poetry; bringing poems to life by reading poetry aloud and dramatising it; encouraging connections to children's personal experience; and exploring many forms of poetry and using it across the curriculum.

The key skills of reading

Anyone new to the field of reading might also reasonably expect that decades of research and scholarly publications would have resulted in a consensual picture of reading skills, that could comfortably inform provision and practice. However, literacy education has been characterised by (some would say beset by) continuing debates about the nature of the reading process and the most effective ways of promoting the reading of children and young people. In the USA, the debates have been characterised as the 'reading wars'; these have continued even after a scientific review of the evidence by a National Reading Panel (NICHHD 2000) in the USA that might have been expected to resolve some contentious issues (Kim 2008). The debates have ranged across the English-speaking world and infiltrated polices and practices in other countries with alphabetic writing systems, such as Brazil (Oliveira 2015).

Some years ago, I was invited to write a chapter in an international handbook on the key skills of reading and found myself confronting these debates (Beard 2003). I attempted to provide an overview of research that has been undertaken to uncover the key skills of reading and the theoretical stances that have tried to reconcile the earlier debates. I also cautioned that, although my chapter focused on certain technical skills of literacy, these skills are developed within social processes in homes, classrooms and the wider world. My conclusion noted that becoming a successful reader involves both key skills and meaningful social practices.

The language base of literacy

It is widely agreed that understanding reading will benefit from a consideration of the structure of language, on which literacy is in some ways 'parasitic'. In attempting to uncover the key skills of reading, the structure of language is a useful starting point. Crystal (1976) has shown how this structure comprises three strands: pronunciation (sounds and spellings), grammar (syntax and morphology) and meaning (words and discourse). Taking the three strands in turn, the letter-sound relationships of unfamiliar words have to be decoded, grammatical sequences have to be followed; words have to be recognised and the meaning attributed to them has to be understood.

The basis for the reading debates have often fallen into one of two groups, often described as 'bottom-up' or 'top-down'. The two groups approach the language base of literacy from different directions. The former gives emphasis to the code that is used in written language (in English, an alphabetic code); the latter emphasises the meaning that is conveyed by the written language. The distinction is clearly made by Jeanne Chall (1983, 28–9). She explains that 'bottom-up' approaches are those that view the reading process as developing from perception of letters, spelling patterns, and words, to sentence and paragraph meaning (e.g. Gough 1972; Laberge and Samuels 1974).

Criticisms of this approach focus on the fact that the perceptions of letters often depend on the surrounding letters and perceptions of words depends on the syntactic and semantic environment in which we encounter them (e.g. Rumelhart 1985). This environment can be seen at work in our perception of homonyms ('*wind* up the clock' c.f. 'the *wind* was blowing') and in resolving ambiguities ('They are eating apples': this could mean either 'The children are eating apples' or 'The apples may be eaten').

'Top down' approaches stress the importance of language and meaning for reading comprehension and also for word recognition. The reader theoretically samples the text to confirm and modify initial hypotheses. The best-known of these approaches is the 'psycholingustic guessing game' model of Kenneth Goodman (1967, 1985) in which he argued that the basis of fluent reading is not word recognition but hypothesis-forming about 'the meanings that lie ahead'. He suggested that reading involves the selection of maximally productive cues to confirm or deny these meanings. Reading was seen as meaning-seeking, selective and constructive. Readers use the least amount of available text information necessary to get meaning.

As with the bottom-up theories, there have been recurrent criticisms of the top-down ones. Gibson and Levin (1975) point out that Goodman's model of reading does not explain how the reader knows when to confirm guesses and where to look to do so. Similarly, Jessie Reid (1993) asks a number of searching questions: how does the reader know which cues will be most productive? Are the criteria fixed for any given word? If the predicted word is not on the page, what then? Can readers sample for the most productive cues in the word they did not expect? Most fundamentally, is the guessing game model optimally efficient?

In confronting what appeared to be an over-polarised debate, Keith Stanovich (1980, 2000) has put forward an 'interactive-compensatory' model of reading. Drawing on over 180 sources, Stanovich argues that fluent reading is an interactive process in which information is used from several knowledge sources simultaneously (letter recognition, letter-sound relationships, vocabulary, knowledge of syntax and meaning). Various component sub-skills of reading can co-operate in a compensatory manner. For example, higher level processes can compensate for deficiencies in lower level processes: the reader with poor word recognition skills may actually be prone to a greater reliance on contextual factors because these provide additional sources of information.

Summarising the reading process

There have been numerous attempts to summarise the reading process in various diagrammatic forms, especially to inform practitioners. In the USA, an overlapping circles diagram has been used (e.g. in the work of Regie Routman 1988), the circles being used to represent semantic, syntactic and grapho-phonic cues. Marilyn Jager Adams (1998) describes the way in which this diagram has been adopted in teacher education and is concerned that it may sometimes be used to under play the role of phonics, as 'grapho-phonic cues' are tucked away at the bottom of the model. She is concerned that such cues may be seen as a last resort in reading. Instead, in her own publications, Adams prefers a triangular model, based on the work of McClelland and Rumelhart (1986), in which the role of the 'phonological processor' in the decoding of unfamiliar words is show by a phonological loop.

In England, another diagrammatic summary became similarly influential, the so-called 'searchlights' model that was used in the non-statutory *Framework for Teaching* in the National Literacy Strategy (Stannard and Huxford 2007). The four sources of 'knowledge' from the national curriculum (phonic, grammatical, context and graphic, including word recognition), were displayed at the four points of the compass around a circle that represents the text. Again, there were concerns that the diagram might not sufficiently illustrate where the intensity of the searchlights should fall at different stages of learning to read.

Following an *Independent review of the teaching of early reading* (Rose 2006) central government policy adopted instead the 'simple view of reading', based on the work of Gough and Tunmer (1986). The simple view suggests that reading is the product of 'decoding' and 'language comprehension'. By 'decoding', the authors mean the ability to recognise words presented singly out of context, with the ability to apply phonic rules being a crucial contributory factor to context-free word recognition ability. By 'linguistic comprehension', they mean the process by which, given word information, sentences and discourse are interpreted. Gough and Tunmer make it clear that word recognition and linguistic comprehension are both necessary but not sufficient for reading. At its most simplistic, the simple view may be summarised by a formula: Decoding (D) x (Oral) Language Comprehension (LC) = Reading Comprehension (RC). There has also been extensive discussion of the simple view.

Catherine Snow (2018), while accepting that the simple view is empirically robust, questions its adequacy for older readers or for 21st century literacy tasks, which require analysis, synthesis and critique. In England, there may also have been some unintended consequences of the adoption of the simple view of reading. The attention given to other related policy elements, such as the issues raised by the implementation of synthetic phonics (e.g. Beard, Brooks, and Ampaw-Farr 2019) and national testing of Year 1 children through a Phonics Screening Check, may have distracted attention from making greater use of reading comprehension research in both curriculum programmes and in teaching approaches. Reading comprehension is a more complex and nuanced phenomenon than is sometimes realised and it warrants a central role in reading studies.

The centrality of reading comprehension

To anyone new to reading studies, reconstructing the author's intended meaning may be assumed to be an integral part of reading. However, the reality is more complex in several ways. The complexities have important implications for teacher education and the components of curriculum provision and assessment.

One complexity is that, even though we can decode the words that we see on the page or screen, we cannot always be sure that, even as 'fluent' readers, we are effectively comprehending the text. This anomaly was recognised many years ago by Frank Smith (1978, 10). We may be able to follow a passage of written text, in which the words and sentence structures are familiar and yet, after several pages, we have to stop and say to ourselves 'What is this all about?' Smith calls this (with due respect to Leo Tolstoy and others), the 'Russian Novel Phenomenon'.

Another complexity is that what we bring to a text affects what we take from it. It is easy to assume (mistakenly) that understanding involves merely the passive extraction of meaning from print. So powerful is the influence of prior knowledge of a topic on reading comprehension that, according to the seminal work of Johnston and Pearson (1982), this knowledge can sometimes be a better predictor of comprehension performance than either an intelligence test score or a reading achievement test score.

A third complexity in reading comprehension is that understanding texts is an interactive process, being in part dependent on the reader making 'an effort after meaning', with prior knowledge being used to interpret what is read in terms of the reader's pre-existing world views, effectively building a mental model of the text.

The idea of a mental model is a key element in investigations of specific difficulties in reading comprehension. In a succession of research council-funded investigations in England, Jane Oakhill and her colleagues have reported that a significant proportion of children (perhaps 10-15%) have specific comprehension difficulties compared with their decoding abilities. Such children tend not to derive the gist as a whole or go beyond the literal meaning of a text. Oakhill's research suggests that inadequate knowledge is unlikely to be the main source of the difficulties.

The role of inferential skills is particularly important to note; authors necessarily leave some links implicit to avoid excessive length and resulting tedium. Effective comprehension depends on an understanding of the main point and sensitivity to the relative importance of other information in the text and also self-monitoring so that any points of difficulty can be remedied (Oakhill, Cain, and Elbro 2014).

Such findings underline the importance of the *Reading for Understanding Initiative* in the USA (Pearson et al. 2020). The report synthesises work both within and across six research teams in reviewing over 200 scholarly articles. The report stresses the importance of emphasising comprehension in pursuit of knowledge and insight, and encouraging collaboration, 'deep' comprehension and critique. The project includes a review of technology-related reading comprehension research, as well as research related to multimodal meaning-making (both digital and nondigital) and reading comprehension in the out-of-school contexts of the 'information age'.

The information age and its manifestations

Leu et al. (2011) have written extensively on the demands of a wide variety of information and communication technologies: Web logs (blogs), word processors, video editors, World Wide Web browsers, Web editors, e-mail, spreadsheets, presentation software, instant messaging, plug-ins for Web resources, bulletin boards, virtual worlds, and other currently 'unenvisioned' new literacies. Leu suggests that, with the Internet in particular, literacy has become 'deictic': its meaning rapidly and continuously changes as new technologies for information and communication continuously appear. Taking up Catherine Snow's views, outlined above, it could be argued that previously unenvisioned aspects of literacy include various manifestations of 'fake news', disinformation and conspiracy theories that social media now spread rapidly across multiple media platforms.

The special features of electronic texts

Among the myriad of features that characterise electronic texts, hypertext has been seen as a quintessential example of how printed and electronic texts differ (Reinking 1998, xxiv). The former is generally linear and hierarchical; the latter is fluid: a set of different potential texts awaiting realisation.

Hypertext's elements are verbal or graphic units and the links that join them. Hypertexts are multi-linear, constructed so that the textual elements can be read in any order. Such distinctions suggest that the key skills in reading hypertext will need to be underpinned by an understanding of the availability of different 'navigational' routes through the material, including points of departure and possible destinations. As with much electronic text, another key requirement is the ability to evaluate and make effective complementary use of visual images. This multi-modality has necessitated reading studies being extended through different theoretical perspectives.

Reading and multimodality

One of the most notable changes in reading studies in recent years is its re-framing within broader theories of communication to include other complementary media, including still and moving images. The work of Gunther Kress (e.g. 2003) has led the way in the use of semiotics, essentially the theory of signs and symbols, in order to address these changes. Kress reminds us how multimodal texts are articulated through the concept of 'arrangement', how the text is framed through its 'affordances' (its action possibilities), its relations and its connections. Arrangements achieve coherence and effect communication, including culturally-based interpretations of colour and gesture.

In this way, multimodality is part of a cultural shift: from an isolated text being used as a primary source of communication, to images being increasingly used to replace writing in many domains of public communication. However, Kress adds the caveat that has enduring significance for educational provision and social mobility: 'writing will remain the preferred mode of the political and cultural elites' (Kress 2003, 1).

This special issue

I realised that the Special Issue would be an opportunity to bring together a collection of articles that build upon recent work in the field and that illustrate the different theoretical approaches that have been drawn upon, including linguistic, psychological, sociological and literary perspectives, as well as some other new or hybrid ones that are found in digital and multi-modal research.

I invited authoritative authors to review the contribution that their discipline/perspective can make to the study of reading, perhaps showcasing some of their own work as appropriate, and spelling out the implications for practice. I am extremely grateful to all the contributors for responding so readily to the remit and for engaging in paired internal reviewing, which helped my task enormously.

The articles

The first article by Greg Brooks summarises the ***linguistic*** base of initial reading (and spelling) in English for the benefit of teachers and others engaged in education. He suggests that an explicit understanding of aspects of the linguistic base is needed in order to teach initial literacy accurately. He discusses the aspects that he deems most relevant to children entering formal schooling. These include spoken language as the foundation of literacy; phonetics and phonology; phoneme-grapheme and grapheme-phoneme correspondences; sequencing in phonics teaching; vocabulary, morphology and syntax; and the linguistic effects of reading to children. Several of these aspects are discussed from two angles, first describing the full system, then summarising where 5-year-olds have reached in their development towards it.

Rhona Stainthorp's article presents an overview of evidence from ***psychological*** research. Her article concentrates on the processes involved in word reading, how children develop word reading skills and the basis for teaching children how to read words successfully. She makes it clear that her focus is on alphabetic writing systems like English, compared with 'whole word' (logographic), syllabic and other writing systems. The article outlines how researchers have proposed two routes to word reading: an indirect route, requiring mapping of letters and sounds using phonological processes, and a direct route, identifying words and mapping them onto meaning using visual processes and memory. The article then discusses how a dual route model fosters an understanding of what children need to achieve to be able to read words. The article concludes by outlining how evidence about how people read words successfully has contributed to effective teaching programmes and to tests for use when the development of word reading is delayed.

Gemma Moss considers the distinctive contribution that ***sociological*** perspectives have made to understanding reading. These perspectives see reading as a profoundly social and cultural activity. Researchers who adopt this perspective have also often incorporated a radical element in their work, seeking to explore, explain and redress inequalities in access to and uses of literacy in its different forms. The article explores how this radical element may create tensions with more skills-based approaches in early reading programmes. The article concludes by exploring how these tensions, which may be intensified in test-based accountability systems, can be navigated in this light.

Sinead Harmey focuses on ***delays and difficulties in learning to read***. She reminds us how, in the twenty-first century, learning to read is an expectation rather than an exception. However, despite years of intensive research and innumerable policy initiatives, some children continue to experience reading difficulties. The article reviews recent and seminal research on reading difficulties through the lenses of three perspectives: (i) cognitive; (ii) social; (iii) cultural-interactive. The article discusses the contribution that these perspectives make to our understandings of how to support children with reading difficulties and the implications for teaching. The article focuses particularly on the contemporary debate about the choice of texts to support reading development. The conclusion argues for a more holistic approach to reading difficulties, with reference to two contemporary assessment tools.

Victoria de Rijke explores the contribution that ***children's literature*** has made to reading, its study, its material world, and the implications for teaching and learning. The article explores particularly the role of picture books in learning to read responsively and imaginatively. The article first explores the category of children's literature as a possible 'lie', in the sense that it assumes possibly misleading boundaries, but also its special contributions to reading studies. These include the animal story or fable as a 'creativity and criticality genre' *par excellence*. The article explores how children's literature has attracted artists and writers of extraordinary talent, frequently breaking boundaries and sometimes taking partisan positions on matters of identity formation and socio-political justice. Distinctive experiments in cross-writing and originality are discussed, and the material poetics, or 'thingness' of books, from the constructivist tradition onwards, as one of children's literature's leading innovations.

The article then engages with the role that children's literature has played in the 'reading wars', including teaching strategies and governmental policies for learning to read; the controversies and competitive tensions inherent in the metrics and mechanisms of reading 'for the test' or for pleasure. The article concludes with a discussion of how, after decades of reader-response theory emphasising the active roles of the reader and the text, reading may now need to be reconceptualised to accommodate new, screen-based, visual literacies that offer linear, radial, and spatial forms of reading and a new identity of the reader-as-player.

Anthony Wilson's article discusses ***poetry for children***. The article is structured around re-examination of Louise Rosenblatt's seminal work of reader-response theory, 'The reader, the text, the poem'. The article argues that poems are essentially social in nature and that they open up a space in which conversation and interpretation can take place. The article takes a similar line to that of Rosenblatt's: that until a reader engages with a poem, bringing to it a combination of the reader's interest and experience, the text will lie dormant.

The article is similar to Victoria de Rijke's in arguing that adopting Rosenblatt's approach implies a model of pedagogy and discourse about poetry that is inimical to the high stakes testing that is currently being used in England and the Anglophone world.

Anthony analyses the cultural and critical frameworks that influenced Rosenblatt's innovations including the tradition of the New Criticism, with its emphasis on empiricism and an assumed reader. He ends the article by offering examples of practice which exemplify the role of talk in aiding a reader's interpretations of poems.

Guy Merchant's article focuses on ***digital literacy*** and the widespread changes in communication associated with new technologies. Although the concept of digital literacy suffers from a lack of agreed definition, the article suggests that reading and writing with technology remains a key point of concern. The written word is now used in new ways and often in combination with other media as new devices and practices are harnessed in meaning making. Different ways of thinking about these new communicative practices have led to the development of a diverse body of research which the article outlines. Various strands of research are used to identify how literacy has both expanded and diversified. Because it is now a significant aspect of full participation in social and cultural life, reading with technology raises important questions for education. The article suggests that current educational policy in England is inadequately articulated; there is a pressing need for more focused classroom research to develop classroom practices that support digital literacy.

Jeff Bezemer and Kate Cowan's article critically reviews how ***social semiotics*** has contributed to the study of reading and outlines an agenda for further research. The article first considers the theoretical and methodological resources that social semiotics has developed to account for contemporary multimodal texts. It goes on to explore how these resources may be used to teach critical reading skills to young people and to support their participation in different social domains.

The discussion reflects on the possibilities and limitations of different analytical frameworks, highlighting barriers and possibilities for advancing social semiotic scholarship on reading and beyond. It ends with a sketch of a new research agenda for social semiotics, in the light of technological change and its implications for reading.

Conclusion

The field of reading is thus a compelling and absorbing one, amenable to investigations through a range of theories and research studies and characterised by many lively debates and discussions. Despite substantial efforts by teachers and researchers, there remain many unresolved issues, including some that are only now beginning to be recognised and addressed. It is hoped that this Special Issue will offer some indications of what still needs to be done to bring more positive rewards from reading to greater numbers of children and young people, as well as celebrating what has already been achieved through bridging research, scholarship and practice.

References

Adams, M. J. 1998. "The three-cueing system." In *Literacy for all: Issues in teaching and learning*, edited by J. Osborn, and F. Lehr, 73–99. New York: The Guilford Press.

Beard, R. 2003. "'Uncovering the key skills of reading'." In *Handbook of early childhood literacy*, edited by N. Hall, J. Larson, and J. Marsh, 199–208. London: Sage.

Beard, R., G. Brooks, and J. Ampaw-Farr. 2019. "'How linguistically-informed are phonics programmes?" ' *Literacy* 53 (2): 86–94. doi:10.1111/lit.12147.

Centre for Literacy in Primary Education. 2018. *Poetry in primary schools – What we know works*. Accessed September 5, 2020. https://clpe.org.uk/library-and-resources/research/poetry-what-we-know-works.

Chall, J. 1983. *Learning to read: The great debate (Updated Edition)*. New York: McGraw-Hill.

Clark, C., and A. Teravainen-Goff. 2020. *Children and young people's reading in 2019: Findings from our annual literacy survey*. London: National Literacy Trust. Online. literacytrust.org.uk/research-services/research-reports/children-and-young-peoples-reading-in-2019/ (Accessed 5 September 2020).

Crystal, D. 1976. *Child language, linguistics and learning*. London: Edward Arnold.

Department of Education and Science. 1975. *A language for life* The Bullock Report. London: Her Majesty's Stationery Office.

Gibson, E. J., and H. Levin. 1975. *The psychology of reading*. Cambridge, MA: MIT Press.

Goodman, K. S. 1967. "Reading: A psycholinguistic guessing game." *Journal of the Reading Specialist* 4 (1): 11–30.

Goodman, K. S. 1985. "Unity in reading." In *Theoretical models and processes of reading*. 3rd ed, H. Singer and R. B. Ruddell, 813–840. Newark, Delaware: International Reading Association.

Gough, P. B. 1972. "One second of reading." In *Language by ear and eye*, edited by J. F. Kavanagh, and I. G. Mattingly, 331–358. Cambridge, MA: MIT Press.

Gough, P. B., and W. E. Tunmer. 1986. "Decoding, reading, and reading disability." *Remedial and Special Education* 7: 6–10.
Gurría, A. 2014. "Introduction to *PISA* 2012 *Results in Focus: What 15-Year-Olds Know and What They Can Do with What they Know*." Organisation for Economic Cooperation and Development. Online. Accessed September 5, 2020. http://www.oecd.org/pisa/keyfindings/pisa-2012-results-overview.pdf5.
Johnston, P., and P. D. Pearson. 1982. *Prior knowledge, connectivity, and the assessment of reading comprehension*. Tech. Rep. No. 245. Urbana: University of Illinois. Center for the Study of Reading.
Kim, J. S. 2008. "Research and the reading wars." *The Phi Delta Kappan* 89 (5): 372–375.
Kress, G. 2003. *Literacy in the new media age*. London: Routlege.
Laberge, D., and S. J. Samuels. 1974. "Towards a theory of automatic information processing in reading." *Cognitive Psychology* 6: 293–323.
Leu, D. J., J. G. McVerry, W. I. O'Byrne, C. Kiili, L. Zawilinski, H. Everett-Cacopardo, C. Kennedy, and E. Forzani. 2011. "The new literacies of online reading comprehension: Expanding the literacy and learning curriculum." *Journal of Adolescent & Adult Literacy* 55 (1): 5–14.
Lewis, N. 1967. "In praise of reading." *Puffin Post* 1 (1): 2.
McClelland, J. L., and D. E. Rumelhart, eds. 1986. *Parallel distributed processing. Vol. 2: Psychological and biological models*. Cambridge, MA: MIT Press.
National Institute of Child Health and Human Development (NICHHD). 2000. *Teaching Children to Read: An evidence-based assessment of the scientific research literature on reading and its implications for reading instruction*. National Reading Panel Report. Washington, DC: National Institute for Child Health and Human Development.
Oakhill, J., K. Cain, and C. Elbro. 2014. *Understanding and teaching reading comprehension: A handbook*. London: Routledge.
Office for Standards in Education. 2007. *Poetry in schools A survey of practice, 2006/07*. London: Ofsted.
Oliveira, J. B. A. 2015. "'Brazil: Why José can't read'." In *Education in South America*, edited by S. Schwartzma, 131–154. London: Bloomsbury.
Olson, D. 2016. *The mind on paper: Reading, consciousness and rationality*. Cambridge: Cambridge University Press.
Pearson, P. D., A. S. Palincsar, G. Biancarosa, and A. I. Berman. 2020. *Reaping the rewards of the reading for understanding initiative*. Washington, DC: National Academy of Education.
Pinker, S. 1994. *The language instinct: How the mind creates language*. New York, NY: Harper.
Reid, J. 1993. "'Reading and spoken language: the nature of the links'." In *Teaching literacy: Balancing perspectives*, edited by R. Beard, 22–34. London: Hodder & Stoughton.
Reinking, D. 1998. "Introduction: Synthesing technological transformations in literacy in a post-typographic world." In *Handbook of literacy and technology*, edited by D. Reinking, M. C. McKenna, L. D. Labbo, and R. D. Keiffer, xi–xxx. Mawah, NJ: L. Erlbaum.
Rose, J. 2006. *Independent review of the teaching of early reading*. London: DfES.
Routman, R. 1988. *Transitions: from literature to literacy*. Portsmouth, NH: Heinemann.
Rudd, D. 2010. *The Routledge companion to children's literature*. London: Routledge.
Rumelhart, D. E. 1985. "Towards an interactive model of reading." In *Theoretical models and processes of reading*. 3rd ed, H. Singer and R. B. Ruddell, 722–750. Newark, Delaware: International Reading Association.
Smith, F. 1978. *Reading*. Cambridge: Cambridge University Press.
Snow, C. 2018. "Simple and not-so-simple views of reading." *Remedial and Special Education* 39 (5): 313–316.
Stannard, J., and L. Huxford. 2007. *The literacy game*. London: Routledge.
Stanovich, K. E. 1980. "Towards an interactive-compensatory model of individual differences in the development of reading fluency." *Reading Research Quarterly* 16: 32–71.
Stanovich, K. E. 2000. *Progress in understanding reading*. New York: Guilford Press.
Styles, M. 1998. *From the garden to the street: Three hundred years of poetry for children*. London: Continuum.

Roger Beard

The linguistic base of initial reading and spelling in English: a tutorial review

Greg Brooks

ABSTRACT

This article summarises the linguistic base of initial reading and spelling in English for the benefit of teachers and others engaged in education who need explicit understanding of parts of the linguistic base in order to teach initial literacy accurately. The aspects covered are those most relevant to children entering formal schooling: spoken language as the foundation of literacy; phonetics and phonology; phoneme-grapheme and grapheme-phoneme correspondences; sequencing in phonics teaching; vocabulary, morphology and syntax; and the linguistic effects of reading to children. Several aspects are discussed from two angles, first describing the full system, then summarising where 5-year-olds have reached in their development towards it.

Prerequisites

International Phonetic Alphabet (IPA) symbols are used in this article; they are explained in Tables 2–4. Phonemes are enclosed in double forward slashes, / /, and graphemes in double angle brackets, < >. 'Vowel' and 'consonant' refer to phonemes, not letters. Long and short vowels are also defined phonetically, and not by the traditional use of those terms in teaching.

Coverage

The purpose of this article is to summarise some of the foundational aspects of the linguistic base of initial reading and spelling in English for the benefit of teachers and others engaged in education who need explicit understanding of parts of the linguistic base in order to teach initial literacy accurately. The aspects covered are those most relevant to children entering formal schooling, namely: spoken language (oracy) as the foundation of literacy; phonetics and phonology; phoneme-grapheme and grapheme-phoneme correspondences; sequencing in phonics teaching; vocabulary; brief notes on morphology and syntax; and the linguistic effects of reading to children (or not). Technical terms are defined in the relevant sections. Some of these aspects are discussed from two angles, first describing the full system, then summarising where 5-year-olds have reached in their development towards it.

Given its focus on the linguistic base and on initial reading and spelling, this article does not attempt to cover the following: aspects of writing other than spelling; higher-order reading skills such as the cognitive complexity of comprehension; the psychology of reading (see Rhona Stainthorp, this issue); reading difficulties, and interventions for those affected by them (see Sinéad Harmey, this issue); historical aspects, including etymology; or, except by implication, how to teach reading and spelling. Only certain cognitive aspects are analysed, and not the affective and psychomotor domains, hugely important though these are.

Also, although the linguistic base of initial reading and spelling in English applies to learners of any age, regardless of whether or not they are already literate in another language, the focus here is on children entering formal schooling at age 5 or thereabouts.

Literacy is founded on oracy

In the most fundamental sense, the linguistic base of literacy is children's understanding and use of their mother tongue, or of another language which they have acquired. As Vygotsky ([1935] 1978, 106) put it:

> A feature of this system [writing] is that it is second-order symbolism, which gradually becomes direct symbolism. This means that written language consists of a system of signs that designate the sounds and words of spoken language, which, in turn, are signs for real entities and relations. Gradually this intermediate link, spoken language, disappears, and written language is converted into a system of signs that directly symbolize the entities and relations between them.

Thus, as analysed in detail in (for example) Brooks and Burton (2016), children need to discover that, and how, the marks on paper or screen relate to the words they already understand in spoken form, and the initial teaching of reading must be designed to help them most efficiently in that discovery. That effort after meaning is paralleled by children's early efforts to communicate on paper – see, for example, Gorman and Brooks (1996).

This reliance on words children already know is why it would be ideal if all children could be educated in their mother tongue, at least to start with. Besides ethical considerations, this principle is partly based on research evidence that children from linguistic minorities who learn to read first in their mother tongue make better progress in the national language when they transfer to it than if they are taught in the national language from the start (Benson 2004). However, this principle often conflicts with practicality: for example, over 300 languages in addition to English are spoken by schoolchildren in London (Von Ahn et al. 2010), so that there is no prospect whatever of the publicly-funded schools in that city attempting to provide initial literacy education in any language but English.

More practical in many circumstances is the principle that every child should enter school speaking the language of the school (European Commission 2012, 24–25). For this to happen, especially for children whose home or mother tongue is not the language of the school, and for children whose language development is delayed, effective preschool provision is the principal precondition. And much of that argument also applies to newly arrived migrants, both older children and adults, who need to acquire the language of their new country speedily, and deserve the support to do so.

This matters because

> The development of reading skills is underpinned by oral language abilities: Phonological skills appear to have a causal influence on the development of early word-level literacy skills, and reading-comprehension ability depends, in addition to word-level literacy skills, on broader (semantic and syntactic) language skills. (Hulme et al. 2015, 1877)

and because

> a range of oral language skills measured in preschool are closely associated with later reading comprehension, and this relationship continues through the primary school years (e.g. Lervåg, Hulme, and Melby-Lervåg 2017) (Castles, Rastle, and Nation 2018, 34)

Phonetics and phonology

Phonetics is the scientific study of speech sounds, and phonology is the study of phonemes, the speech sounds that differentiate words of different meanings in a particular language. In English,

Table 1. Categories of phonemes in the RP and General American accents.

		RP	GA
Consonants	Voiced	16	16
	Voiceless	8	8
Pure vowels	Short	7	6
	Long	5	3
Diphthongs		8	5
Retroflex ('R-coloured') vowels		0	6

for example, *bat, pat* are different words, so /b, p/ are phonemes of spoken English. The (mainly but not exclusively southern) British accent often called Received Pronunciation (RP) has 44 phonemes (see Gimson's *Pronunciation of English*, various editions, 1962–2014). The most widespread accent in the USA, General American (GA), also has 44 phonemes.

The 44 phonemes of RP and GA fall into the categories shown in Table 1.

The 24 consonant phonemes of both RP and GA, and the IPA symbols for them, are shown in Table 2.

Of the 24 consonant phonemes, the 16 with no entry in the penultimate column of Table 2 are voiced, that is, pronounced with vibration of the vocal cords, and the eight marked 'voiceless' are pronounced with little or no such vibration. The distinction is important for understanding the variations in how certain noun and verb endings are pronounced (see below under 'Morphology' for that, and under 'Children's phonological development' for the significance of 'fricative').

As Table 1 implies, differences in vowel phonemes constitute the differences between the RP and GA accents; hence it is impossible to list these phonemes in one Table. Table 3 shows the 20 vowel phonemes of RP, and Table 4 the 20 vowel phonemes of GA, with their IPA symbols in both cases. Notes to both Tables follow Table 4.

There is no short pure vowel entry for letter <o> in Table 4, despite there being one in Table 3. The absence of such an entry in Table 4, and the use of *ox* to illustrate /ɑː/ instead, arise because, despite the intuitions and pretty constant tradition of many teachers in the United States, there is no

Table 2. The International Phonetic Alphabet symbols for the 24 consonant phonemes of the Received Pronunciation and General American accents of English.

/b/	as in the first sound of	*by*	/baɪ/		
/d/	as in the first sound of	*dye*	/daɪ/		
/g/	as in the first sound of	*goo*	/guː/		
/m/	as in the first sound of	*my*	/maɪ/		
/n/	as in the first sound of	*nigh*	/naɪ/		
/p/	as in the first sound of	*pie*	/paɪ/	voiceless	
/t/	as in the first sound of	*tie*	/taɪ/	voiceless	
/r/	as in the first sound of	*rye*	/raɪ/		
/k/	as in the first sound of	*coo*	/kuː/	voiceless	
/ʧ/	as in the first sound of	*chew*	/ʧuː/	voiceless	
/f/	as in the first sound of	*few*	/fjuː/	voiceless	fricative
/ʤ/	as in the first sound of	*jaw*	/ʤɔː/		
/l/	as in the first sound of	*law*	/lɔː/		
/s/	as in the first sound of	*sue*	/suː/	voiceless	fricative
/v/	as in the first sound of	*view*	/vjuː/		fricative
/z/	as in the first sound of	*zoo*	/zuː/		fricative
/h/	as in the first sound of	*who*	/huː/		fricative
/ŋ/	as in the last sound of	*ring*	/rɪŋ/		
/ʃ/	as in the third sound of	*fission*	/ˈfɪʃən/	voiceless	fricative
/ʒ/	as in the third sound of	*vision*	/ˈvɪʒən/		fricative
/θ/	as in the first sound of	*thigh*	/θaɪ/	voiceless	
/ð/	as in the first sound of	*thy*	/ðaɪ/		
/w/	as in the first sound of	*well*	/wel/		
/j/	as in the first sound of	*yell, union*	/jel, ˈjuːnjən/		fricative

The IPA symbols used in Tables 2 and 3 are identical to those used in the *Cambridge English Pronouncing Dictionary* (2003) and in my *Dictionary of the British English Spelling System* (Brooks 2015)

Table 3. The International Phonetic Alphabet symbols for the 20 vowel phonemes of the RP accent of English, plus /juː/.

Short pure vowels			
/æ/	as in the first sound of	*ant*	/ænt/
/e/	as in the first sound of	*end*	/end/
/ɪ/	as in the first sound of	*ink*	/ɪŋk/
/ɒ/	as in the first sound of	*ox*	/ɒks/
/ʌ/	as in the first sound of	*up*	/ʌp/
/ʊ/	as in the second sound of	*pull*	/pʊl/
/ə/ (schwa)	as in the first sound of	*about*	/ə'baʊt
Long pure vowels			
/ɑː/	as in the first sound of	*aardvark*	/'ɑːdvɑːk/
/ɜː/	as in the first sound of	*earl*	/ɜːl/
/ɔː/	as in the whole sound of	*awe*	/ɔː/
/uː/	as in the first sound of	*ooze*	/uːz/
/iː/	as in the first sound of	*eel*	/iːl/
Special 2-phoneme sequence *			
/juː/	as in the first two sounds of	*union*	/'juːnjən/
Diphthongs			
/eɪ/	as in the first sound of	*aim*	/eɪm/
/aɪ/	as in the first sound of	*ice*	/aɪs/
/əʊ/	as in the first sound of	*oath*	/əʊθ/
/aʊ/	as in the first sound of	*ouch*	/aʊʧ/
/ɔɪ/	as in the first sound of	*oyster*	/'ɔɪstə/
/eə/	as in the whole sound of	*air*	/eə/
/ɪə/	as in the whole sound of	*ear*	/ɪə/
/ʊə/	as in the second sound of	*rural*	/'rʊərəl/

Table 4. The International Phonetic Alphabet symbols for the 20 vowel phonemes of the General American accent of English, plus /juː/.

Short pure vowels			
/æ/	as in the first sound of	*ant*	/ænt/
/ɛ/	as in the first sound of	*end*	/end/
/ɪ/	as in the first sound of	*ink*	/ɪŋk/
/ʌ/	as in the first sound of	*up*	/ʌp/
/ʊ/	as in the second sound of	*pull*	/pʊl/
/ə/ (schwa)	as in the first sound of	*about*	/ə'baʊt
Long pure vowels			
/ɑː/	as in the first sound of	*ox*	/ɑːks/
/uː/	as in the first sound of	*ooze*	/uːz/
/iː/	as in the first sound of	*eel*	/iːl/
Special 2-phoneme sequence *			
/juː/	as in the first two sounds of	*union*	/'juːnjən/
Diphthongs			
/eɪ/	as in the first sound of	*aim*	/eɪm/
/aɪ/	as in the first sound of	*ice*	/aɪs/
/oʊ/	as in the first sound of	*oath*	/oʊθ/
/aʊ/	as in the first sound of	*ouch*	/aʊʧ/
/oɪ/	as in the first sound of	*oyster*	/'oɪstɚ/
Retroflex ('r-colored') vowels			
/ɑɚ/	as in the whole sound of	*are*	/ɑɚ/
/eɚ/	as in the whole sound of	*air*	/eɚ/
/ɪɚ/	as in the whole sound of	*ear*	/ɪɚ/
/ʊɚ/	as in the second sound of	*rural*	/'rʊɚrəl/
/ɚ/	as in the second sound of	*bird*	/bɚd/
/oɚ/	as in the whole sound of	*ore*	/oɚ/

*In order to analyse English spelling rigorously, including accounting for the spelling of words like *union*, the 2-phoneme sequence /juː/ has to be given quasi-phoneme status (Brooks 2015; Carney 1994).

In order to represent the vowel phonemes of the GA accent, the phonetic symbols used in Table 4 are (with minor modifications) those used in the *Advanced Learner's English Dictionary* (Merriam-Webster, 2008: 1994).

phonetically short vowel phoneme corresponding to <o> in the GA accent. Nevertheless, the long pure vowel /ɑː/ spelt <o> still patterns with the predominant 'short' sounds of <a, e, i, u>, namely /æ, e, ɪ, ʌ/.

Children's phonological development

As Cruttenden (1979, xii) points out, many children have acquired the full vowel system by age 2½, but that, even at age 5, some still have difficulty with:

- fricative consonants (see Table 2). The classic example here is the 'lisp' that may precede full mastery of /s/;
- consonant clusters, e.g. pronouncing *spot* as 'pot', or *please* as 'peas'; and
- /r/, which may be replaced by a different phoneme /ʋ/ which is produced with the upper teeth touching the lower lip. This is often misheard as /w/ and 'regarded as a speech defect in adults' (Cruttenden in Gimson, 7th edition, 2008, 221).

While much of this will resolve without intervention, speech and language therapists can help with persisting problems. However, some regional variations (e.g. London and London-influenced /f, v/ instead of /θ, ð/) are better handled through sensitive teaching of spelling.

Even though rather few children have not acquired the full set of phonemes by school entry, it is essential for teachers to know the phonetic details listed above because of their key importance for fully understanding the complexities of English spelling and for teaching phonics.

Orthography: the spelling system

Since there are 44 phonemes in both RP and GA, but only 26 letters in the alphabet in which both British and US English are written, letters and phonemes cannot be in one-to-one relationship, so sequences of more than one letter are used as extra symbols. These sequences, and the 26 letters of the alphabet used singly, make up the graphemes, or 'spelling choices', of English orthography. However, the correspondences between phonemes and graphemes in English are notoriously complex: every phoneme can be spelt by more than one grapheme (sometimes several), graphemes can consist of one, two, three or four letters (e.g. <u, oo, oeu, ough> spelling /uː/ in *super, moon, manoeuvre, through*, plus the 'split digraph' <u-e> (one of six in English orthography) spelling /uː/ in *rule*), and many graphemes have more than one pronunciation (often several; the average has been calculated as 2.4 – Gontijo, Gontijo, and Shillcock 2003).

In their seminal study of children learning to read in 14 languages in 15 European countries, Seymour, Aro, and Erskine (2003) found that their sample of English-speaking children acquired initial reading much more slowly than any of the other groups. They noted that the orthographic complexity of English was at one end of the scale (Finnish, with 100% regularity, was at the other), and hypothesised that this was one of the two main determinants of English-speaking children's much slower progress (for the other, see below under 'Vocabulary').

The complex web of correspondences between the phonemes of RP and the graphemes of British spelling has been analysed in great detail by Carney (1994) and in my *Dictionary of the British English Spelling System* (Brooks 2015). (No comparable reliable analysis of the relationships between the GA accent and the US English spelling system has yet appeared.) Both analyses cover both phoneme-grapheme correspondences (sound to symbol) and grapheme-phoneme correspondences (symbol to sound). For convenience, both forms of correspondence will be referred to here (as in many other sources) as GPCs. My analysis produced totals of 284 graphemes and 543 GPCs – but only obsessives need to know about all of them, especially since children need only be taught enough phonics for them to 'crack the code' and launch themselves as independent readers.

Table 5. Solity and Vousden's (2009) 65 grapheme–phoneme correspondences.

Single-letter grapheme	Pronunciation	Multiple-letter grapheme	Pronunciation	Suffix grapheme	Pronunciation
b	/b/ bed	ai	/eɪ/ aid	ed	/t/ or /d/
c	/k/ kiss	air	/eə/ chair	s	/s/ or /z/
d	/d/ dog	ar	/ɑː/ barn		
f	/f/ fish	au	/ɔː/ cause		
g	/g/ golf	aw	/ɔː/ claw		
h	/h/ help	ay	/eɪ/ bay		
j	/ʤ/ jump	ea	/iː/ beam		
k	/k/ kite	ear	/ɪə/ clear		
l	/l/ lamp	ee	/iː/ creek		
m	/m/ man	er	/ɜː/ fern		
n	/n/ nip	ew	/uː/ screw		
p	/p/ pad	ey	/iː/ key		
q	/k/ quick	igh	/aɪ/ fight		
r	/r/ run	ir	/ɜː/ bird		
s	/s/ sun	oa	/əʊ/ float		
t	/t/ tap	oi	/ɔɪ/ foil		
v	/v/ van	oo	/uː/ food		
w	/w/ wet	oor	/ɔː/ door		
x	/ks/ ox	or	/ɔː/ born		
y	/j/ young	ou	/aʊ/ bound		
z	/z/ zap	oy	/ɔɪ/ toy		
Pronounce geminates as single *		ur	/ɜː/ blur		
		ch	/ʧ/ chip		
		ck	/k/ buck		
		kn	/n/ know		
		ph	/f/ photo		
		qu	/kw/ quick		
		sh	/ʃ/ shop		
		th	/θ/ thin		
		wh	/w/ what		
a	/æ/ cat	a_e	/eɪ/ make		
e	/e/ bed	e_e	/iː/ eve		
i	/ɪ/ sit	i_e	/aɪ/ life		
o	/ɒ/ log	o_e	/əʊ/ code		
u	/ʌ/ sun	u_e	/juː/ mute		

Source: Adapted by permission of Jonathan Solity from Solity and Vousden (2009), Table 5, *p.*485, with IPA symbols added and omissions corrected: in the original Table, letter <s> and its example word are missing, and the example word opposite grapheme <ir> is *float*, so here <s>, *sun*, grapheme <oa> and *bird* as the example word for <ir> have been inserted.

* The 'pronounce geminate consonant letters as single' rule has very few exceptions, e.g. <gg> pronounced /ʤ/ and not /g/ in *exaggerate, suggest* and a few other words; <zz> pronounced /ts/ in *pizza*. This is therefore a strong reading rule – but it provides no help towards knowing when to **write** consonant letters double. Chapter 4 of my *Dictionary* tackles that topic in depth.

For practical purposes, teachers only need to know that there are 89 graphemes and 138 GPCs in what I have called the main system, plus some of the rarer graphemes which nevertheless occur in common words, e.g. <st> spelling /s/ in *castle*. Tables laying out this much of the system can be found in the Appendix to the *Letters and Sounds* materials published by the British government some years ago (DfES 2007), in Burton (2011), and in Appendix B of my *Dictionary*. They are reproduced again in the Appendix to this article.

An alternative analysis of which graphemes and GPCs children and their teachers need to know is based on the frequency of graphemes in children's reading books. Solity and Vousden (2009) identified 76 key graphemes, which consist of: the 26 letters of the alphabet; 33 digraphs; three trigraphs (<air, igh, oor>); <qu> treated as a single item representing /kw/; and 2 'suffix graphemes' (<ed, s>). By adding the rule that the 12 geminate consonant letters (<bb, dd, ff, gg, ll, mm, nn, pp, rr, ss, tt, zz>) are to be pronounced as though they are single, Solity and Vousden reduced their list to 65 GPC rules, as shown in Table 5.

Of Solity and Vousden's 77 graphemes (including the 12 geminates), all but five (<ey, kn, oa, oor, qu>) are also in my main system; and 20 less frequent graphemes in my main system (<are, ce, ci, dg,

dge, eer, ere, ge, ie, le, ng, ore, ow, se, si, ssi, tch, ti, ue, ve>) are not in their list. Almost all of the latter group are certainly not needed in the initial stages (<ci, dg, le, si, ssi, ti> in particular because they do not occur in monosyllables), but <ng, tch> definitely are needed quite early, and are surprising omissions from Solity and Vousden's list. However, their analysis suggests that, even within my 'main system', it should be possible to prioritise a subset of GPCs for great utility and effectiveness when teaching beginners to read.

Sequencing

It is all very well knowing which GPCs are the most frequent and useful – but no learner can absorb them all at once, so initial teaching must organise them in some sequence or other. Even those who avoid phonics and stick with non-phonics-based reading schemes and/or 'real books' try to ensure that early reading books have simple vocabulary and syntax. In such cases, however, the rationale for the sequencing choices seems very rarely to be stated, if ever, and any sequencing of graphemes and GPCs may happen more by chance than intention.

Those who produce materials for systematic phonics teaching adopt some form of progression from an initial set of very restricted graphemes and GPCs (and start introducing high-frequency irregular words, e.g. *the*, quite early). Traditional analytic phonics teaching apparently used the alphabet as the sequence, working from <a> to <z> and devoting one week to each letter and its predominant pronunciation, so that most of a school year was used up. I have argued (Brooks 2002) that analytic phonics, because it bans sounding-out (at least in the early stages), relies too much on children's ability to make inferences, and that, if phonics is to be taught, it should be done explicitly. Another objection to analytic phonics might be that the second most frequent letter in English, <t>, would supposedly only be encountered at week 20.

Synthetic phonics schemes, by contrast, teach sounding-out for both reading and spelling right from the start. Many begin with some variant of *satpin* because a greater number of simple (and mostly regularly-pronounced) monosyllabic words can be generated from the letters <s a t p i n> and their most regular correspondences /s æ t p ɪ n/ than from any other set of six letters: at least 40 such words (but ignoring *pint*). The *Letters and Sounds (L&S)* scheme (DfES 2007), for example, began with *satpin*. The complete sequence of introduction of the 44 RP phonemes (and three 2-phoneme sequences: /ks, kw, juː/) and their most frequent graphemes in *L&S* is not tabulated as such anywhere in *L&S* itself, but can be deduced to be as shown in Table 6. One refinement is mentioned in the note on sources below the Table.

Devisers of new schemes today would need strong reasons for not following this example, unless they adopt a sequence which has a similar rationale and advantages.

Vocabulary

As shown above, both the RP and GA accents have 44 phonemes; many other accents with which English is spoken have a similar number. On this limited resource the English language has created a vast vocabulary:

> As of 30 November 2005, the *Oxford English Dictionary* contained approximately 301,100 main entries. Supplementing the entry headwords, there are 157,000 bold-type combinations and derivatives; 169,000 italicized-bold phrases and combinations; 616,500 word-forms in total. (https://en.wikipedia.org/wiki/Oxford_English_Dictionary accessed 2/8/19)

One of the features of spoken English which underpins that diversity is its complex syllable structure. Whereas many languages have simple syllable structures, often of CV (consonant–vowel) type, English syllables can consist of 0–3 consonants at the start (onset), and 0–4 consonants at the end (coda), the only obligatory element being the medial vowel. Thus English monosyllables range from *a, I* /eɪ, aɪ/ to (e.g.) *strengths* /streŋkθs/. If there were no restrictions on which phonemes

Table 6. Sequence of phonemes and their principal graphemes in *Letters and Sounds* (DfES 2007).

Phase	Set	Phoneme(s)	Grapheme(s)
2	1	s	s
		æ	a
		t	t
		p	p
	2	ɪ	i
		n	n
		m	m
		d	d
	3	g	g
		ɒ	o
		k	c
		k	k
	4	k	ck
		e	e
		ʌ	u
		r	r
	5	h	h
		b	b
		f	f, ff
		l	l, ll
		s	ss
3	6	ʤ	j
		v	v
		w	w
		ks	x
	7	j	y
		z	z, zz
		kw	qu
			(further) Digraphs and trigraphs
	8	ʧ	ch
		ʃ	sh
		θ, ð	th
		ŋ	ng
	9	eɪ	ai
		iː	ee
		aɪ	igh
		əʊ	oa
	10	ʊ, uː	oo
		ɜː	ur
		ɔɪ	oi
		eə	air
		(j)ʊə	ure
	11	aʊ	ow
		ɪə	ear
		ɔː	or
		ɑː	ar
		ə	er
5		ʒ	(zh)

Sources: DfES (2007, 48 for Sets 1–5, p.74 for Sets 6 and 7 and the list of further digraphs and trigraphs, and p.132 for /ʒ/). Burton et al. (2008, 46) for the suggested division of the further digraphs and trigraphs into sets 8–11.

could appear in which position, possible English monosyllables would total many billions – but there are only (only!) 9,000 or so (Moser, Dreher, and Oyer 1957). A couple of the restrictions are that long vowels hardly ever occur before /ŋ/; and that where a syllable begins with three consonants, the first must be /s/, the second must be one of /k, p, t/, and the third must be one of /l, r/, yielding just five sequences, as in *sclerosis, scream, split, spray, string* (/stl/ does not occur).

In their study of children learning to read in 14 languages in 15 countries, already mentioned, Seymour, Aro, and Erskine (2003) noted that the syllabic complexity of English was at one end of the scale (Finnish, with almost entirely CV syllables, was again at the other), and hypothesised that this was the other main determinant of English-speaking children's much slower progress.

Children's spoken vocabulary

Most children entering school who speak the language of the school already have quite a wide vocabulary, both receptive and expressive. According to Shipley and McAfee (2015), at age 5 native English-speaking children **recognise** at least 10,000 words. According to an Australian website summarising data from English-speaking countries (https://www.education.vic.gov.au/childhood/professionals/learning/ecliteracy/interactingwithothers/Pages/conceptsdevelopmentandvocabulary.aspx accessed 4/8/19) the average **expressive** vocabulary of a 5-year-old is 5000+ words.

However, two caveats are necessary. First, Treffers-Daller and Milton (2013) show that estimates of English-speaking adults' vocabulary sizes vary widely, if not wildly, by as much as a factor of 20, and that this is due to significant differences in the methods by which the estimates are arrived at; the same is likely to be true also of estimates of English-speaking children's vocabulary sizes. By the method they use, Treffers-Daller and Milton arrive at a figure of about 10,000 word families for first-year undergraduates at three British universities, and infer an average rate of acquisition of about 500 word families a year since birth; for 5-year-olds this would imply about 2,500 word families. (Here a word family comprises a root word and all its inflected and derived forms, e.g. *work, working, worked, worker, rework*, etc., and not the alternative sense of a set of words with a common sound and spelling pattern. 'Root word meanings' in the next quotation are word families in the first sense just given.)

Secondly, all such averages conceal great variability. According to Grøver (2017, 286):

> By the time children enter elementary school, there is already considerable variability in the breadth and depth of their vocabularies. For example, Biemiller (2005) estimated that lower-quartile English-speaking children begin kindergarten with a thousand fewer root word meanings than average children and continue to acquire fewer words during the first years of schooling, resulting in 2000 fewer root words by the end of second grade.

Though cause-and-effect studies in this area would be unethical, it seems likely that a powerful source of these differences is very young children's experiences in the home. In their classic study in the USA, Hart and Risley (1995) recorded one hour a week of all the exchanges in 42 families for 2½ years, from when the focus child was 7–9 months old to his/her 3rd birthday or soon after. This study gave rise to the notion of the '30 million word gap', i.e. that over a few years a child from a professional family would be exposed to three times as many words on average as a child from a poor family: 42 million words v. 13 million words.

Details of this research have proved contentious (Kamenetz 2018): all the families lived in one area of one town, Kansas City; 17 of the 20 'welfare' and 'working class' families were black, while 9 out of 10 of the 'professional' families were white; only by wild extrapolation is it possible to estimate vocabulary growth from small samples of speech, particularly when the samples don't contain the same number of words; the low-income families may have been intimidated into silence by the presence of a researcher, especially someone of another race, whereas the educated parents may have been more likely to show off by talking more when the observer was present. Sperry, Sperry, and Miller (2019) reported a 'failure to replicate' Hart and Risley in a study of a similar size but weighted more heavily to lower SES families, and analysing speech from all family members rather than just the focus child's primary caregiver. They found no 'word gap'.

Despite all this, the general thesis that SES differences in children's exposure to speech affect children's vocabularies is plausible. Gilkerson et al. (2017) conducted a large replication of Hart and Risley using a much less intrusive recording method, with 329 families, and 49,765 hours of recording, from children aged 2 months to 4 years. They concluded that the 'word gap' between high-income and low-income groups was about 4 million words by the time the children turned 4. Focused interventions can help prevent the differences becoming disadvantages.

Children's early vocabulary sizes matter both for their ability to communicate clearly and effectively, and because vocabulary size is one of the strongest predictors of success in learning to read (Storch and Whitehurst 2002). Lee (2011, 83), using data on 1,071 children from nine US states studied and repeatedly tested from age 2 to age 11, found that 'expressive vocabulary at age 2 can significantly predict … 16 language and literacy outcomes such as letter identification, phonological awareness, vocabulary, and reading comprehension over the span of 9 years.'

Sequencing of vocabulary in early reading books

As implied above, all theories of how children learn to read, and therefore of how to teach them, are predicated on the assumption that, when a child succeeds in producing a word-sound in response to a printed word, if that word-sound corresponds to a word in the child's receptive aural vocabulary, the word will be recognised and understood. A further tacit assumption is that the ease of early printed word recognition and comprehension will correlate with the frequency with which the child has heard various words.

One would imagine, therefore, that the words that authors of children's early reading books choose would be based (in part) on lists of the frequency of words in young children's receptive and expressive vocabularies – but this does not appear to be the case. There are numerous studies of young children's vocabularies which provide lists of the words which occur – there is a list of such corpora at https://childes.talkbank.org/access/ (accessed 2/10/19) – but only one study, it seems, and it is not included on that website, which ranks the children's own spoken words by frequency of occurrence. Hopkins (1979) showed that previous researchers had studied small and/or unrepresentative samples of children, and in some cases had based their frequency lists wholly or partly on studies of *adults'* vocabularies, presumably on the assumption that the words adults use most frequently will be among those that young children hear most frequently, and thus learn to understand early in life. It would be interesting to know whether this assumption has ever been investigated empirically.

In her own research Hopkins (1979, 242) studied

> 125 first-grade children who … were randomly selected from sixteen classrooms in nine public elementary schools in the [US] Midwest. All students were monolingual Caucasian children who, in the opinion of superintendents, principals, and teachers, lived in neighborhoods at the middle socioeconomic level.

Her database eventually contained 100,549 running words (tokens), which included a total of 3,928 different words (types). When the word types were ranked by frequency, there emerged a feature that would cast doubt on using the results to inform the vocabulary of children's books: of the 100 most frequent words, 82 were function words, and only 18 were content words. Among the latter the first definite noun was 'house', at no.72. No record has been found of Hopkins' data being used by authors.

Instead, many authors take account of word frequency lists derived from printed texts rather than from children's vocabularies. In the UK perhaps the most famous is *Key words to literacy* (McNally and Murray 1962), which gave rise to the *Ladybird Key Words Reading Scheme*, launched in 1964. In the United States the corresponding source used to be *The American Heritage Word Frequency Book* (Carroll, Davies, and Richman 1971), which was based on a corpus of 5 million running words from written texts used in US schools. Both are now very out-of-date. A more recent US resource is Zeno et al. (1995), which was based on 6000 texts spanning kindergarten to university, and indicates the frequency of words that appear in written texts in grades 1–13 in the United States.

The British research team of Masterson et al. (2010, 222) pointed out that 'American counts … may be inappropriate for UK children', and had therefore created the Children's Printed Word database (Masterson et al. 2003) for use in psycholinguistic experiments with British children, and potentially by UK authors of children's books. The database provides 'information regarding the contents and nature of the reading vocabulary to which 5- to 9-year-old children are exposed in the UK' (Masterson et al. 2010, 222). It is based on 1011 books, and 'contains 12,193 different words (types), and 995,927 occurrences of these words (tokens). The 100 most frequent words (just under 1% of all types) account for 51.9% of all tokens' (Masterson et al. 2010, 227). The feature which limited the usefulness of Hopkins' (1979) data recurs here: of the 100 most frequent words, 89 are function words, and only 11 are content words.

However, Masterson et al.'s list of the 100 most frequent words was used in *Letters and Sounds* (DfES 2007, 194) to show which of the words were to be taught in Phases 2–5 of that scheme, and to categorise the words in each Phase as 'decodable' by children using the phoneme-grapheme correspondences introduced up to that point, or 'tricky' – not yet decodable. A note under Phase 5 points out that 'some of the words that were tricky in earlier phases become fully decodable in Phase Five.' According to the criteria used to judge the 100 words, 59 are decodable and 41 tricky. The latter category comprises *the, to, I, go, no, into* (Phase 2), *he, she, we, me, be, was, you, they, all, are, my, her* (Phase 3), *said, have, like, so, do, some come, were, there, little, one, when, out, what* (Phase 4), and *oh, their, people, Mr, Mrs, looked, called, asked, could* (Phase 5). The high utility (matching their frequency) of most of these words would in many authorities' eyes justify some sight-word teaching from the start alongside *satpin* synthetic phonics.

However well-constructed such databases may be, using them to choose words for children's books would involve at least an element of a self-perpetuating circle: some words in new books would be used because they appear in lists of words used in books that already exist.

To break out of that limitation, authors of children's books of course rely on intuition and inspiration. It would obviously be silly to include words like 'antediluvian' or 'sesquipedalian' in books for 5-year-olds, so authors on the whole select and sequence the initial vocabulary they use carefully, sometimes in the interests of decodability (see below), more often to enthuse and engage their young readers. In either case, they need to, or should, take account of the usefulness of the words they choose. Sufficient repetition of words can help children to build up a sight word vocabulary, though some words and some children require large amounts of repetition (Masidlover 2014; Stuart, Masterson, and Dixon 2000), but in particularly interesting books children may not see the new words they come across for some time:

> The problem is that most words are not commonly seen. Primary grade children are hit with an avalanche of printed words. Whilst some words are seen a lot, the most meaningful words (the content words) are not. After encountering, for example, *'hen'* and *'haystack'* in *Rosie's Walk*, it will be miles of print before children again encounter *'hen'*, let alone *'haystack'*. (Juel and Minden-Cupp 2000, 462)

Conversely, books that rely on frequent repetition of just a few words, as in some 'look-and-say' schemes, may have 'the result … that this method, so full of promise for brighter material, usually succeeds in producing dull repetitive stuff' (Daniels and Diack 1960, 17–18).

A similar fate has befallen some writers of 'decodable' schemes, those in which authors begin with repeated rehearsal of just a few GPCs. Historical examples include the nineteenth-century reader beginning 'Can a pig jig in a wig?', Bloomfield's 'can Dan fan man Nan … ', and Fries's 'AT-CAT CAT-RAT A CAT-A RAT … ' (for details see Brooks 1993). Both Bloomfield and Fries seem to have subscribed to the Gestalt psychology thesis that written words are recognised as wholes, and therefore to have believed that sub-word teaching, as in sounding-out, was wrong. But since children learning to read had somehow to deduce the connections between letters and sounds, the massive repetitions of rimes in their materials seem to have been meant to enable children to work out the relevant GPCs without being explicitly taught them. Happily, repetition in decodable texts need not be mind-numbingly tedious, but can be fun, as is proved by the Dr Seuss books, among others. But the case for explicit phonics teaching remains.

Morphology

This is the branch of grammar which analyses the internal structure of words and how their various forms encode differences of meaning. It has two branches:

- derivational morphology, which covers how the meanings of words change when prefixes such as in-, un-, re- are attached; also suffixes which change the word class ('part of speech') a word belongs to, e.g. -less, -ness, -ation. Rather little of this complexity has been acquired by age 5, and this topic is therefore not tackled here;
- inflectional morphology, which covers the word endings which indicate verb tense, noun plural, etc.

Compared to many other languages, English has remarkably little inflectional morphology, in fact just nine such endings (shown here in conventional written form rather than in IPA):

- <(e)s> marking the plural of regular nouns
- <'s> marking the possessive of singular and irregular plural nouns, e.g. *Foyle's war, the geese's cackling*
- <s> marking the third person singular present tense of all verbs except the modals *can, may, must, shall, will* and sometimes *dare, need*
- <ing> marking the present participle of all verbs
- <(e)d> marking the past tense and past participle of all regular verbs
- <t> marking the past tense of some irregular verbs, e.g. *learnt, spelt*
- <en> marking the past participle of some irregular verbs, e.g. *beaten, forbidden*
- <er, est> marking the comparative and superlative of most monosyllabic adjectives and of disyllabic adjectives ending in <-y>, e.g. *hotter, hottest, happier, happiest* (though such forms seem to be being replaced by alternatives using *more, most*).

Some irregular plural nouns and past forms of verbs are instead marked by changes of vowel, e.g. *man, men; swim, swam, swum*, and a few by no change at all, e.g. *sheep, hit*.

The plural, possessive and third person singular endings all have three pronunciations:

/ɪz/ after any sibilant consonant /s, z, ʃ, ʒ, ʧ, ʤ/
/s/ after any of the non-sibilant voiceless consonants /p, t, k, θ, f/
/z/ after any of the non-sibilant voiced consonants /b, d, g, l, m, n, ŋ, ð, v/ or a vowel.

Similarly, the regular past tense and participle ending has three pronunciations:

/ɪd/ after /t, d/, e.g. *wanted, intended*
/t/ after any voiceless consonant except /t/
/d/ after any voiced consonant except /d/ or a vowel.

Some regional dialects, for example African-American English, differ markedly from Standard English in these respects.

Brown (1973) is the classic text showing which grammatical morphemes normally-developing children have acquired by age 5. These include <ing, ed>, all three regular endings involving <s> (in writing), and some irregular past tenses. Few 5-year-olds would still be producing regularised versions of irregular past tenses such as 'We goed to the seaside and I buyed an ice-cream', or reduplicated irregulars, e.g. *wented*.

Syntax

This is the branch of grammar which studies sentence structure and word order. Again, Brown (1973) showed that normally-developing children have by age 5 acquired at least the definite and indefinite articles *the, a(n)*, and both main and auxiliary verb uses of present tense forms of *be, have*. Development of syntax continues well into the school years: over 50 years ago Carol Chomsky (1969) showed that many children are still acquiring certain complex structures between the ages of 5 and 10, especially those that characterise written language but rarely occur in everyday speech. For example, she presented children with a blindfolded doll, and asked them 'Is the doll easy to see or hard to see?', and then 'Would you make her easy/hard to see?' Most of the younger children thought the doll was 'hard to see' and made it 'easy to see' by taking off the blindfold. The older children did not make this mistake. There are also (very rare) cases of children (and adults) whose spoken language is normal except for a seemingly intractable inability to acquire the full syntactic system, e.g. not producing modal verbs such as *may, ought*.

In both branches of grammar, the 'normal' course of development conceals great variability. To give just one example: Brown (1973) found that mastery of the regular third person singular verb ending <s>, or rather of its three pronunciations, could occur at any point between the ages of 28 and 50 months. Children at the slower end of the developmental range in either branch of grammar are at serious risk of having difficulty in learning to be literate. Again, speech and language therapists specialise in helping children whose development here is delayed or abnormal.

The linguistic effects of reading to children (or not)

As with vocabulary growth, here too preschool experience, especially of being read to, is key. For example, Farrant and Zubrick (2012) show that parental reading to young children influences the children's vocabulary development. Logan et al. (2019) summarise their study as follows:

> [It] uses data from 60 commonly read children's books to estimate the number of words that children are exposed to during book reading sessions. We estimated the total cumulative word exposure for children who are read to at varying frequencies corresponding to [US] nationally representative benchmarks across the first 5 years of life ... Parents who read 1 picture book with their children every day provide their children with exposure to an estimated 78,000 words each a year. Cumulatively, over the 5 years before kindergarten entry, we estimate that children from literacy-rich homes hear a cumulative 1.4 million more words during storybook reading than children who are never read to.

Some *Young Fluent Readers*, the title of Margaret Clark's (1976) classic study, seem to learn to read almost without being taught, while others lag well behind. Similar findings arose from a more recent study of children who learn to read before going to school (Stainthorp and Hughes 1999). As with preschool oral interactions, variations in parental reading to children have consequences. The title of Shirley Brice Heath's classic study, *What No Bedtime Story Means* (Heath, 1982), alludes to those at one extreme, the other has been very ably summed up here:

> Children who experience years of listening to written stories implicitly learn the linguistic differences between oral discourse and written storybook discourse, particularly the literate vocabulary, complex grammatical constructions and ... decontextualised nature of written language. Children with the Big Picture of literacy functions (knowledge that print 'means' linguistically and that it serves many purposes in people's lives) take more intentionally and successfully from instruction. (Purcell-Gates and Waterman 2000, 215)

When all that is in place, and children have cracked the code, the world lies all before them.

Disclosure statement

No potential conflict of interest was reported by the author(s).

ORCID

Greg Brooks http://orcid.org/0000-0002-9054-5156

References

Benson, C. 2004. *The Importance of Mother Tongue-Based Schooling for Educational Quality*. (Commissioned Study for EFA Global Monitoring Report 2005). Stockholm: Stockholm University Centre for Research on Bilingualism.

Biemiller, A. 2005. "Size and Sequence in Vocabulary Development: Implications for Schooling Words for Primary Grade Vocabulary Instruction." In *Teaching and Learning Vocabulary: Bringing Research to Practice*, edited by I. E. H. Hiebert, 223–235. New York: Routledge.

Brooks, G. 1993. "Psychological Influences on Bloomfield's "Linguistic" Method." In *Further Studies in the History of Reading*, edited by G. Brooks, A. K. Pugh, and N. Hall, 67–81. Widnes: UK Reading Association.

Brooks, G. 2002. "Phonemic Awareness is a Key Factor in Learning to be Literate: How Best Should it be Taught?" In *Perspectives on the Teaching and Learning of Phonics*, edited by M. Cook, 61–83. Royston, Herts: UK Reading Association.

Brooks, G. 2015. *Dictionary of the British English Spelling System*. Cambridge: Open Book Publishers. http://www.openbookpublishers.com/reader/325.

Brooks, G., and M. Burton. 2016. *ELINET Analytic Glossary of the Initial Teaching and Learning of Literacy*. Cologne: European Literacy Policy Network. http://www.eli-net.eu/fileadmin/ELINET/Redaktion/user_upload/Elinet_analytic_glossary.pdf.

Brown, R. 1973. *A First Language: The Early Stages*. Cambridge, MA: Harvard University Press.

Burton, M. 2011. *Phonetics for Phonics*. Leicester: National Institute of Adult Continuing Education.

Burton, M., J. Davey, M. Lewis, L. Ritchie, and G. Brooks. 2008. *Improving Reading: Phonics and Fluency. Practitioner Guide*. London: National Research and Development Centre for Adult Literacy and Numeracy. http://www.nrdc.org.uk/?p=254.

Cambridge University Press. 2003. *Cambridge English Pronouncing Dictionary*. 16th ed. Cambridge: CUP.

Carney, E. 1994. *A Survey of English Spelling*. London: Routledge.

Carroll, J.B., P. Davies, and B. Richman. 1971. *The American Heritage Word Frequency Book*. Boston, MA: Houghton Mifflin.

Castles, A., K. Rastle, and K. Nation. 2018. "Ending the Reading Wars: Reading Acquisition From Novice to Expert." *Psychological Science in the Public Interest* 19: 5–51. doi:10.1177/1529100618772271.

Chomsky, C. 1969. *The Acquisition of Syntax in Children from 5 to 10*. Cambridge, MA: MIT Press.

Clark, M.M. 1976. *Young Fluent Readers*. London: Heinemann.

Cruttenden, A. 1979. *Language in Infancy and Childhood*. Manchester: Manchester University Press.

Daniels, J.C., and H. Diack. 1960. *The Royal Road Readers. Teachers' Book*. 2nd ed. London: Chatto and Windus.

DfES (Department for Education and Skills). 2007. *Letters and Sounds: Principles and Practice of High Quality Phonics*. London: DfES.

European Commission. 2012. *EU High Level Group of Experts on Literacy. Final Report*. Luxembourg: Publications Office of the European Union. http://ec.europa.eu/education/literacy/what-eu/high-level-group/documents/literacy-finalreport_en.pdf.

Farrant, B.M., and S.R. Zubrick. 2012. "Early Vocabulary Development: The Importance of Joint Attention and Parent-Child Book Reading." *First Language* 32 (3): 343–364.

Gilkerson, J., J.A. Richards, S.F. Warren, J.K. Montgomery, C.R. Greenwood, D. Kimbrough Oller, J.H.L. Hansen, and T.D. Paul. 2017. "Mapping the Early Language Environment Using All-Day Recordings and Automated Analysis." *American Journal of Speech-Language Pathology* 26 (2): 248–265.

Gimson, A.C. 1962. *An Introduction to the Pronunciation of English*. London: Edward Arnold. (8th edn.) (Gimson's Pronunciation of English, edited by A. Cruttenden). 2014. doi:10.4324/9780203784969.

Gontijo, P.F.D., I. Gontijo, and R. Shillcock. 2003. "Grapheme-phoneme Probabilities in British English." *Behavior Research Methods, Instruments, and Computers* 35 (1): 136–157. doi:10.3758/bf03195506

Gorman, T.P., and G. Brooks. 1996. *Assessing Young Children's Writing: a Step by Step Guide*. London: Basic Skills Agency.

Grøver, V. 2017. "Fostering Vocabulary in Early Childhood Education." In *The Routledge International Handbook of Early Literacy Education*, edited by N. Kucirkova, C. E. Snow, V. Grøver, and C. McBride, 284–295. Abingdon, UK: Routledge.

Hart, B.M., and T.R. Risley. 1995. *Meaningful Differences in the Everyday Experience of Young American Children*. Baltimore, MD: Brookes.

Heath, S.B. 1982. "What no Bedtime Story Means: Narrative Skills at Home and at School." *Language and Society* 11 (2): 49–76.

Hopkins, C.J. 1979. "The Spontaneous Oral Vocabulary of Children in Grade 1." *The Elementary School Journal* 79 (4): 240–249.

Hulme, C., H.M. Nash, D. Gooch, A. Lervåg, and M.J. Snowling. 2015. "The Foundations of Literacy Development in Children at Familial Risk of Dyslexia." *Psychological Science* 26: 1877–1886. doi:10.1177/0956797615603702.

Juel, C., and C. Minden-Cupp. 2000. "Learning to Read Words: Linguistic Units and Instructional Strategies." *Reading Research Quarterly* 35: 458–492.

Kamenetz, A. 2018. 'Let's Stop Talking about the "30 Million Word Gap". *All Things Considered, National Public Radio Education, How Learning Happens* (1st June). Accessed November 20, 2019. https://www.npr.org/sections/ed/2018/06/01/615188051/lets-stop-talking-about-the-30-million-word-gap?t=1574266154138.

Lee, J. 2011. "Size Matters: Early Vocabulary as a Predictor of Language and Literacy Competence." *Applied Psycholinguistics* 32 (1): 69–92. doi:10.1017/S0142716410000299.
Lervåg, A., C. Hulme, and M. Melby-Lervåg. 2017. "'Unpicking the Developmental Relationship between Oral Language Skills and Reading Comprehension: It's Simple, but Complex.'." *Child Development* 89 (5): 1821–1838. doi:10.1111/cdev.12861.
Logan, J.A.R., L.M. Justice, M. Yumus, and L.J. Chaparro-Moreno. 2019. "When Children are not Read to at Home: The Million Word gap." *Journal of Developmental and Behavioral Pediatrics* 40 (5): 383–386.
Masidlover, M. 2014. "Acquisition is Not Spongelike: Investigating the Level of Book Exposure Required for Reliable Recognition of Content Words by Year 1 English Children." Unpublished Ed. D. (Educational Psychology) thesis, University of Sheffield, Sheffield, UK.
Masterson, J., M. Stuart, M. Dixon, and S. Lovejoy. 2003. *The Children's Printed Word Database*. www.essex.ac.uk/psychology/cpwd.
Masterson, J., M. Stuart, M. Dixon, and S. Lovejoy. 2010. "Children's Printed Word Database: Continuities and Changes Over Time in Children's Early Reading Vocabulary." *British Journal of Psychology* 101: 221–242.
McNally, J., and W. Murray. 1962. *Key Words to Literacy and the Teaching of Reading: A Basic Word List for Developing Early Reading and Writing Skills*. London: Schoolmaster Publishing. (Further editions in 1968, 1984).
Merriam-Webster. 2008. *Advanced Learner's English Dictionary*. Springfield, MA: Merriam-Webster.
Moser, H.M., J.J. Dreher, and H.I. Oyer. 1957. *One-syllable Words*. Columbus, OH: Ohio State University Research Foundation, Technical Report No. 53.
Purcell-Gates, V., and R.A. Waterman. 2000. *Now We Read, We See, We Speak*. Mahwah, NJ: Lawrence Erlbaum.
Seymour, P.H.K., M. Aro, and J.M. Erskine. 2003. "Foundation Literacy Acquisition in European Orthographies." *British Journal of Psychology* 94: 143–174.
Shipley, K.G., and J.G. McAfee. 2015. *Assessment in Speech–Language Pathology: A Resource Manual*. 5th ed. Boston, MA: Cengage Learning.
Solity, J., and J. Vousden. 2009. "Real Books vs Reading Schemes: A New Perspective from Instructional Psychology." *Educational Psychology* 29 (4): 469–511. doi:10.1080/01443410903103657.
Sperry, D.E., L.L. Sperry, and L.E. Miller. 2019. "Reexamining the Verbal Environments of Children From Different Socioeconomic Backgrounds." *Child Development* 90 (4): 303–1318.
Stainthorp, R., and D. Hughes. 1999. *Learning From Children Who Read at an Early Age*. London: Routledge.
Storch, S.A., and G.J. Whitehurst. 2002. "Oral Language and Code-Related Precursors to Reading: Evidence from a Longitudinal Structural Model." *Developmental Psychology* 38 (6): 934–947.
Stuart, M., J. Masterson, and M. Dixon. 2000. "Spongelike Acquisition of Sight Vocabulary in Beginning Readers?." *Journal of Research in Reading* 23: 12–27.
Treffers-Daller, J., and J. Milton. 2013. "Vocabulary Size Revisited: The Link Between Vocabulary Size and Academic Achievement." *Applied Linguistics Review* 4 (1): 151–172. doi:10.1515/applirev20130007.
Von Ahn, M., R. Lupton, C. Greenwood, and D. Wiggins. 2010. *Languages, Ethnicity, and Education in London*. London: Institute of Education, University of London.
Vygotsky, L.S. 1935. "The Prehistory of Written Language." In *Mental Development of Children During Education*, 20–32. Moscow-Leningrad: Uchpedgiz. Translated in *Mind in Society: The Development of Higher Psychological Processes*. In: Cole, M., John-Steiner, M.V., Scribner, S. and Souberman, E. (1978). Cambridge, MA: Harvard University Press, pp. 105–119.
Zeno, S.M., S.H. Ivens, R.T. Millard, and R. Duvvuri. 1995. *The Educator's Word Frequency Guide*. Brewster, NY: Touchstone Applied Science Associates.

Appendix: Pedagogically selected lists of phoneme-grapheme and grapheme-phoneme correspondences

These lists are intended to be useful to teachers and to writers of early reading books. Similar tables (also largely devised by me) appeared in the *Notes of Guidance* to *Letters and Sounds* (DfES 2007). As far as possible I have ensured that all words within the 1000 most frequent words in English whose correspondences are not covered by the major correspondences are listed in the right-hand columns of Tables A1–2 and in Tables A.6 and A.8. My source for the 1000 most frequent words was: https://simple.wiktionary.org/wiki/Wiktionary:Most_frequent_1000_words_in_English [accessed 22/9/2020].

For guidance on the phonetics underpinning the application of these lists in phonics teaching see Burton (2011), which also contains versions of these lists.

Table A1. The phoneme-grapheme correspondences of British English spelling, by RP phoneme, 1: Consonants.

	Grapheme(s)			
Phoneme	Basic	Other	As in …	Common words with rare graphemes for the phoneme
/b/	b	bb	bed rabbit	<bu> build buy
/k/	c	ck k q ch	come back look queen Christmas	<cu> biscuit
/ʧ/	ch	tch	children match	<t> nature picture <ti> question
/d/	d	dd ed	dad teddy called	
/f/	f	ff ph	from off elephant	<ft> often soften <gh> cough enough laugh rough tough
/g/	g	gg	get jogging	<gh> ghost <gu> guess guy
/h/	h		horse	<wh> who whole whose
/ʤ/	j	dg dge g ge	just budgie bridge giant orange	
/l/	l	ll	leg ball	
/m/	m	mm	my mummy	<mb> climb lamb thumb <me> come some <mn> autumn column
/n/	n	nn	now dinner	<gn> gnome sign <kn> knife knock knot know <ne> done engine none
/ŋ/	ng	n	sing sink	<ngue> tongue
/p/	p	pp	pen apple	<ph> shepherd
/r/	r	rr	red berry	<rh> rgyme rhythm <wr> write wrong
/s/	s	c ce se ss	sit city once horse grass	<sc> science scissors <st> castle Christmas listen whistle
/ʃ/	sh	ti	ship station	<ch> machine <ci> special <s> sugar sure <ss> issue pressure tissue <ssi> permission
/ʒ/	si		vision	<s> measure pleasure treasure usual
/t/	t	tt ed	but little looked	<pt> receipt <th> Thomas <tw> two
/θ/	th		thing	
/ð/	th		that	<the> breathe
/v/	v	ve	very have	<bv> obvious <f> of
/w/	w	u	went queen	<wh> what when (etc.) wheel whistle white wʌ/ spelt <o> once one
/j/	y		yellow	onion view
/z/	z	s se ze zz	zoo is please sneeze puzzle	<si> business <ss> scissors

Table A2. The phoneme-grapheme correspondences of British English spelling, by RP phoneme, 2: Vowels.

	Grapheme(s)			
Phoneme	Basic	Other	As in …	Common words with rare graphemes for the phoneme
/æ/	a		and	
/ə/	a	e er o	a the butter button	<ar> sugar possible <our> colour favour honour <re> centre <ure> nature picture
/eɪ/	a.e	a ai ay	came bacon paint day	<aigh> straight <ea> break great steak <eigh> eight <ey> they
/eə/	air	are ar	fair fare parent	<ear> bear pear tear wear <ere> there where <eir> their
/ɑː/	ar	a	far ask	<al> half <are> are aunt laugh <ear> heart
/e/	e	ea	went bread	<a> any many <ai> again(st) said <ay> says <ie> friend
/iː/	ee	e ea ey ie y	see he beach key field city	<e.e> these <eo> people <i.e> police
/ɪə/	eer	ear er ere	cheer hear hero here	<ier> fierce
/ɜː/	er	ir or ur	her girl word fur	<ear> early earth heard learn <ere> were <our> journey
/ɪ/	i	e y	is England gym	<a> language sausage <o> women <u> business minute
/aɪ/	i.e	i igh y	like I night my	<ei> either <eigh> height <eye> eye <ye> goodbye /aɪe/ spelt <ir, ire, yre> biro fire wire tyre
/ɒ/	o	a	not was	because sausage <ho> honest honour <ou> cough
/əʊ/	o	o.e ow	so bone blow	<oa> approach boat <oh> oh <ough> although

(*Continued*)

Table A2. Continued.

Phoneme	Grapheme(s) Basic	Grapheme(s) Other	As in …	Common words with rare graphemes for the phoneme
/ɔɪ/	oi	oy	boil boy	
/ʊ/	oo	u	book put	<o> woman <oul> could should would
/uː/	oo	ew u u.e	too blew super rule	<o> do to two who <oe> shoe <o.e> lose move prove whose <ou> you <ough> through <ue> blue true <ui> fruit
/ʊə/	oor	ure	poor sure	<our> tour
/ɔː/	or	a ar au aw ore	for all warn sauce saw before	<augh> caught naughty <oar> board <oor> door floor <ough> bought brought fought ought thought <our> course four your
/aʊ/	ou	ow	out down	/aʊə/ spelt <hour> hour /aʊə/ spelt <our, ower> flour flower
/ʌ/	u	o	but some	<oo> blood flood <ou> country couple double encourage enough rough tough trouble young /wʌ/ spelt <o> once one

Table A3. The phoneme-grapheme correspondences of British English spelling, 3: 2-phoneme sequences frequently spelt with single graphemes.

2-phoneme sequence	Grapheme(s) Basic	Grapheme(s) Other	As in …	2-grapheme spellings for same sequence
/əl/ (only word-final)	le		little	anim**al** lab**el** penc**il** car**ol** beautif**ul**
/juː/	u	eau ew ue u.e	union beauty few argue cute	v**iew you**
/ks/	x		box	ban**ks** tri**cks** politi**cs**

N.B. The 2-phoneme sequence /kw/ is almost always spelt <qu> and should also be taught as a unit.

Table A4. The grapheme-phoneme correspondences of British English spelling, 1: Single graphemes frequently pronounced as 2-phoneme sequences.

Grapheme(s)	2-phoneme sequence	Other phonemes	As in …
eau ew u ue u.e	/juː/		beauty few union argue cute
le (only word-final)	/əl/	(too many to list)	little
X	/ks/		box

N.B. The 2-grapheme sequence <qu> is almost always pronounced /kw/ and should also be taught as a unit.

Table A5. The grapheme-phoneme correspondences of British English spelling, 2: Major correspondences for consonant graphemes.

Grapheme(s)	Phoneme(s) Basic	Phoneme(s) Other	As in …
b bb	/b/		bed rabbit
c	/k/	/s/	come city
ce	/s/		once
ch	/ʧ/	/k/	children Christmas
ck	/k/		back
d dd	/d/		dad teddy
dg(e)	/ʤ/		budgie bridge
ed	/d/	/t/	called looked
f ff	/f/		from off
g	/g/	/ʤ/	get giant
ge	/ʤ/		orange
gg	/g/		jogging
h	/h/		horse
j	/ʤ/		just
k	/k/		look
l ll	/l/		leg ball
m mm	/m/		my mummy
n	/n/	/ŋ/	now sink
ng	/ŋ/		sing
nn	/n/		dinner
p pp	/p/		pen apple
ph	/f/		elephant
q	/k/		queen
r rr	/r/		red berry
s se	/s/	/z/	sit is horse please

(*Continued*)

Table A5. Continued.

Grapheme(s)	Phoneme(s) Basic	Other	As in …
sh	/ʃ/		ship
si	/ʒ/		vision
ss	/s/		grass
t tt	/t/		but little
tch	/ʧ/		match
th	/θ/	/ð/	thing that
ti	/ʃ/	/ʧ/	station question
u	/w/		queen
v ve	/v/		very have
w	/w/		went
y	/j/		yellow
z ze zz	/z/		zoo sneeze puzzle

Table A6. The grapheme-phoneme correspondences of British English spelling, 3: Minor correspondences for consonant graphemes.

Grapheme(s)	Phoneme(s)	As in …
bu	/b/	build buy
bc	/v/	obvious
ch ci	/ʃ/	machine special
cu	/k/	biscuit
f	/v/	of
ft	/f/	often soften
gh	/f g/	cough enough laugh rough tough; ghost
gn	/n/	gnome sign
gu	/g/	guess guy
i	/j/	onion view
kn	/n/	knife knock knot know
mb me mn	/m/	climb lamb thumb; come some; autumn column
ne	/n/	done engine none
ngue	/ŋ/	tongue
o	/wʌ/	once one
ph	/p/	shepherd
pt	/t/	receipt
rh	/r/	rhyme rhythm
s ssi	/ʃ/	sugar sure; permission
s	/ʒ/	measure pleasure treasure usual
sc	/s/	science scissors
si	/z/	business
ss	/ʃ z/	issue pressure tissue; scissors
st	/s/	castle Christmas listen whistle
t	/ʧ/	nature picture
th tw	/t/	Thomas two
the	/ð/	breathe
wh	/h w/	who whole whose; what when (etc.) wheel whistle white
wr	/r/	write wrong

Table A7. The grapheme-phoneme correspondences of British English spelling, 4: Major correspondences for vowel graphemes.

Grapheme(s)	Phoneme(s) Basic	Other	As in …
a	/æ/	/eɪ ɑː ɒ ɔː ə/	and bacon ask was all about
a.e ai ay	/eɪ/		came paint day
air are	/eə/		fair fare
ar	/ɑː/	/eə ɔː/	far parent warn
au aw	/ɔː/		sauce saw
e	/e/	/iː ɪ ə/	went he England the
ea	/iː/	/e/	beach bread
ear eer ere	/ɪə/		hear cheer here
ee ey	/iː/		see key
er	/ɜː/	/ɪə ə/	her hero butter

(Continued)

Table A7. Continued.

Grapheme(s)	Phoneme(s) Basic	Phoneme(s) Other	As in …
ew	/uː/		blew
i	/ɪ/	/aɪ/	is I
ie	/iː/		field
i.e igh	/aɪ/		like night
ir	/ɜː/		girl
o	/ɒ/	/ʌ əʊ ə/	not some so button
o.e	/əʊ/		bone
oi oy	/ɔɪ/		boil boy
oo	/uː/	/ʊ/	too book
oor	/ɔː/	/ʊə/	door poor
or	/ɔː/	/ɜː/	for worm
ore	/ɔː/		before
ou	/aʊ/		out
ow	/aʊ/	/əʊ/	down blow
u	/ʌ/	/ʊ uː/	but put super
u.e	/uː/		rule
ur	/ɜː/		fur
y	/aɪ/	/ɪ iː/	my gym city

Table A8. The grapheme-phoneme correspondences of British English spelling, 5: Minor correspondences for vowel graphemes.

Grapheme(s)	Phoneme(s)	As in …
a	/e ɪ/	any many; language sausage
ai ay	/e/	again(st) said says
aigh	/eɪ/	straight
al are	/ɑː/	half; are
ar	/ə/	sugar
au	/ɑː ɒ/	aunt laugh; because sausage
augh	/ɔː/	caught naughty
ea ey	/eɪ/	break great steak; they
ear	/eə ɑː ɜː/	bear pear tear wear; heart; early earth heard learn
e.e eo	/iː/	these; people
ei	/aɪ/	either
eigh	/eɪ aɪ/	eight; height
eir	/eə/	their
ere	/eə ɜː/	there where; were
eye	/aɪ/	eye
ho	/ɒ/	honest honour
hour	/aʊə/	hour
i	/ə/	possible
ie	/e/	friend
i.e	/iː/	police
ier	/ɪə/	fierce
ir ire	/aɪə/	biro fire wire
o	/ʊ ɪ wʌ/	woman; women; once one
o oe o.e	/uː/	do to two who; shoe; lose move prove whose
oa oh	/əʊ/	approach boat oh
oar	/ɔː/	board
oo	/ʌ/	blood flood
oor	/ɔː/	door floor
ou	/ɒ uː ʌ/	cough; you; country couple double encourage enough rough tough trouble young
ough	/əʊ uː ɔː/	although; through; bought brought fought ought thought
oul	/ʊ/	could should would
our	/ə ɜː ʊə ɔː aʊə/	colour favour honour; journey; tour; course four your; flour our
ower	/aʊə/	flower
re	/ə/	centre
u	/ɪ/	business minute
ue ui	/uː/	blue true fruit
ure	/ə/	nature picture
ye	/aɪ/	goodbye
yre	/aɪə/	tyre

How psychology helps us to understand word reading

Rhona Stainthorp

ABSTRACT
This paper presents an overview of evidence from psychological research, which enables us to understand the processes involved in word reading, how children develop word reading skills and how to teach them to read words successfully. Psychological models of reading in alphabetic orthographies propose two routes to word reading: an indirect route requiring mapping of letters and sounds using phonological processes and a direct route, mapping visual identities of words onto meaning using visual processes and memory. The dual route paves the way to an understanding of what children need to achieve to be able to read words. Evidence about how people read words successfully has led to the development of effective teaching programmes and of tests to identify deficits when word reading does not develop optimally.

How psychology helps us to understand word reading

Reading is a highly complex applied human cognitive activity. Psychologists recognise the contribution that other disciplines make to the study of reading and to teaching reading, but the unique contribution of psychology is to generate objective evidence about the processes needed to identify print, which in turn has led to evidence-based theories and models about how people read. Psychologists study how people process the squiggles on the page, what may go wrong with that and how to ameliorate difficulties. This also has implications for how to teach reading.

Definitions of reading

What is reading and reading behaviour? A fairly basic definition would be that reading means accessing language through the eyes rather than through the ears. Language processes are recruited for reading because writing systems were developed to present verbal information in a permanent visual form. Listeners comprehend speakers' communications. Therefore, analogously, readers comprehend writers' texts.

Language is a biologically determined human capacity and we can feel confident in saying that language is a behaviour that is part of 'normal' human development and functioning (Pinker 2009). Given language input from the environment, and an intact brain, all human babies acquire language and they do it in roughly the same timeframe as others in their society. They do not need a curriculum for learning to communicate and comprehend.

It is this human ability that is capitalised upon for reading. At some point in human history, there was the insight that spoken language could be represented in visual form. The Chinese did this with their logographic system, which began pictorially but which is now stylised with the characters being abstract representations of language at the level of words and concepts; and the Phoenicians did it with their set of symbols: letters that represented language at the level of the consonant phonemes of their language. Orthographies (writing systems) are culturally, not biologically determined. Unlike speaking and listening, writing and reading do not emerge through the developmental process. All societies have language, but not all societies have been literate. Humans *learn* to read and write. They learn something that has been invented by other humans. These are behaviours that are dependent on cognitive processes that develop through the maturational process. These processes are applied to the act of learning to read and write in cultural settings where learning can take place so that reading and writing become skillful.

Unlike language, achieving reading and writing skills does not have a biologically determined timescale. Individual societies legislate about when children start reading instruction. This impacts on expectations of success. In England, national tests assess word reading skill at age 6 years, and text reading competence at age 7 years. However, in Finland, children do not begin primary school until the August of the year they turn 7, and only then do they receive reading instruction. This does not compromise performance. Finland has consistently been one of the highest performing countries in the international Progress in Reading Literacy Studies (PIRLS) since the initial study in 2001 (Mullis et al. 2003). This serves to illustrate the cultural nature of this applied cognitive skill.

Cognitive processes and reading

The field of the psychology of reading is vast including different branches of the discipline, but for the purposes of this paper, a small coherent subsection is considered, namely the cognitive processes that are involved in word reading. Most of the evidence cited comes from research in alphabetic scripts with a skew towards English. Here, English is used as the basis for discussion of the contribution that psychology has made to understanding word reading, with an acknowledgement of evidence from other orthographies.

Alphabetic writing systems are based on a cipher whereby the individual sounds of a language (phonemes) are represented by graphic symbols (letters). Some orthographies are *transparent:* e.g. Finnish, Greek, Turkish. Their mappings from sound-to-letter (phoneme–grapheme correspondences: PGCs), and letter-to-sound (grapheme–phoneme correspondences: GPCs) are very simple, regular and consistent. By contrast, English orthography is characterised as deep, opaque and inconsistent in the way the graphemes represent the phonemes. Some words do have regular transparent mappings and can be read by the application of GPC rules: e.g. *dog, fish.* Such words are called *regular.* Others, like *friend, mother, rough* are called *exception* or *irregular* words because they cannot be accurately read through the application of rules. Their spelling deviates from regular grapheme–phoneme mappings.

English is an outlier orthography relative to most alphabetic systems (Share 2008) because of the higher number of the exception words. Thus, the nature of English orthography has provided a 'natural' experimental setting for studying how people read words, and what they need to learn to achieve fluent word reading skills. Studies of English have then spawned studies across the world in many different orthographies: e.g. Chinese, German, Greek, Arabic, Hebrew, Turkish, Japanese. Though English has an opaque, inconsistent orthography, the level of inconsistency is not uniform. Coltheart et al. (2001) estimated that 80% of monosyllabic English words could be read accurately by the application of a small set of GPC rules. The remaining 20% generally only had one non-regular grapheme: e.g. *said.* There are very few written English words where the application of regular GPCs does not lead to a spoken approximation of the intended word.

The focus on word reading in this paper does not mean that psychologists have not studied comprehension (see, for example, Perfetti, Oakhill, and Landi 2005). Indeed, the raison d'etre of reading is to access the language locked up in the page. We read to understand. However, most adult readers are skilled, fluent, accurate, word readers. The cognitive processing needed for identifying words is minimal relative to that required for understanding text. Thus, by being able to read words accurately, the goal of reading for comprehension becomes more readily attainable. Hence, the extensive research by psychologists into word reading skills, which are the basis of reading.

The simple view of reading

The *Simple View of Reading* (SVR) developed by psychologists Gough and Tunmer (1986) proposed that reading could be encapsulated as the interaction between two sets of exceptionally complex processes: Word Decoding and Linguistic Comprehension. They proposed that **R**eading resulted from **D**ecoding written words: i.e. recognising and understanding them individually, and **C**omprehending texts at word, sentence and text level. This they illustrated by an equation: $\mathbf{R} = \mathbf{D} \times \mathbf{C}$. 'Simple' does not imply that the processes are themselves simple. The evidence from psychology is that both sets are complex, necessary and separable-but-linked.

Hoover and Gough (1990) further clarified the term *decoding*. They stated: 'Skilled decoding is simply efficient word recognition: the ability to rapidly derive a representation from printed input that allows access to the appropriate entry in the mental lexicon, and this, the retrieval of semantic information at the word level' (Hoover and Gough 1990, 130). This is important because, in education circles in the UK, *decoding* has tended to be synonymous with using phonics to identify words: phonics being a system of instruction to learn GPCs in order to learn how to read words. This was not intended by Gough and Tunmer. By decoding they meant going from print to word identification through the utilisation of word recognition processes not just phonics. Evidence from psychology has helped us to understand what these word recognition processes are. There is now a wealth of evidence which accounts for *how* we read the words using word recognition processes.

The Rose Review (2006) into the *Effective Teaching of Early Reading* presented the SVR in the following cross-diagram (Figure 1).

Word recognition processes (horizontal axis) and linguistic comprehension processes (vertical axis) are presented orthogonally (at right-angles) to show they *essential* but *independent*. This cross-diagram highlights the implications of any individual differences in decoding and comprehension since individuals can vary in competence along both dimensions. The readers we want to produce are those in the top right quadrant. Their word recognition processes are so good that the words spring off the page effortlessly. For them, the largest proportion of their processing capacity is devoted to understanding the language that is being unlocked.

Some children have difficulty identifying written words (left-hand side). For these, the label *dyslexic* is sometimes used. Some of this group will also have language comprehension difficulties

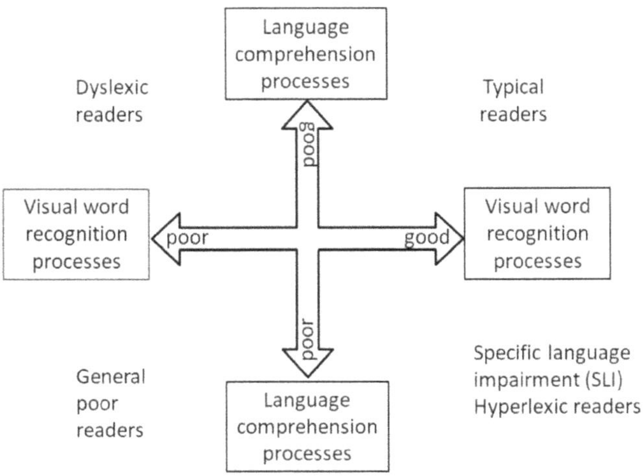

Figure 1. The simple view of reading: cross-diagram.

(bottom left) making reading exceptionally challenging. Others have intact comprehension skills (top left). Their comprehension of the *texts* can be compromised too because of their difficulty identifying the words.

Some children can read words accurately and fluently but have poor comprehension skills (bottom right). They might sound like skilled readers when reading aloud but their understanding of what is being decoded is compromised. These children may be classified as being *hyperlexic,* or found to have specific language impairment (Nation 1999).

The SVR framework is helpful for determining where the difficulties lie for a child not making acceptable progress in learning to read despite appropriate teaching.

Models of word reading

The SVR draws attention to the necessity for identifying words on the page in order to read for comprehension. There are a number of theoretical and computational models of word reading (e.g. Coltheart et al. 2001; Harm and Seidenberg 2004; Grainger et al. 2012; Perry, Ziegler, and Zorzi 2007) which are designed to specify the processes involved. These are some of the best-specified models of human processing in psychology. They vary in detail, but at heart, all models propose two sets of key cognitive processes to be involved in word reading. One set involves processes whereby there is translation of the letters of a word into its component sounds leading to the identification of the phonological identity linked to its meaning. This is the *indirect* or *phonological* route to word reading. The other set involves processes that enable decoding via direct recognition of the word's orthographic identity (its spelling), which further enables direct access to meaning and phonology. This is the *direct* or *lexical-semantic* (word-meaning) route to word reading.

Figure 2 illustrates the dual route model of adult word reading proposed by Forster and Chambers in 1973 and since developed and refined by Coltheart and colleagues. It provides a highly accessible explanation of human performance that maps on to effective teaching.

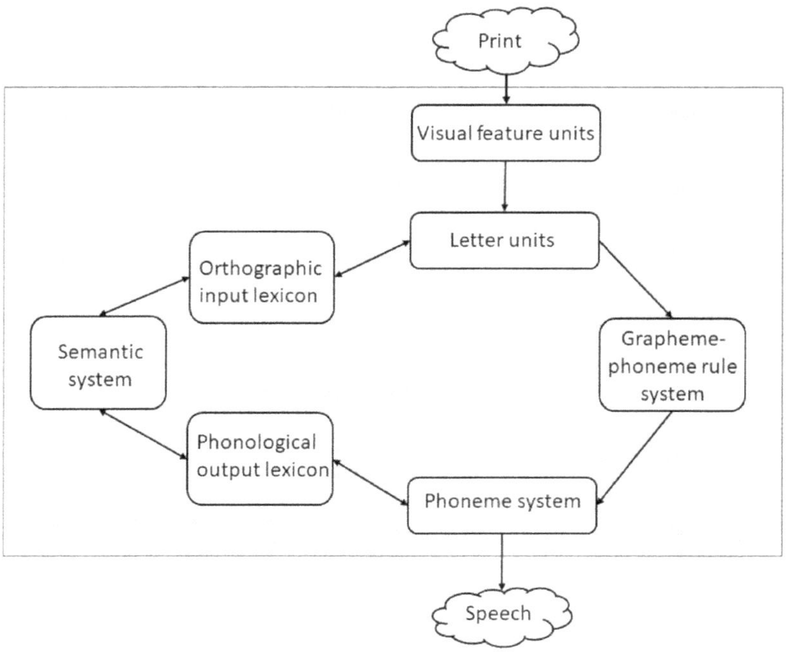

Figure 2. The dual route model of word reading after Forster and Chambers (1973).

At the start, reading involves visual processing. Print enters the brain via the eyes leading to the generation of a word's visual identity. In alphabetic reading, this happens by extracting visual features that are used to build up abstract letter identities. Skilled readers extract abstract information about the letters regardless of size, case or font: a A ɑ (Bigsby 1988; Bowers, Vigliocco, and Haan 1998). Evidence for adults being able to do this comes from studies of cross-case matching where people judge whether pairs of stimuli such as G g or S s are the same letter. Performance is not compromised when the upper- and lower-case allographs (forms of the letter) are visually distinct (Gg), or similar but of different size (Ss) (Kinoshita and Kaplan 2008; Norris and Kinoshita 2008).

Once abstract letter identities are available, two sets of processes are activated. One is represented by the right-hand route of Figure 2. Abstract identities are mapped onto phonemes via a rule system utilising GPC knowledge. The result of this process activates a phonemic sequence. If the word is composed of regular GPCs then this phonemic sequence activates a real word phonological identity, which is linked to meaning. This does not work for exception words like *once* or *choir*.

The other set of processes are depicted in the left-hand route of the model. They involve mapping the sequence of abstract letter identities against entries in an orthographic lexicon. These are the orthographic identities of words whose abstract visual identity has been memorised. Orthographic identities are linked to semantic identities of words. These are also linked to phonemic identities, leading to the phonology of the written words becoming available.

Word identification is conceived of as a 'horse race'. When the letter units are identified, both routes get activated. Then, once the word is identified, activation along both routes is terminated. There is no conscious decision. Typical adults with no adverse brain injuries show that they have the two routes available. They can read non-words like *negtop* or *flintworth* accurately. These have no orthographic identities so can only be read by using GPCs. This demonstrates that adults have a functioning indirect route. Since they also read exception words accurately, they demonstrate a functioning direct route. Regular words are generally read faster than exception words, but this relationship breaks down with high-frequency words where there is no difference in reading speed between regular and exception words. High-frequency words have been seen many times leading to orthographic identities being stored in the orthographic lexicon, thereby rendering them accessible via the direct route even when they are regular. Known regular words could be read by either route, but, because the direct route does not require additional grapheme–phoneme mapping, this is the faster route (Paap and Noel 1991).

Learning to read

The dual route model provides an excellent evidence-based account of the processes involved in word reading, and hence the goal to be reached when teaching children to read. It is not a route map for reaching that goal. We need to understand how children *learn* to read words. This means understanding how, through teaching and experience, they use their cognitive processes to identify words by 'setting up' the two routes.

The indirect route is predicated on knowledge of the letters of the alphabet, knowledge of the phonemes that these represent, awareness of the phonemic structure of words, and ability to map letters onto sounds. None of this is trivial. The phonological system is integral to the language system. It is involved in the acquisition of vocabulary both in terms of production and comprehension. This involves *implicit* phonological processing. The sounds and the meanings of words are entwined. However, *explicit* awareness of the phonemic structure of words is necessary for the functioning of the indirect route. Children generally need explicit teaching to gain insights about sound as a separate dimension of words from their meaning. If they are taught about letters in the absence of having explicit phonemic awareness, they only have half of the cipher needed for establishing the indirect route. Phonics teaching involves learning about letters and their phonemes both of which are necessary for mapping. This provides a link between the acoustic identity of a word and its visual identity. This knowledge facilitates working out the phonological identities of printed words and thereby access their meanings. Without this knowledge, establishing the indirect route is compromised.

Teaching word reading

The National Reading Panel report in the United States (National Institute of Child Health and Human Development 2000), the Rowe report in Australia (Rowe 2005) and the Rose Review in England (Rose 2006) all evaluated the evidence on teaching word reading and concluded that systematic synthetic phonics teaching was the most effective way to begin teaching children to read words independently. It is not coincidental that these reviews all took place in English-speaking jurisdictions. There is compelling evidence that it takes longer for children to learn to read words in English than in other European alphabetic systems. This relates to the deep inconsistent orthography (Seymour, Aro, and Erskine 2003). Seymour et al. also suggested that the complex syllabic nature of spoken English may also compromise early word reading. A study by Babayigit and Stainthorp (2007) investigated the development of literacy skills in Turkish. Turkish is an almost perfectly transparent orthography with each phoneme being represented by a single letter, and that letter always representing only that phoneme. Children learn to read words faster in Turkish than in English. However, Turkish is also an agglutinating language with very long multisyllabic words. This feature of the spoken language did not compromise learning to read words.

In the past, claims were made that, because English has such a complex orthography, it was not possible to teach children to read using phonics (Goodman 1967; Smith 1971). The evidence is to the contrary. Children can certainly learn to read words by being taught phonics (e.g. Byrne and Fielding-Barnsley 1989, 1990; Johnston and Watson 2004; Brooks in press). In addition, claims made about the complexity of English orthography have been exaggerated (see Coltheart et al. 2001, cited above). Take *friend*. The <ie> vowel grapheme is the only source of irregularity. The consonant frame is regular and transparent. The overwhelming number of irregularities in English relate to the spelling of vowel phonemes. This is because there are 20 different vowel phonemes in English, but only 5 vowel letters plus Y. Orthographic devices such as using a second vowel letter: e.g. *ea, ee;* or a consonant letter: *aw, al,* have been developed over the centuries to represent vowel phonemes. There are very few English words where the application of GPCs does not lead to a close approximation of the spoken word to the word on the page. Even highly 'strange' words, which are often cited as reasons for not using GPCs can be worked out by the initial use of phonics plus vocabulary knowledge. *Yacht* maybe unique and strange, but Y at the beginning of words is almost always /j/ as in *you*, and T at the end is always /t/ as in *coat*. Children taught phonics, on first encountering *yacht*, may map Y onto /j/, A onto / æ / as in *cat*, CH onto /tʃ/ as in *chip* and T onto /t/. This leads to the incorrect /j æ tʃ t/. However, it is a strategy-based solution which is a close approximation to the target, not a random guess. Phonics facilitates establishment of the direct route to word reading (Stuart, Masterson, and Dixon 2000). Even if, through the application of GPCs, irregular words are regularised, the resulting attempt gives something to work on to support the correct identification of words. Children who encounter *yacht* for the first time, but who have never been taught phonics have no strategy for working out the word. Children who have not begun to develop the indirect route to word reading are reliant on asking for help and not developing independence.

What about the direct route? Establishing this is dependent on multiple encounters with written words and being told what word each letter sequence represents. The processes involved are visual and phonological memory: remembering the unique letter sequence and pairing this with meaning and phonology. During learning, children require someone to tell them what the word is so the orthographic-semantic-phonological linkages can be remembered. This is not based on the application of rules, but rote learning based on multiple visual encounters with words, which are paired with phonology. Just looking at an unknown word does not lead to phonology. Evidence from Stuart, Masterson, and Dixon (2000) suggests that in the early stages of learning to read children need at least 32 supported encounters with words in order to remember them. However, at the age when children begin to learn to read in England working memory capacity is less than optimal, which reduces the efficiency of memorising (Gathercole and Alloway 2008). How we store verbal material is through phonological repetition, yet under about the age of 7 years, children do not engage in strategic repetition for memorisation. This means they need adult help to support them in their attempts to remember exception words and enter them in the orthographic lexicon.

It would theoretically be possible to establish the complete orthographic lexicon by memorising every word, but it would take a long time. It would also seem implausible since the basis of the alphabetic system is the use of a cipher and not simple rote learning. The point about alphabetic writing systems is that they are composed of a small number of graphic symbols that map onto a small set of phonemes. The demands on memory for learning the letters, the sounds and their mappings are considerably less than the demands for rote learning of all the orthographic identities. By being taught and learning the cipher and establishing the indirect route to word reading, multiple letter–sound mappings of words leads to the formation of orthographic identities for thousands of words, thereby establishing the direct route. Thus, both routes to word reading in an alphabetic system are necessary and need to be set up during the learning phase.

It is the responsibility of education systems to teach children to read effectively. With the SVR as a framework, the logical conclusion is that teachers need to teach children both to read the words accurately and to understand the texts. This would seem to be uncontroversial, but over the years, there has been considerable debate particularly about how to teach and even whether to teach word reading directly. The evidence from psychological research about how people read words has informed this debate. The reviews from the US, Australia and England cited above all evaluated the evidence from psychological research into word reading and all came to similar conclusions that a programme of systematic, synthetic phonics teaching at the start of literacy instruction appeared to be the most effective. This is in marked contrast to authors who maintained that learning to read is similar to learning to talk and since we do not teach children to talk, we do not need to take an analytic approach to teaching them to read (Goodman 1967; Smith 1971; Waterland 1985). This whole-language approach to teaching reading placed an emphasis on the discovery of meaning through texts with reading being considered to be a 'psycholinguistic guessing game' whereby readers were said to use any graphic, syntactic and semantic knowledge they had to guess at the identity of the printed words on the page. The evidence underpinning the dual route model shows that adult skilled readers and competent child readers do not guess at the identity of words on the page because they have strategies and lexical knowledge enabling them to identify them accurately.

Approaches to teaching word reading based on phonics articulate well with the establishment and functioning of the indirect route to word reading and obviate the need for guessing. This means that children must be taught GPCs. They also must be taught how to synthesise (blend) phonemes into words. The rationale for a systematic approach is that most GPCs, and certainly all the regular and most frequent ones, are taught cumulatively rather than serendipitously, enabling progress to be charted. Phonics teaching means children are taught *how* to read words. They are given a tool enabling them to attempt any word that they do not yet know. Phonics teaching facilitates the setting up of the indirect route.

This approach is mandatory in England with the National Curriculum (NC) (DfE 2013) requiring a phonics first approach. Fortunately, whether by accident or design, the NC appears to have been influenced by the dual route model, because teachers are also required to provide a whole-word, look–say, memorisation approach for high-frequency exception words. This supports the setting up of the orthographic lexicon, thereby ensuring that both routes to word reading are supported through teaching.

Individual differences in cognitive processes underlying word reading

Phonological awareness

The indirect route is dependent on readers having insights about the phonemic structure of words. In 1964, Bruce reported a series of experiments investigating the development of the ability to make a simple phonetic [*sic*] analysis of the spoken word in children between the ages of 5:1 and 7:6 years.

We would now call this an investigation of individual differences in phonological awareness. He found a gradual increase in children's ability to give the word that would result from the removal of a specified letter sound. For example: 'what word would be left if you take the Buh off BEAR?' This is phoneme deletion. Over the subsequent decades, psychologists have studied the development of many aspects of phonological awareness. The types of tasks used at the level of the phoneme are blending, deletion, identification, phoneme counting, spoonerisms and phonological memory.

Phonological awareness is defined as a metacognitive skill requiring conscious awareness of, and ability to manipulate the sounds of language. This metacognition may be at the level of the syllable, the rime or the phoneme, with awareness of the phoneme being the last to be achieved (Stainthorp and Hughes 1998). As identified by Bruce (1964), this is a skill that takes time to develop. Preschool children with typical language skills can comprehend and make themselves understood, showing evidence of a functioning language system based on sounds, but they have difficulty introspecting on the sound structure of words divorced from meaning. Explicit, conscious awareness of phonemic structures is something that '… .depends on metalinguistic abilities that do not come free with the acquisition of language' (Shankweiler and Crain 1986, 142).

Research into the development of phonological awareness has intrinsic interest. However, the *relationship* between phonology and word reading has rapidly become an area of study. An implication of the functioning of the indirect route to word reading is that readers must have insight into the phonemic structure of words, since, without this, mapping sounds onto letters is compromised.

Individual differences in phonological processing have been found to be related to normal acquisition of word reading skills (Bradley and Bryant 1983; Ellis and Large 1987; Lundberg, Frost, and Petersen 1988; Stanovich 1986); to compromised acquisition of word reading skills which is a marker of people identified as having dyslexia (Muter et al. 2004; Snowling 1981, 1991; Snowling and Hulme 1989) and to precocious reading skills (Stainthorp and Hughes 1998, 1999, 2004a, 2004b).

The finding that poor phonological processing is a characteristic of some people identified as having dyslexia is directly predicted from the dual route model. A deficit in phonological processing, particularly at the level of the phoneme, compromises word reading skills because children with this deficit have difficulty with explicit phonology and therefore learning the GPCs. This leads to difficulty establishing the indirect route.

A practical outcome of these findings of a phonological core deficit in some people with word reading difficulties has been the development of standardised assessments of phonological awareness designed to support the diagnosis of reading difficulties: e.g. the Phonological Abilities Test (Muter, Hulme, and Snowling 1997), the Phonological Assessment Battery (Frederickson, Frith, and Reason 1997), and the Comprehensive Test of Phonological Processing (Wagner, Torgesen, and Rashotte 1999). These were designed to identify whether children giving cause for concern in their reading acquisition had a deficit in phonological processes which might be causal in their word reading development. They involve manipulation of phonemes from simple to more complex tasks taking account of changes relating to age. Thus, they support diagnosis of reading difficulties and provide pointers to intervention in relation to the indirect route.

Rapid automatised naming

In addition to research into phonology and word reading, evidence has been amassed showing that slow performance on rapid automatised naming tasks is also associated with poor word reading (Denckla and Rudel 1976; Spring and Capps 1974). Rapid automatised naming (RAN) is assessed by requiring participants to name stimuli presented in matrix array going first across and then down as quickly as possible. It can be alphanumeric RAN with small sets of letters or numerals, or non-alphanumeric RAN with small sets of colours or objects. RAN tasks require rapid access to the phonological identity of the stimuli and fast scanning across and down. Thus, RAN tasks appear to involve processes that are involved in oral reading.

Competing views about the nature and impact of RAN have been advanced. Wagner and Torgesen and colleagues (Torgesen et al. 1997; Wagner and Torgesen 1987) proposed that slow RAN is an index of an underlying deficit in phonological processing and therefore related to the functioning of the indirect route. This view led to RAN being included phonological assessments.

There is no gainsaying that phonological processes must be involved in RAN performance since the behavioural requirement is for phonological output. However, Kail and colleagues (Kail 1991; Kail and Hall 1994; Kail, Hall, and Caskey 1999) suggested that RAN is an index of a general speed of processing not specific to word reading. A third alternative account has been given by Wolf and Bowers (Bowers and Wolf 1993; Wolf and Bowers 1999). They suggested that RAN indexes processes that are, at least in part, independent of phonology. They proposed the *Double Deficit* theory of dyslexia whereby there are three groups of children with word reading problems who show different deficit profiles. Some exhibit a single deficit profile in cognitive processing: either a phonological deficit or a RAN deficit. A third group show deficits in both and have much more severe problems in learning to read words.

This view is dependent on there being evidence that there are children who have a RAN deficit in the absence of a phonological deficit. In a series of studies Powell and Stainthorp and colleagues identified just such a group and investigated their reading and spelling performance (Powell et al. 2007; Stainthorp, Powell, and Stuart 2013; Stainthorp et al. 2010). Relative to age and phonological awareness matched children, RAN deficit children were found to be significantly slower to make same/different judgements to simple visual features like single lines and curves of different orientation, non-nameable letter-like forms, and letters. However, the speed differences to judging letter-like forms and letters disappeared once reaction times to simple visual features were controlled. They concluded that children with a single RAN deficit have difficulty discriminating simple visual features that cannot be explained in terms of a more general speed of processing deficit, a deficit in making same/different judgments, or to differences in word reading ability. The impact that this deficit might have on word reading was investigated and it was found that the group with a single RAN deficit showed poorer orthographic knowledge at both word and subword level (Powell, Stainthorp, and Stuart 2014). Further analyses showed that the participants with low naming performance were significantly poorer spellers overall and had a specific difficulty in spelling exception words. These findings support the view that RAN may be indexing processes that are implicated in the establishment of fully specified orthographic representations. Thus, a RAN deficit may differentially affect establishing the direct route.

Assessing word reading ability

In education systems, it is necessary periodically to assess children's learning in order to establish how well they have learnt what has been taught, and to identify those whose progress is problematic. Quality assessments provide objective measures of progress without bias or personal agendas and psychologists have long been involved in developing these.

Assessment of word reading has a long history: e.g. Burt (1922), Schonell (1950). However, it is only more recently that word reading assessments have been developed in the light of our understanding of orthography and how people read words. Assessments of word reading should be designed to shed light on the extent to which both routes to word reading have been established or are compromised.

Where there are concerns about word reading skills, it is appropriate to use assessments which have been developed specifically to identify the source of difficulties and arise out of empirical evidence about word reading processes. The Diagnostic Test of Word Reading Processes (DTWRP) (Forum for Research in Literacy and Language 2012) is a norm-based standardised test developed to do just this. It involves two-word reading scales: 30 regular words and 30 exception words, and a further non-word reading scale of 30 non-words. The items in each scale get progressively harder to account for normal improvement as children age. The guiding principle is that assessment of both general word reading performance and of the efficiency of the indirect and the direct routes is enabled.

Performance on the regular word reading scale gives an indication of overall word reading skill, but as argued above, which route is activated cannot be determined. Performance when reading exception words identifies the efficiency and extent of the orthographic lexicon, and performance when reading non-words identifies the efficiency of the indirect route.

By comparing performance on the three scales, it is possible to generate a profile of word reading ability. The test was standardised and normed for children between 6 and 12 years, but the earlier it is administered, the better because early intervention is more likely to facilitate progress.

The DTWRP was designed to measure accuracy, but there is another dimension of word reading that impacts on progress: namely speed. If the phonological and orthographic processes are efficient, then word reading should be fast as well as accurate, allowing for maximum processing capacity to be available for comprehension. The Test of Word Reading Efficiency (TOWRE) (Wagner, Torgesen, and Rashotte 2011) was designed to assess the efficiency of phonological processing and sight word reading by requiring children to read as many items from lists of real words and non-words in 45 seconds.

If there are concerns about the development of the word reading processes, administration of the DTWRP and the TOWRE provides information about the source of the difficulty and pointers to potential interventions. This information can then be combined with assessments of phonological processing and RAN performance to further identify the potential underlying causation.

Psychology and word reading

The argument presented in this paper is that in the last few decades, psychologists have mapped how adults read words and how children learn to read them. The description of the two routes to word reading provides a powerful framework for developing evidence-based approaches to teaching word reading and for diagnosing where children might have deficits. The work of psychologists has been capitalised on by educationalists who are able to draw practical implications from empirical research. This leads to a creative synergy whereby the learners benefit.

Disclosure statement

No potential conflict of interest was reported by the author(s).

References

Babayigit, S., and R. Stainthorp. 2007. "Preliterate Phonological Awareness and Early Literacy Skills in Turkish." *Journal of Research in Reading* 30(4): 394–413. doi:10.1111/j.1467-9817.2007.00350.x.

Bigsby, P. 1988. "The Visual Processor Module and Normal Adult Readers." *British Journal of Psychology* 79(4): 455–469. doi:10.1111/j.2044-8295.1988.tb02746.x.

Bowers, J. S., G. Vigliocco, and R. Haan. 1998. "Orthographic, Phonological, and Articulatory Contributions to Masked Letter and Word Priming." *Journal of Experimental Psychology: Human Perception and Performance* 24: 1705–1719. doi:10.1037/0096-1523.24.6.1705.

Bowers, P. G., and M. Wolf. 1993. "Theoretical Links among Naming Speed, Precise Timing Mechanisms and Orthographic Skill in Dyslexia." *Reading and Writing: An Interdisciplinary Journal* 5(1): 69–85.

Bradley, L., and P. E. Bryant. 1983. "Categorising Sounds and Learning to Read – A Causal Connection." *Nature* 301(5899): 419–421.

Brooks, G. in press. "Currrent Debates Over the Teaching of Phonics." In *Oxford Research Encyclopedia of Education*, edited by A. Luke and P. Freebody. Oxford University Press.

Bruce, D. J. 1964. "The Analysis of Sounds by Young People." *British Journal of Educational Psychology* 34: 158–170. doi:10.1111/j.2044-8279.1964.tb00620.x.

Burt, C. 1922. *Mental and Scholastic Tests*. King and Son Ltd.

Byrne, B., and R. Fielding-Barnsley. 1989. "Phonemic Awareness and Letter Knowledge in the Child's Acquisition of the Alphabetic Principle." *Journal of Educational Psychology* 81(3): 313–321. doi:10.1037/0022-0663.81.3.313.

Byrne, B., and R. Fielding-Barnsley. 1990. "Acquiring the Alphabetic Principle: A Case for Teaching Recognition of Phoneme Identity." *Journal of Educational Psychology* 82(4): 805–812. doi:10.1037/0022-0663.82.4.805.

Coltheart, M., K. Rastle, C. Perry, R. Langdon, and J. Ziegler. 2001. "DRC: A Dual Route Cascaded Model of Visual Word Recognition and Reading Aloud." *Psychological Review* 108(1): 204–256.

Denckla, M. B., and R. G. Rudel. 1976. "Rapid Automatized Naming (RAN) – Dyslexia Differentiated from Other Learning Disabilities." *Neuropsychologia* 14(4): 471–479.

DfE [Department for Education]. 2013. *English programmes of study: Key stages 1 and 2 National Curriculum in England.* https://assets.publishing.service.gov.uk/government/uploads/system/uploads/attachment_data/file/335186/PRIMARY_national_curriculum_-_English_220714.pdf.

Ellis, N., and B. Large. 1987. "The Development of Reading: As You Seek so Shall You Find." *British Journal of Psychology* 78: 1–28. doi:10.1111/j.2044-8295.1987.tb02222.x.

Forster, K. I., and S. Chambers. 1973. "Lexical Access and Naming Time." *Journal of Verbal Learning and Verbal Behavior* 12 (6): 627–635.

Forum for research in literacy and language. 2012. *Diagnostic Test of Word Reading Processes.* Brentford: GL-Assessment.

Frederickson, N., U. Frith, and R. Reason. 1997. *Phonological Assessment Battery.* Brentford: GL-Assessment.

Gathercole, S. E., and T. P. Alloway. 2008. *Working Memory and Learning: A Practical Guide for Teachers.* London: Sage Ltd.

Goodman, K. S. 1967. "Reading: A Psycholinguistic Guessing Game." *Journal of the Reading Specialist* 6(4): 126–135. doi:10.1080/19388076709556976.

Gough, P. B., and W. E. Tunmer. 1986. "Decoding, Reading, and Reading Disability." *Remedial and Special Education* 7(1): 6–10.

Grainger, J., B. Lété, D. Bertand, S. Dufau, and J. Ziegler. 2012. "Evidence for Multiple Routes in Learning to Read." *Cognition* 123(2): 280–292.

Harm, M. W., and M. S. Seidenberg. 2004. "Computing the Meanings of Words in Reading: Cooperative Division of Labor Between Visual and Phonological Processes." *Psychological Review* 111: 662–720. doi:10.1037/0033-295X.111.3.662.

Hoover, W. A., and P. B. Gough. 1990. "The Simple View of Reading." *Reading and Writing: An Interdisciplinary Journal* 2(2): 127–160.

Johnston, R., and J. Watson. 2004. "Accelerating the Development of Reading, Spelling and Phonemic Awareness Skills in Initial Readers." *Reading and Writing: An Interdisciplinary Journal* 17(4): 327–357. doi:10.1023/B:READ.0000032666.66359.62.

Kail, R. 1991. "Development of Processing Speed in Childhood and Adolescence." *Advances in Child Development and Behaviour* 23: 151–185.

Kail, R., and L. K. Hall. 1994. "Processing Speed, Naming Speed, and Reading." *Developmental Psychology* 30(6): 949–954.

Kail, R., L. K. Hall, and B. J. Caskey. 1999. "Processing Speed, Exposure to Print, and Naming Speed." *Applied Psycholinguistics* 20(2): 303–314.

Kinoshita, S., and L. Kaplan. 2008. "Priming of Abstract Letter Identities in the Letter Match Task." *Quarterly Journal of Experimental Psychology* 61(12): 1873–1885.

Lundberg, I., J. Frost, and O.-P. Petersen. 1988. "Effects of an Extensive Program for Stimulating Phonological Awareness in Preschool Children." *Reading Research Quarterly* 23(3): 263–284.

Mullis, I. V. S., M. O. Martin, E. J. Gonzalez, and A. M. Kennedy. 2003. *PIRLS 2001 International Report: IEA's study of reading literacy in primary schools in 35 countries.* Chestnut Hill, MA: TIMSS & PIRLS International Study Center, Boston College.

Muter, V., C. Hulme, and M. Snowling. 1997. *Phonological Abilities Test.* London: Psychological Corporation.

Muter, V., C. Hulme, M. Snowling, and J. Stevenson. 2004. "Phonemes, Rimes, Vocabulary, and Grammatical Skills as Foundations of Early Reading Development: Evidence from a Longitudinal Study." *Developmental Psychology* 40(5): 665–681. doi:10.1037/0012-1649.40.5.665.

Nation, K. 1999. "Reading Skills in Hyperlexia: A Developmental Perspective." *Psychological Bulletin* 125: 338–355. doi:10.1037/0033-2909.125.3.338.

National Institute of Child Health and Human Development. 2000. *Report of the National Reading Panel: Teaching Children to Read: An Evidence Based Assessment of the Scientific Research Literature on Reading and Its Implications for Reading Instruction: Reports of the subgroups.* Rockville, MD: NICHD Clearinghouse.

Norris, D., and S. Kinoshita. 2008. "Perception as Evidence Accumulation and Bayesian Inference: Insights from Masked Priming." *Journal of Experimental Psychology: General* 137(3): 434–455.

Paap, K. R., and R. W. Noel. 1991. "Dual-route Models of Print to Sound: Still a Good Horse Race." *Psychological Research* 53 (1): 13–24.

Perfetti, C., J. Oakhill, and N. Landi. 2005. "'The Acquisition of Reading Comprehension Skill'." In *The Science of Reading: A Handbook (Part III),* edited by M. Snowling and C. Hulme, 227–247. Oxford: Blackwell Publishing.

Perry, C., J. C. Ziegler, and M. Zorzi. 2007. "Nested Incremental Modeling in the Development of Computational Theories: The CDP+ Model of Reading Aloud." *Psychological Review* 11: 273–315. doi:10.1037/0033-295X.114.2.2732010.

Pinker, S. 2009. *Language Learnability and Language Development.* Cambridge, MA: Harvard University Press.

Powell, D., R. Stainthorp, and M. Stuart. 2014. "Deficits in Orthographic Knowledge in Children Poor at Rapid Automatized Naming (RAN) Tasks." *Scientific Studies of Reading* 18(3): 192–207.

Powell, D., R. Stainthorp, M. Stuart, H. Garwood, and P. Quinlan. 2007. "An Experimental Comparison Between Rival Theories of Rapid Automatized Naming Performance and Its Relationship to Reading." *Journal of Experimental Child Psychology* 98(1): 46–68.

Rose, J. 2006. *Independent Review of the Teaching of Early Reading*. London: Department for Education and Skills.

Rowe, K. 2005. *Teaching Reading: National Inquiry into the Teaching of Literacy*. Canberra, Australia: Department of Education. Science and Training, Australian Council for Educational Research.

Schonell, F. J. 1950. *The Graded Word Reading Test*. Edinburgh: Oliver and Boyd.

Seymour, P. H. K., M. Aro, and J. M. Erskine. 2003. "Foundation Literacy Acquisition in European Orthographies." *British Journal of Psychology* 94(2): 143–174.

Shankweiler, D., and S. Crain. 1986. "Language Mechanisms and Reading Disorder: A Modular Approach." *Cognition* 24(1–2): 139–168.

Share, D. L. 2008. "On the Anglocentricities of Current Reading Research and Practice: The Perils of Overreliance on an 'Outlier' Orthography." *Psychological Bulletin* 134(4): 584–615. doi:10.1037/0033-2909.134.4.584.

Smith, F. 1971. *Understanding Reading: A Psycholinguistic Analysis of Reading and Learning to Read*. New York: Holt: Rinehart and Winston.

Snowling, M. J. 1981. "'Phonemic Deficits in Developmental Dyslexia." *Psychological Research* 43(2): 219–234.

Snowling, M. J. 1991. "Developmental Reading Disorders." *Child Psychology & Psychiatry & Allied Disciplines* 32(1): 49–77.

Snowling, M., and C. Hulme. 1989. "A Longitudinal Case Study of Developmental Phonological Dyslexia." *Cognitive Neuropsychology* 6: 379–401. doi:10.1080/02643298908253289.

Spring, C., and C. Capps. 1974. "Encoding Speed, Rehearsal, and Probed Recall of Dyslexic Boys." *Journal of Educational Psychology* 66(5): 780–786.

Stainthorp, R., and D. Hughes. 1998. "Phonological Sensitivity and Reading: Evidence from Precocious Readers." *Journal of Research in Reading* 21(1): 53–68.

Stainthorp, R., and D. Hughes. 1999. *Learning from Children Who Read at an Early age*. London: Routledge.

Stainthorp, R., and D. Hughes. 2004a. "An Illustrative Case Study of Precocious Reading Ability." *Gifted Child Quarterly* 48 (2): 107–120.

Stainthorp, R., and D. Hughes. 2004b. "What Happens to Precocious Readers' Performance by the age of 11 Years?" *Journal of Research in Reading* 27(4): 357–372.

Stainthorp, R., D. Powell, and M. Stuart. 2013. "The Relationship Between Rapid Naming and Word Spelling in English." *Journal of Research in Reading* 36: 371–388.

Stainthorp, R., D. Powell, M. Stuart, P. Quinlan, and H. Garwood. 2010. "Visual Processing Deficits in Children with Slow RAN Performance." *Scientific Studies of Reading* 14(3): 266–292.

Stanovich, K. E. 1986. "Matthew Effects in Reading: Some Consequences of Individual Differences in the Acquisition of Literacy." *Reading Research Quarterly* 21(4): 360–407.

Stuart, M., J. Masterson, and M. Dixon. 2000. "'Spongelike Acquisition of Sight Vocabulary in Beginning Readers?" *Journal of Research in Reading* 23(1): 12–27.

Torgesen, J. K., R. K. Wagner, C. A. Rashotte, S. Burgess, and S. Hecht. 1997. "Contributions of Phonological Awareness and Rapid Automatic Naming Ability to the Growth of Word-Reading Skills in Second- to Fifth-Grade Children." *Scientific Studies of Reading* 1(2): 161–185.

Wagner, R. K., and J. K. Torgesen. 1987. "The Nature of Phonological Processing and Its Causal Role in the Acquisition of Reading Skills." *Psychological Bulletin* 101(2): 192–212.

Wagner, R. K., J. K. Torgesen, and C. A. Rashotte. 1999. *The Comprehensive Test of Phonological Processing*. Austin, TX: PRO-ED Inc.

Wagner, R. K., J. K. Torgesen, and C. A. Rashotte. 2011. *Test of Word Reading Efficiency 2*. London: Pearson.

Waterland, L. 1985. *Read with Me: An Apprenticeship Approach to Reading*. Stroud: Thimble Press.

Wolf, M., and P. G. Bowers. 1999. "The Double-deficit Hypothesis for the Developmental Dyslexias." *Journal of Educational Psychology* 91(3): 415–438.

Literacies and social practice: sociological perspectives on reading research

Gemma Moss

ABSTRACT
This article considers the distinctive contribution that sociological perspectives have made to understanding reading as a profoundly social and cultural activity, differentiated by the specifics of time and place. Literacy researchers, using a social lens, have sought to explore, explain and redress inequalities in access to and uses of literacy in its different forms. This has often meant championing pedagogies premised on dialogue and connection. Yet this may conflict with an emphasis in current policy on children mastering a relatively narrow skills-based definition of literacy as they begin to learn to read. The article explores how the tension points in the literacy curriculum, intensified in test-based accountability systems, can be navigated in this light.

Introduction

> Viewed sociologically, literacy training is not a matter of who has the right or truthful theory of mind, language, morality or pedagogy. It is a matter of how various theories and practices shape what people do with the technology of writing – and of how, once institutionalised, these selections and constructions serve particular class, cultural and gendered formations. (Luke 1997, 308)

This paper sets out to explore what sociological approaches contribute to understanding reading from a socially-situated perspective. It reviews some of the key ideas that have shaped thinking about literacy as a social practice and what they can contribute to understanding inequalities in literacy attainment and how they might be addressed.

Literacy as a social practice

The distinctive and sizeable body of work on *literacy as a social practice* (sometimes known as the New Literacy Studies) has developed from foundational studies in social anthropology and sociolinguistics (Heath 1983; Street 1984; Michaels 1986; Prinsloo and Baynham 2008). This literature focuses on how acts of reading and writing are shaped by the social contexts in which they take place. The presumption is that reading and writing are best understood as culturally mediated activities rather than as discrete and decontextualised cognitive skills.

The disciplines of anthropology and sociolinguistics give the literature two key concepts that have become integral to the exploration of variation within and between communities in their uses of literacy: the *literacy event* and *literacy practices*. The *literacy event* is defined by Shirley Brice Heath as 'any occasion in which a piece of writing is integral to the nature of the participants' interactions and their interpretative processes' (Heath 1982, 93). Making the event central to data collection, rather than restricting study, as psychology might, to the cognitive processes involved at an individual level, draws attention to how the broader social context helps shape what goes on, through the social interactions between participants that render any event meaningful, as well as the affordances of any material and discursive resources that participants draw on. Studying literacy through the literacy event decentres the role of the written text in meaning making, drawing attention to what else helps define 'what counts as reading' here (See Heap 1991). Reading in school thus instantiates a different logic than reading in the home; and reading in a religious context makes different requirements of readers than reading as part of informal social interactions online. Different roles and resources make things turn out differently.

Studying socially-situated events means taking account of what is particular to this event, involving these participants, in these interactions, taking place at this specific moment in time. But it also means exploring how that event is connected in time and space to other events that participants will already be familiar with, and other settings the resources in this event have travelled through (Brandt and Clinton 2002). Each particular event taps into broader material and discursive histories, acting as a pivot point between past, present and future. Stretching the frame in this way leads to questions about what travels across from one event to another. How do participants recognise the roles they are expected to play here? How do prior knowledge and the constituent resources shape what happens this time round? How does the unexpected or new in this event add to and reformulate what has gone before? In all these ways, studying the event, rather than isolating the individual's response to a particular text, opens up the possibilities of reviewing how literacy functions as part of a broader communicative repertoire, alongside other modes (visual, oral, gestural) and potentially other languages and different scripts too. Elsewhere, the terms multimodality and multiliteracies have helped bring these issues into focus.

The generalised conceptions of reading and writing that participants form through the range of social events in which they participate constitute *literacy practices*. These are the regularities in ways of conceptualising and using literacy that become part of a group or community's cultural repertoire and which they navigate between (Street 1984; Barton and Hamilton 1998). For those using the concepts of literacy events and practices, this is less a matter of identifying a fixed number of stable forms that remain the same across time and place, so much as researching the possibilities that events offer to remake what it means to read and to write each time. Accounts are dynamic. Although the language used to describe events and practices has altered over time, this conception of the ebb and flow to the social dimensions to literacy remains at the core of the literature.

Re-describing what counts as reading: ethnography and multimodality

Literacy as social practice perspectives generated early interest from educationalists, not least because they made visible conflicting definitions of what counts as literacy in and out of school. Research was able to demonstrate the routine privileging of (selective) social norms within the school which led to the marginalising or exclusion of other ways of doing literacy, particularly those associated with disadvantaged communities. Shirley Brice Heath's *Ways with Words* (1983) remains the seminal work here. In her study of children growing up in the two communities of Trackton and Roadville in the south-eastern United States, one black and one white, Heath drew out the very different orientations to the business of language and literacy learning within each community. She showed how these in turn created different kinds of disjuncture for each communities' children as they encountered a very different set of practices in school, while their own went largely unrecognised.

By revealing the logic to each communities' 'ways with words' Heath's research data became a way of prompting schools to think again about presumptions of similarity, based on the school's own values and preferences, that she characterised as much more fully aligned with 'mainstream' or middleclass communities. Her work helped shift the debate over literacy attainment from looking for deficits within marginalised communities to challenging the lack of recognition that schools afford children who bring very different 'funds of knowledge' with them to school (Moll et al. 1992).

To challenge and widen teachers' perceptions of how else literacies can be constituted and mobilised within communities, researchers have adopted a variety strategies. Eve Gregory, Charmian Kenner and colleagues began to study more closely how multi or bilingual children navigate between different scripts as well as different languages in the process of learning to read and write (Gregory et al. 2004). This meant documenting the literacy practices of children and their families in the multilingual and diverse communities of East London. These studies revealed the differently literate worlds that helped shape children's literacy learning in bi or trilingual family settings. Gregory's work in particular highlighted the important role that siblings play in supporting school literacy, something that has often been overlooked in the case of bilingual children (Gregory et al. 2004). Kenner (2004) drew attention to young children's visualisation of different scripts as part of learning to read and write in more than one language, an observation that was taken up by Gunter Kress. Researching in a very different context, Kress himself in his work with Kress and Theo van Leeuwen (1996) on *Reading Images* re-framed how to think about texts by taking into account the varied role that combinations of images and written language play in constructing reading pathways and guiding meaning making, whether in print or online. The concept of multimodality that emerged from this research has laid the groundwork for an increasing number of studies of the changing pattern to literacy practices that combine visual, oral and written modes in new ways (Bezemer, Jewitt, and Van Leeuwen 2019).

Identifying forms of text that have value for children and young people outside of school and that may be marginalised in school raises questions about the kinds of texts schools privilege as the object of school pedagogy. (See, for instance, Kress and Rowsell's discussion of Snapchat and Instagram, where image carries more of the meaning than the written language (Kress and Rowsell 2019, 41–46)). Are these necessary or arbitrary selections, when it comes to the business of teaching literacy? These questions become more urgent as policy becomes much more central in determining literacy curriculum design and delivery.

Many researchers adopting literacy as social practice perspectives are committed to the view that revealing and respecting differences in literacy practices can act as a vehicle for engineering educational change, enabling home and school practices to become more interconnected, and in this way more meaningful to students (Pahl and Rowsell 2006). Yet whether such acts of re-description can actively challenge and reorder literacy teaching in school in ways that substantially advantage marginalised communities has turned out to be much less straightforward than at first thought (Rios-Aguilar et al. 2011). Not least because, as policymakers increasingly emphasise education as a one-way delivery system in which teachers are expected to follow a set curriculum with fidelity, so the space in which to validate other texts and other ways of reading beyond the bounds of the formal curriculum shrinks too (See for instance, (Dernikos and Thiel 2020)). In this context, the kinds of exchanges given value by teachers and by students alters also.

Reconceptualising policy and pedagogy

Policy-driven education reform has brought about changes to teachers' professional standing, a reshaping of teachers' professional knowledge and expertise, as well as the re-ordering of schools' relationships to their local communities. Through the policy tools deployed in high stakes accountability regimes, education has become simultaneously a focus for investment *and* a vehicle for generating stories of comparative failure (Greany and Waterhouse 2016). This combination of attention and blame may help contain the stresses and strains that economic re-structuring brings. It does not solve them.

Keeping this context in mind, this kind of analysis of the interdependent relationship between education and wider social structures leads to a different perspective on what can be changed in and through the literacy curriculum and what cannot. By looking more specifically at the precise economic and material contexts in which schools function locally, the ways in which these wider social conditions impact on pupils' and families' experience of and relationship to education become all too apparent (Hayes et al. 2009; Fine and Weis 2003). The weight of material and social disadvantage that marginalised communities carry, especially when they are disconnected from routes out of deep poverty and can only find limited opportunities for meaningful and well paid employment (Weis 2004) all matter. Indeed, in many respects the distributive principles underpinning education accountability systems only exacerbate matters, leading to schools serving the most deprived communities being the most heavily penalised. High staff turnover and high-pressure management may well follow, resulting in a much poorer curriculum offer for the children concerned (Biesta 2004). Changing curriculum content or emphasising meaning-making at the heart of the literacy curriculum cannot be enough on its own to substantially alter these wider circumstances.

To try and turn this broader state of affairs around, researchers have made concerted efforts to imagine more 'productive pedagogies' that will better meet the needs of economically marginalised communities (Lingard, Hayes, and Mills 2003; Munns 2007; Singh, Märtsin, and Glasswell 2013). The hope is that by reclaiming and rearticulating what constitutes worthwhile pedagogy, it might be possible to create more socially just outcomes for pupils from socially disadvantaged communities that can be sustained over time. Such re-imaginings take into account 'the policy and structural conditions that work against the valuing of teachers and their work' (Lingard, Hayes, and Mills 2003) recognising also the challenges that poverty poses marginalised communities.

Re-framing pedagogic practice

Buried behind different approaches to making literacy pedagogies more productive for socially disadvantaged communities lie the works of two different theorists: the social psychologist, Vygotsky and the sociologist, Bernstein. Both theorise education as profoundly social processes but through different lenses (Daniels 2004). Vygotsky's theoretical framework emerged from his studies of child development and in particular his focus on the role that language, as a culturally-mediated tool, plays in reordering children's thinking and ultimately their knowledge of the world, in and through social interaction with others (Vygotsky 2012). By contrast, Bernstein's theoretical framework developed through studying the principles that underpin the social organisation of education (Bernstein 1996). He focused on how instructional and regulative dimensions interact in the formation of pedagogic discourse, the relay system that produces education as a socially differentiated practice. For Bernstein, the distributive rules pedagogic discourse creates can be seen in the social organisation of the curriculum and in particular the principles of selection, sequencing, pacing and evaluation that any given curriculum might embody.

Both Vygotsky and Bernstein have helped shape thinking about how to create more socially just pedagogies, though their insights have been variously interpreted in the process of transfer into educational contexts at different moments in time. Different readings of the implications of their theoretical frameworks for the social organisation of teaching and learning depend upon: differing conceptions of student agency within educational settings, and their connection to generating purposeful learning environments; how equitable access to valued forms of intellectual inquiry is conceived, when what counts as valuable knowledge and ways of knowing are matters of debate; and the terms under which the school curriculum benefits from being connected to community practices outside its formal structures (Ladwig 2007; Mills et al. 2009). Despite these differences some shared principles have emerged. For instance, Luke (2010), based on a large corpus of systematic lesson observations and a review of the school reform literature, comments that sustained achievement gains among the most 'at risk' students require:

(1) An everyday focus on curriculum content and issues of substantive intellectual demand and depth;
(2) Sustained scaffolded student talk and dialogue around issues of cultural and intellectual substance; and

(3) Visible connections of school knowledge to everyday civic, cultural, political and social life. (Luke 2010)

The Queensland Productive Pedagogies Framework proposed four dimensions, three of which substantially overlap with Luke's: intellectual quality, connectedness, supportive classroom environment, and valuing and working with difference (Mills et al. 2009). The consensus thus rests with a balance of challenge and engagement in the curriculum as enacted in classrooms, such that students are motivated to engage with and at the same time are stretched by the teaching and learning environment. In fact, all too often observational studies have found that regardless of the orientation of teachers to the business of teaching and learning, whether as progressivists or traditionalists, there are many lessons where students complete worksheets, copy from the board, answer questions at the end of chapters and engage in 'busy work'. Further, the assessable tasks set by teachers often focus on lower order domains of activity, such as recall, reassembly of existing and provided information, and skill repetition. The overall picture counters the Vygotskian axiom of stretching students beyond what they can readily do. (Luke 2010)

Lingard, in a review of the Queensland Productive Pedagogies model in action, similarly comments

> What we saw were very supportive and caring teachers, teachers practising an almost social worker version of teachers' work; teacher work as therapy. We believe that teachers should be praised for this, their commitments to social support for students, but that the absence of intellectual demand, connectedness, and working with and valuing difference carries significant social justice implications. (Lingard 2007, 257)

The diagnosis is the reverse of what many policy makers seem to think. The issues are not to do with teaching the basics, still less the question of which particular method of teaching children to read in the early years should prevail – as if that choice alone will make all the difference. Rather it is about opening up what Luke calls 'improved achievement and engaged life pathways, especially amongst the lower performing groups and cohorts' (Luke 2003). Looking over the long term, he argues these pathways should offer students opportunities to meaningfully engage with teaching and learning in the present, and equip them with the resilience to navigate successfully from education into fruitful futures. Creating resourceful, active and engaged students is serious work.

Redesigning the reading curriculum

The challenges of developing more productive pedagogies in schools that can better serve disadvantaged communities rest with the possibilities of creating sustainable pathways through schooling that can combine intellectual challenge with engagement. Work backwards from the texts already in circulation outside school, and this puts the emphasis on finding ways to include students' interests in the literacy classroom. Work backwards from the existing curriculum to generate better outcomes, and this may place more emphasis on making accessible to a wider range of students the kinds of 'powerful genres' that formal education systems value (Hicks 1997). These logics arise and are developed in different contexts. In their own terms both can be understood as inclusive strategies. From a Bernsteinian perspective it is also possible to read them as operating with contrasting modes of social regulation and control: the different forms of pedagogic discourse they deploy imagine the responsibilities and obligations of teachers and pupils differently. Neither is innocent, both will have costs. They will simply fall in different ways. This is as true for literacy as for other areas of the curriculum.

The outside-in approach to shaping productive pedagogies – steering by the objective of incorporating children's interests into the literacy curriculum – fits well with teaching writing. After all, children's intentions as meaning-makers are expected to shape what they write, even in a literacy curriculum dedicated to teaching children powerful forms whose rules they are expected to acquire in order to participate fully within their society – the hope expressed for a curriculum predicated on genre theory (See Luke 1997 for a critical account of the latter). Anne Haas Dyson and

Barbara Comber's attempts to reimagine socially just pedagogies start very much from the bottom up, with what children might have to say (Comber 2016; Dyson 2013). But they also work from an acute sense of how the experience of growing up in poverty shapes the resources that children bring to that task, highlighting the need to create times and spaces where matters of concern for pupils can be listened to and respected within school settings. Their work stretches how we might understand those starting points. A vignette in Dyson's (2013) work shows this dynamic vividly at work: she recalls a school trip to an abandoned building with a large parking lot which the teacher wants pupils to reimagine as a garden. The pupils imagine it as housing – a much more acute need in their lives. The terms of the conversation change.

Being able to acknowledge and articulate the impacts of deprivation in the communities children belong to is as vital for productive literacy-based activities as celebrating the multimodal resources that pupils draw on and can share. Both Dyson and Comber use the full range of children's experience as jumping off points to build 'new ways of talking, new vocabularies and, most importantly, new ways to harness language and other symbolic modes ... for critical ends', as Dyson puts it (Dyson in Comber 2016, xi). Place-based pedagogies of the kind that Comber advocates stress the importance of reflecting on the resources in the immediate locality and using them to design curriculum activities that are conceptually rich. These are ways of working that incorporate agendas that matter to children into the warp and weave of the literacy classroom. They may be particularly important to hang on to in teaching contexts that privilege a skills-based curriculum, where what children have to say is increasingly being drowned out by the long lists of what they need to learn.

The reading curriculum often seems more resistant to being reworked in this way, particularly in the early years. In part this is because many education systems now exercise considerable external control over pace and sequencing in the teaching of reading in the early years, through the tools of assessment and curriculum specification. The reading process is broken down into its component skills, isolated one from another, with the sequence and pace in which each set of skills should be taught tightly specified. This seems to be a consequence of following experimental research traditions in psychology that theory build through studying individual aspects of the reading process separately, then model how they come together and interact (Kendeou, Savage, and Broek 2009). It also fits with the pedagogic assumptions of a synthetic phonics lobby fully convinced that phonics taught in the sequence it specifies, and followed with fidelity, is not only the necessary but also sufficient approach to teaching children to read. The strong version of this belief – that synthetic phonics teaching must take precedence over every other approach or children's futures as competent readers will be jeopardised – is at odds with the wider research literature that recognises that systematic phonics teaching is an important element in learning to read as part of a rich literacy curriculum, but cannot do it all on its own (Savage and Cloutier 2017; Suggate 2016).

When the strong version of the value of synthetic phonics teaching gets taken up in policy, unintended consequences can follow. In the case of the early years literacy curriculum in England, it risks marginalising children's own reading interests in favour of the limited diet of the school's reading scheme, 'closely matched to their developing phonic knowledge' (DfE 2013, 11). This can lead to an increasing push towards restricting reading not just to a reading scheme but to decodable texts where the vocabulary introduced is limited to the phoneme-grapheme correspondences already taught. This is reading as reinforcement for synthetic phonics teaching. Yet, there is little research evidence for the benefits of restricting reading in this way (Cheatham and Allor 2012). Indeed, there are risks that decodable texts may limit comprehension through the contorted syntax they deploy in order to meet their lexical constraints (Price-Mohr and Price 2020). The emphasis on fluent decoding skills as the essential preliminary to reading, rather than a by-product of exercising the skill, leads to an odd positioning of comprehension and reading for pleasure in the curriculum for KS1. These are kept apart from 'word reading' in the National Curriculum with comprehension represented as best supported by listening to the teacher read aloud, on the assumption that this act alone will help pupils learn new vocabulary and understand the structure to written language:

> listening frequently to stories, poems and non-fiction that they cannot yet read for themselves, pupils begin to understand how written language can be structured in order, for example, to build surprise in narratives or to present facts in non-fiction. (DfE 2013)

This is very much a literacy curriculum divided into its constituent parts, each taught in isolation, using different modes. Deviation from the compartmentalisation of the literacy curriculum, and the specified pace and sequence in each of its parts are seen as undesirable. The founding assumption seems to be that the unexpected and unforeseen might disturb the learning process:

> The meaning of some new words should be introduced to pupils before they start to read on their own, so that these unknown words do not hold up their comprehension. (DfE 2013)

This exhortation implies that the meanings of words are fixed, can be known outside of context and can be usefully taught in this way. This departs some way from the radically different theory of learning that Vygotskian social-constructivist perspectives adopt and the radically different theories of language developed in sociolinguistics, psycholinguistics and social semiotics. Here children are understood to actively appropriate and then refashion, through use, the forms of language they acquire in social interaction with others. This is a necessary part of development. The exercise of pupil agency forms an essential part of learning.

From a Bernsteinian perspective, the approach to literacy teaching in the English National Curriculum exemplifies strong classification and framing, through the visibility of curriculum boundaries and the barriers to access they sanction. Synthetic phonics teaching in the prescribed manner is enforced through a phonics screening check with a mandatory pass mark, coupled with the requirement that pupils re-sit the same test in the following year if they fail. Testing decoding skills by asking children to read nonsense words strengthens the belief that skills must be decontextualised to be fully mastered. In all these ways, phonics knowledge becomes the gate-keeper to other reading experiences. Reinforced in England by the high-stakes accountability regime, the reading curriculum narrows. This is not to underestimate the importance of children acquiring good decoding skills. Getting to grips with phoneme-grapheme correspondences in the English writing system is an important part of developing fluent reading. Phonics benefit from being taught systematically, but the evidence does not support fidelity to any specific sequence of segmentation and blending, coupled with restrictions on what children can read for themselves (See Moss et al. 2019 for a very different approach to phonics instruction designed for use with adult learners). This is a policy choice, not a necessity.

Reviewing the tension points in the reading curriculum: proficiency and choice

In tracking the impact of the early reading curriculum in England, there are distinctions to be drawn between phonics research, as a body of knowledge about phoneme-grapheme correspondences and the role they play in developing children's reading fluency; the role that policy plays in shaping phonics pedagogy through curriculum specifications and assessment tools; the reinterpretation that follows in reading schemes and in guidance to teachers; and what actually happens on the ground. Classrooms are themselves dynamic contexts and teachers play an important part in mediating policy and pedagogy in situ. The ways in which the curriculum is enacted, through the social interactions of which it is composed, will help shape how children perceive and understand what it means to read and to be a reader.

Literacy as social practice perspectives provide a useful set of tools through which to capture children's experience of the literacy curriculum. They do so by making central to analysis the literacy events of which the curriculum is composed and the forms of social interaction they sanction in the classroom setting (Moss 2007). Rather than evaluate the merits of a particular method or check the convergence between what policy or a reading scheme stipulates should happen and what actually does, this orientation to research focuses on what the boundaries to practice in each event make visible, and how in their totality these produce different understandings of what it means to be a reader or a writer here (Moss 2007) with consequences for the social dynamic to learning.

Ahead of recent phonics policy, I and fellow researcher Dena Attar used this approach to develop a social explanation for boys' comparative underachievement in reading (Moss 2007). By auditing the terms under which different kinds of texts were mobilised in different literacy events over the course of the day, it was possible to identify three different orientations to the business of reading in class which seemed relatively stable across time and place. These were

- Reading for proficiency – in which how well children read is paramount, often evidenced by the teacher or other adult recording a measure of the child's proficiency as a formal part of the event.
- Reading for choice – in which concepts such as enjoyment or interest were mobilised to justify the choice of text. Choice could be very differently exercised by teacher or child, and with some children's choices restricted by their perceived proficiency
- Procedural reading – reading to get things done. Often little commented on in the classroom, although an important element in keeping the business of teaching and learning going on, this included reading worksheets or reading instructions written on the board, so that other things could happen. The reading itself was not evaluated.

We observed that reading for proficiency was most dominant in terms of how children understood 'what counts as reading here' (Heap 1991). Indeed, children's perceived competence at reading is fundamental to the social geography of the classroom right through the primary school. This predates the introduction of phonics first and fast as policy for literacy pedagogy in English schools. It is reflected in how children are grouped on entry to school, the kinds of texts they are given access to and the choices they can make about what to read, when and how. Language used in the classroom to describe readers – free readers, independent readers – and to describe books – readers, reading scheme, read alones, chapter books – all reflect the hierarchical organisation of reading in the classroom, a reading ladder which positions children in comparison to their peers.

Not only were children fully aware of this, it mattered in terms of how they engaged with the curriculum. In particular, boys placed at the bottom of the proficiency ladder reacted quite differently to that designation from girls. Struggling girl readers were more likely to accept that status, and live with the designation of books that matched their competence, even in contexts where free choice was allowed. Outside of 'proficiency events' – events where the teacher listened to children read texts matched to their competence – some would willingly read 'easy books' with friends much higher up the proficiency ladder. Boys would not. Instead, we documented that struggling boy readers consistently exercised a preference for highly visual non-fiction, whenever they could in the classroom. In distinct contrast to children's fiction texts, such texts created picture-led reading paths on the page in which size of typeface signalled salience of image or commentary, not the reading skill required to deal with the text. These texts became the focus for shared conversations with more able boy readers, with the pictures acting as prompts for what each knew about the topic. In essence this strategy preserved struggling boy readers' self-esteem but at the expense of getting to grips with the skills they lacked. Looking across the dataset it became apparent that the conflict between preserving self-esteem and accepting that they needed help hindered this group from making progress. (See also Moses and Qiao 2018; Solsken 1993; Scherer 2016). Gender and the designation of ability intersected to create different pathways through the literacy curriculum.

Re-orchestrating the parts: building challenge *and* engagement in reading

Studying the events that constitute the enacted curriculum and paying attention to what children make of it, as well as what the teacher intends, are all ways of making sense of literacy learning from a social perspective. It remains an open question how far the changes in the policy environment and a new curriculum settlement have impacted on what children take reading to be and how they react to the hierarchies the reading curriculum creates now. Hierarchies in the reading curriculum are in-built through the formal specifications that control pace and sequencing in the teaching of reading and determine how quickly children will make their way up the reading ladder, via what route. The reading curriculum in the early years instantiates most visibly the modes of social control Bernstein sees running through pedagogic discourse. This is so, regardless of the particular pedagogic approach adopted. Some set out to mask differences between learners, as Basil Bernstein argued invisible pedagogies try to do; others render them highly visible, as the old monitorial system and the division of the student body into ability groups for teaching purposes does. The question is not so much whether such hierarchies exist as how children navigate them.

Certainly, the literacy curriculum in England in its current instantiation risks marooning those who do not acquire phonic decoding skills quickly enough, in line with curriculum expectations, in a decoding cul-de-sac, with fewer and fewer possibilities for finding any other way out. Endlessly repeating what hasn't yet been learnt can only put this group at further and further distance from their peers who plough on. The National Literacy Strategy, through its emphasis on whole class teaching and differentiated group work, tried harder to keep everyone moving along at the same pace, and certainly went to some lengths to ensure that those struggling most with basic decoding weren't shut out from other opportunities to reflect and engage in the rest of the literacy curriculum. Yet it did not work for everyone (Moss 2004).

Moses and Qiao's account (Moses and Qiao 2018) of how a particular teacher 'made space for positive identity negotiations for students with strong or emerging decoding skills' shifts the focus back to the enacted curriculum – what actually happens in the moment by moment interactions between children and teachers in classrooms. From documenting such moments, they show how two focus students were acutely aware of their status as struggling or successful readers in class, and that this influenced how they interacted with their peers. Yet the teacher kept open the possibility of their being more than that by drawing on the struggling reader's meaning-making skills in talking about texts shared in the whole class. Children do not have to be imprisoned by what they cannot yet do. The dosage metaphor in teaching – that children only learn according to the precisely measured inputs they are given – fundamentally obscures how challenge and engagement work as levers for change.

Conclusion

In the introduction to *Pedagogy, Symbolic Control and Identity*, Bernstein (1996) argued for three pedagogic rights: the right to individual enhancement; the right to be included; and the right to participate. He glossed the right to individual enhancement as 'a condition for experiencing boundaries, be they social, intellectual or personal, not as prisons, or stereotypes but as tension points condensing the past *and* opening possible futures' (Bernstein, 1996). The boundaries to current curriculum specifications are amenable to change. We can do this through research, through teachers' mediating actions and most importantly by offering pupils more than the curriculum imagines for them. There is certainly more space to flex teaching and learning in this way in what Luke et al. (2013) call a 'low definition' curriculum. That is a curriculum that anticipates and encourages local adaptation by virtue of being 'less elaborated, detailed and constrained' (Luke et al. 2013, 7). This helps create conditions that ensure broad areas of the curriculum are opened up to all pupils, as matters of equity and inclusion. These are principles worth remembering in policy-constrained times. We should put them into practice where we can.

Disclosure statement

No potential conflict of interest was reported by the author(s).

ORCID

Gemma Moss http://orcid.org/0000-0003-4441-2974

References

Barton, D., and M. Hamilton. 1998. *Local Literacies: Reading and Writing in one Community*. London: Routledge.

Bernstein, B. 1996. *Pedagogy, Symbolic Control and Identity*. London: Taylor & Francis.

Bezemer, J., C. Jewitt, and T. Van Leeuwen. 2019. "Tribute to Gunther Kress (1940–2019): Reflecting on Visuals That Shaped his Work." *Visual Communication* 19 (1): 3–11.

Biesta, G. J. J. 2004. "Education, Accountability, and the Ethical Demand: Can the Democratic Potential of Accountability be Regained?" *Educational Theory* 54 (3): 233–250. doi:10.1111/j.0013-2004.2004.00017.x.

Brandt, D., and K. Clinton. 2002. "Limits of the Local: Expanding Perspectives on Literacy as a Social Practice." *Journal of Literacy Research* 34 (3): 337–356.

Cheatham, J. P., and J. H. Allor. 2012. "The Influence of Decodability in Early Reading Text on Reading Achievement: A Review of the Evidence." *Reading and Writing* 2223–2246. doi:10.1007/s11145-011-9355-2.

Comber, B. 2016. *Literacy, Place, and Pedagogies of Possibility*. New York, NJ: Routledge.

Daniels, H. 2004. "Activity Theory, Discourse and Bernstein." *Educational Review* 56 (2): 121–132. doi:10.1080/0031910410001693218.

Dernikos, B. P., and J. J. Thiel. 2020. "Literacy Learning as Cruelly Optimistic: Recovering Possible Lost Futures Through Transmedial Storytelling." *Literacy* 54 (2): 31–39. doi:10.1111/lit.12207.

DfE (Department for Education). 2013. *English Programmes of Study: Key Stages 1 and 2 National Curriculum in England*. London: HMSO.

Dyson, A. 2013. *Rewriting the Basics: Literacy Learning in Children's Cultures*. New York: Teachers College Press.

Fine, M., and L. Weis. 2003. *Silenced Voices and Extraordinary Conversations: Re-Imagining Schools*. New York: Teachers College Press.

Greany, T., and J. Waterhouse. 2016. "Rebels Against the System." *International Journal of Educational Management* 30 (7): 1188–1206. doi:10.1108/IJEM-11-2015-0148.

Gregory, E., S. Long, and D. Volk, eds. 2004. *Many Pathways to Literacy: Young Children Learning with Siblings, Grandparents, Peers, Communities*. London: Routledge.

Hayes, D., R. Hattam, B. Comber, L. Kerkham, P. Thomson, and R. Lupton. 2009. *Literacy, Leading and Learning: Beyond Pedagogies of Poverty*. New York, NY: Routledge.

Heap, J. 1991. "A Situated Perspective on What Counts as Reading." In *Towards a Critical Sociology of Reading: Papers of the XII World Congress on Reading*, edited by A. Luke and C. Baker. Amsterdam: John Benjamins.

Heath, S. B. 1982. "What no Bedtime Story Means: Narrative Skills at Home and School." *Language and Society* 11 (1): 49–76.

Heath, S. B. 1983. *Ways with Words*. Cambridge: Cambridge University Press.

Hicks, D. 1997. "Working through Discourse Genres in School." *Research in the Teaching of English* 31 (4): 459–485.

Kendeou, P., R. Savage, and P. Broek. 2009. "Revisiting the Simple View of Reading." *British Journal of Educational Psychology* 79 (2): 353–370. doi:10.1348/978185408X369020.

Kenner, C. 2004. *Becoming Biliterate: Young Children Learning Different Writing Systems*. Stoke on Trent: Trentham Books.

Kress, G., and J. Rowsell. 2019. "Literacy as a Social Practice: New Realities and New Models." In *Re-theorizing literacy practices: complex social and cultural contexts*, edited by D. Bloome, M. L. Castanheira, C. Leung, and J. Rowsell. New York: Routledge.

Kress, G., and T. Van Leeuwen. 1996. *Reading Images*. London: Routledge.

Ladwig, J. G. 2007. "Modelling Pedagogy in Australian School Reform." *Pedagogies: An International Journal* 2 (2): 57–76. doi:10.1080/15544800701343919.

Lingard, B. 2007. "Pedagogies of Indifference." *International Journal of Inclusive Education* 11 (3): 245–266. doi:10.1080/13603110701237498.

Lingard, B., D. Hayes, and M. Mills. 2003. "Teachers and Productive Pedagogies: Contextualising, Conceptualising, Utilising." *Pedagogy, Culture and Society* 11 (3): 399–424. doi:10.1080/14681360300200181.

Luke, A. 1997. "Genres of Power: Literacy Education and the Production of Capital." In *Literacy in Society*, edited by R. Hasan and G. Williams, 308–338. London: Longman.

Luke, A. 2003. "After the Marketplace: Evidence, Social Science and Educational Research." *Australian Educational Researcher* 34 (2): 87–107. doi:10.1007/bf03216792.

Luke, A. 2010. "Will the Australian Curriculum up the Intellectual Ante in Primary Classrooms?" *Curriculum Perspectives* 30 (3): 59–64.

Luke, A., A. Woods, and K. Weir. 2013. "Curriculum Design, Equity and the Technical form of the Curriculum." In *Curriculum, Syllabus Design, and Equity: A Primer and Model*, edited by A, Luke, A. Woods, and K. Weir. New York: Routledge.

Michaels, S. 1986. "Narrative Presentations: An Oral Preparation for Literacy with First Graders." In *The Social Construction of Literacy*, edited by J. Cook-Gumperz. Cambridge: Cambridge University Press.
Mills, M., M. Goos, A. Keddie, E. Honan, D. Pendergast, R. Gilbert, K. Nichols, P. Renshaw, and T. Wright. 2009. "Productive Pedagogies: A Redefined Methodology for Analysing Quality Teacher Practice." *Australian Educational Researcher* 36 (3): 67–87. doi:10.1007/BF03216906.
Moll, L. C., C. Amanti, D. Neff, and N. González. 1992. "Funds of Knowledge for Teaching: Using a Qualitative Approach to Connect Homes and Classrooms." *Theory Into Practice* 31 (2): 132–141.
Moses, L., and X. Qiao. 2018. "Literate Identity Development in First Grade: A Cross-Case Analysis of Students with Strong and Emerging Decoding Skills." *Journal of Language and Literacy Education* 14 (2): 1–30.
Moss, G. 2004. "Changing Practice: The National Literacy Strategy and the Politics of Literacy Policy." *Literacy* 38 (3): 126–133.
Moss, G. 2007. *Literacy and Gender, Researching Texts, Contexts and Readers*. Abingdon: Routledge.
Moss, G., G. Brooks, J. Brown, M. Burton, C. Collins, A. Convery, S. Duncan, T. Millar, B. Read, and I. Schwab. 2019. *Post-16 Phonics Approaches: A Toolkit*. London: Education and Training Foundation.
Munns, G. 2007. "A Sense of Wonder: Pedagogies to Engage Students who Live in Poverty." *International Journal of Inclusive Education* 11 (3): 301–315. doi:10.1080/13603110701237571.
Pahl, K., and J. Rowsell. 2006. *Travel Notes from the New Literacy Studies: Instances of Practice*. Clevedon: Multilingual Matters.
Price-Mohr, R., and C. Price. 2020. "A Comparison of Children Aged 4–5 Years Learning to Read Through Instructional Texts Containing Either a High or a low Proportion of Phonically-Decodable Words." *Early Childhood Education Journal* 48 (1): 39–47. doi:10.1007/s10643-019-00970-4.
Prinsloo, M., and M. Baynham, eds. 2008. *Literacies, Global and Local*. Amsterdam: John Benjamins.
Rios-Aguilar, C., J. Marquez Kiyama, M. Gravitt, and L. Moll. 2011. "Funds of Knowledge for the Poor and Forms of Capital for the Rich? A Capital Approach to Examining Funds of Knowledge." *Theory and Research in Education* 9 (2): 163–184. doi:10.1177/1477878511409776.
Savage, R., and E. Cloutier. 2017. "Early Reading Interventions: The State of the Practice, and Some New Directions in Building Causal Theoretical Models." In *Theories of Reading Development*, edited by K. Cain, D. Compton, and R. Parrila. Amsterdam: John Benjamins.
Scherer, L. 2016. "'I am not Clever, They are Cleverer Than Us': Children Reading in the Primary School." *British Journal of Sociology of Education* 37 (3): 389–407. doi:10.1080/01425692.2014.948989.
Singh, P., M. Märtsin, and K. Glasswell. 2013. "Knowledge Work at the Boundary: Making a Difference to Educational Disadvantage. Learning." *Culture and Social Interaction* 2: 102–110. doi:10.1016/j.lcsi.2013.02.001.
Solsken, J. W. 1993. *Literacy, Gender, and Work in Families and Schools*. Norwood, NJ: Ablex.
Street, B. 1984. *Literacy in Theory and Practice*. Cambridge: Cambridge University Press.
Suggate, S. P. 2016. "A meta-Analysis of the Long-term Effects of Phonemic Awareness, Phonics, Fluency, and Reading Comprehension Interventions." *Journal of Learning Disabilities* 49 (1): 77–96.
Vygotsky, L. 2012. *Thought and Language*. Cambridge, MA: MIT Press.
Weis, L. 2004. *Class Reunion: The Remaking of the American White Working Class*. Routledge Taylor & Francis Group. doi:10.4324/9780203311578.

Perspectives on dealing with reading difficulties

Sinéad Harmey

ABSTRACT
Learning to read is an expectation rather than an exception in society today. Despite this, some children experience reading difficulties. The purpose of this article is to review recent and seminal research on reading difficulties through the lenses of three perspectives: cognitive, social and cultural and interactive. The three perspectives are reviewed and the contribution they make to our understandings of how to support children with reading difficulties are considered. The implication of these perspectives on instruction is explored by examining one contentious contemporary debate in the field of reading instruction; choice of texts to support reading development. To conclude, an argument for a more holistic approach to reading difficulties is provided with reference to two contemporary assessment tools.

Learning to read is a fundamental skill. In 1820, only 12% of the world's population could read, whereas today only approximately 14% of the population are unable to read (Roser and Ortiz-Ospina 2016). Learning to read, therefore, is an expectation rather than an exception and standards of literacy across the world have risen exponentially in the last two centuries. Despite this, some children do experience difficulties learning to read and these difficulties can persist into adulthood (Every Child a Chance Trust 2009).

Given that reading is an expectation, difficulties in reading can have profound effects that span social, emotional, and economic spheres. Childhood reading is linked to later cognitive progress in teenage years (Sullivan and Brown 2013). Early difficulties in reading are also associated with risks for mental health illnesses in adulthood (Boyes et al. 2016). There is, however, substantial evidence that early literacy intervention can reduce the incidences of reading difficulties and improve later life circumstances (Brooks 2016; Mathes and Denton 2002; Stanovich 1986; Vellutino et al. 2004).

In this article, I provide an argument as to why it is important to consider the theoretical foundations of perspectives about reading difficulties. I then review why children might have reading difficulties through the lens of three different theoretical perspectives. To do this I:

- Provide a summary of the perspective, discussing how difficulties might be framed;
- Review some seminal and contemporary pieces of research about reading and reading difficulties by researchers from each respective perspective;
- Critique the affordances and limitations of each perspective;
- Consider the implications adopting each perspective has for instruction of children experiencing reading difficulties.

I explore the implications diverse perspectives have on policy and practice through an exploration of the case of choice of texts to support reading development; a key contemporary and contentious issue in the field of reading, particularly in England. To conclude, an argument for a more holistic approach to reading difficulties is provided with reference to two contemporary assessment tools.

Perspectives on reading difficulties: controversy and consensus

Why might some children have difficulty learning to read? This is a complex issue as answers will always be framed, consciously or unconsciously, by the theories of reading held by literacy researchers or teachers (Alexander and Fox 2013). This shapes the foci of studies, how findings are interpreted and, ultimately, has implications for how children are taught.

While the field of literacy research has come far in terms of understanding why children might have difficulty learning to read, the field also remains divided in terms of what factors are thought to underlie reading difficulties and how best to ameliorate these difficulties through intervention and instruction. Few would be unfamiliar with the notion of the 'Reading Wars', which persists in the popular press with headlines like *'Reading Taught the Wrong Way'* (Hanford 2018) and *'An old and contested solution to boost reading scores'* (Goldstein 2020) and in even in peer reviewed journals with titles like *'Ending the Reading Wars: Reading Acquisition from Novice to Expert'* (Castles, Rastle, and Nation 2018).

The recent to and fro between the International Literacy Association (ILA) and the International Dyslexia Association (IDA) on the subject of dyslexia is a good example of the lack of agreement in the field. In 2016, the expert panel of the ILA (2016a) issued a research brief on dyslexia. The panel concluded that when instruction is responsive to students' individual needs, the percentage of children with persistent difficulties is small (below 2%) (c.f. Vellutino et al. 2004). They suggested that while genetics and neurology 'played a role in reading difficulties … environment and instruction moderate that role' (2). They stated that dyslexia is not a result of visual difficulties (for example, letter reversals), agreed that the analysis and manipulation of sounds is a key factor in dyslexia and severe reading difficulties but that there was no empirically proven preferred method to teach children with dyslexia. The key focus of the ILA recommendation was on the instructional experiences of the learner.

The International Dyslexia Association (IDA) (2016) issued a position statement in response to the ILA research brief that refuted some of the conclusions of the ILA, in particular the conclusion that there was no preferred way to teach children with reading difficulties. Rather the IDA suggested that interventions must have a clear focus on phonological coding. The IDA, in contrast to the ILA, focused on the cognitive factors underpinning reading difficulties and set foci for instruction. In response, the ILA (2016b) published an addendum refuting and discussing the IDA response in more detail.

While debate is important, lack of consensus creates confusion for those who teach children. It follows, therefore, that answering the question 'why might some children have difficulty learning to read' is not straightforward. Instead of looking for consensus, I propose to address the issues at stake by considering how researchers operating from different perspectives answer this question.

Cognitive perspectives

I begin by considering research into reading framed by cognitive perspectives. Theories, models, and frameworks of reading like the Simple View of Reading (Gough and Tunmer 1986; Hoover and Gough 1990), the interactive model of reading (Rumelhart 2013), dual-route model of reading (see Coltheart 2005), literacy processing theory (Clay 2001), and the phase theory of sight word reading (Ehri 2005) all consider what occurs 'in the head' of the reader as they process written text.

Taken together, these theories establish that there is a range of cognitive skills that, in early childhood, are either precursors to later reading ability, underlie reading ability in later schooling, or are used or orchestrated as a reader extracts meaning from text. How development occurs or proceeds is described differently within these models. Some focus exclusively on the development of word reading (Ehri 2005), the processing of visual, semantic, and syntactic information (Doyle 2013; Rumelhart 2013), how the processes of decoding and listening comprehension result in reading comprehension (Gough and Tunmer 1986), or how text is comprehended (Kintsch 2013). Some describe development as stage like (c.f. Ehri 2005), whereas others describe the interactive nature of development (Clay in Doyle 2013) as it changes over time. Others point to the factors involved in skilled reading or deficient in those with reading difficulties (Gough and Tunmer 1986). Taken together, the main areas of consensus from this perspective are the importance of phonological awareness, decoding, and reading comprehension.

Phonological awareness

Phonological awareness is defined as 'an awareness of sounds in spoken (not written) words' (Stahl and Murray 1994, 221) and treated as a key underlying cognitive skill in the development of skilled reading. Research shows it to both be a prerequisite to and consequence of becoming literate (Snowling and Hulme 2012; Duff and Clarke 2011). Al Otaiba and Fuchs (2002) in a review of research that investigated children who did not respond to literacy intervention, found that in 70% of the studies, the children had difficulties in phonological awareness.

Decoding

In an alphabetic system, learning how to map sounds to print is essential if children are to decode successfully and derive meaning from print. In English, children need to map phonemes to graphemes (sounds to individual letters) as well as a groups of letters (see Castles, Rastle, and Nation 2018 for a full discussion). Difficulties in word identification are associated with more basic difficulties in alphabetic coding which underlie most reading difficulties (Vellutino et al. 2004). Word identification constitutes a reader's ability to access knowledge of the orthographic, phonological, semantic, and morpho-syntactic properties of the word and is also essential. For example, Murphy and Farquharson (2016) found in a recent longitudinal study, children's ability to access these sources of knowledge was related to later reading difficulties.

Language and reading comprehension

Text is language in written form. Language skills, and the ability to comprehend and understand written language, in addition to the code related skills described above are an essential part of skilled reading (Oakhill *et al.* 2014; Perfetti, Landi, and Oakhill 2005). Oral language skills, working memory, vocabulary knowledge and comprehension monitoring and meaning-making skills like inference are all related to reading ability (Castles, Rastle, and Nation 2018). Research suggests that children with difficulties in reading comprehension demonstrate unique profiles (Cain and Oakhill 2006, 694) rather than having a single cause. In a study examining the profiles of children with poor comprehension but accurate word reading, Cain and Oakhill (ibid) concluded that difficulties in reading comprehension are complex but that, in general poor vocabulary and cognitive ability are closely related to poor word reading and reading comprehension respectively. In sum, this body of research suggests that typical reading development depends upon a range of cognitive skills that are both code-related and language related (Storch and Whitehurst 2002). Difficulties in reading development may stem from difficulties in any one of these areas and these are, in many ways, related and dependent upon each other.

Implications of this perspective

Framing reading difficulties from this perspective identifies the different cognitive processes that underlie reading development and difficulties. Such attention, provides invaluable information for teachers on the foci for literacy assessment, instruction, and intervention. Given the importance of decoding, phonological awareness, vocabulary, alphabet knowledge and language it is essential that any early literacy curriculum or reading intervention addresses these areas (Foorman et al. 2016).

How are these best taught? The National Reading Panel (National Institute of Child Health and Development [NICHD]) (2000), The National Early Literacy Panel (National Institute for Literacy 2008) and, more recently, the expert panel of the What Works Clearinghouse (Foorman et al. 2016) all recommended that children need to be taught how to listen for, identify, and segment individual sounds in speech. Indeed, in a recent meta-analysis, Suggate (2016) found that pure phonemic awareness interventions (as opposed to phonics and phonemic awareness) demonstrated greater effect sizes at follow-up.

Teaching children how to decode and link letter-sound knowledge is also essential and is best taught via systematic phonics instruction (Brooks 2016; Education Endowment Foundation 2017; NICHD 2000; Torgerson et al. 2019). What is less clear, however, is the best way to teach phonics. While many advocate for systematic synthetic phonics (see Rose 2006) empirical evidence identifying a 'best method' (see Torgerson et al. 2019 for a full discussion) is mixed. As Castles, Rastle, and Nation (2018) concluded, 'the evidence is not yet sufficient that a synthetic phonics approach should be preferred over an analytic one' (13). This stands in contrast to the OFSTED (2017) assertion that 'systematic synthetic phonics is the route to reading' (7).

Understanding text read is a complex process and some with reading difficulties struggle to gain meaning from text read (Duff and Clarke 2011). While decoding is necessary it is not sufficient and the development of language (Education Endowment Foundation 2017; Hulme et al. 2020) and comprehension skills, particularly in academic language and talk that supports the use of inferential language (Foorman et al. 2016) must be encouraged (EEF 2017). Readers need to be able to make inferences, monitor their understanding of text read, apply background knowledge, and develop coherence between words and ideas at sentence, paragraph, and text level (Cain 2010). Instruction, therefore, must also maintain a focus on making meaning. Brooks (2016) concluded that there is evidence that the comprehension skills of struggling readers can be improved if targeted.

Framing reading difficulties from a cognitive perspective permits teachers to consider what needs to be assessed and taught to support reading development. However, attending to cognitive factors only neglects the factors that lie outside the child. Research on the cognitive factors involved in reading difficulties foregrounds what goes on in the head of readers as they interact with text. This foreshadows the emotional, cultural, and instructional factors that are involved in the reading process.

Social and cultural perspectives

While it may be more typical to frame reading in terms of the cognitive factors that underlie the difficulties children may have in reading, there is a body of research that frames reading in terms of the social and cultural factors that can also contribute to our knowledge about reading difficulties. A range of researchers study reading as both a social practice (Heath 1982) and a cultural event (Dyson 1993; Freebody and Luke 1990; Kress 2003; Rowe 1994). In terms of reading difficulties, researchers operating from this perspective propose that literacy teachers should focus less on skill development and instead consider whether school culture and teaching practices may limit the opportunities students have to develop as readers (Alvermann 2001). For example, Freebody and Luke (1990), argue that reading is more than decoding and that readers need to learn to become active text participants, users, and analysts. Readers bring cultural and social backgrounds to the interpretation of any text. What they comprehend and infer will be influenced by readers active participation in the negotiation of meaning, their use of knowledge gained from elsewhere as well as prior reading and their critical analysis of the text.

The negotiation of meaning is dependent on culture and culture is reflected in language use bound by culture and history (Lee 2013). Differences in language can act as barriers to participation in literacy for both second language learners and those who speak non-mainstream dialects of English (Cazden 1988; Lee 2006). This was clearly illustrated by Heath's (1982) seminal ethnographic study of the development of language and literacy in three communities (middle class, a white Appalachian community, and a black rural community) and the dichotomies she found between ways of using language at home and at preschool for some of these communities. As Kress (2003) argued, 'the more pronounced the cultural differences, the greater are the differences in the resources of representations and in the practices of their use' (27). In other words, how readers access text (traditional written text or multimodal texts) is mediated by the differences between the cultural background of the meaning maker and the author.

Reading difficulties influence student identity (Hall 2012). In a recent case study, (Kabuto and Harmey 2020) a student defined by his teacher as struggling with reading and writing defined himself in the same terms. This impacted his ability to engage with text. The levels and labels assigned by the teacher acted as gatekeepers to whether he would attempt to read a book, regardless of whether he could read it accurately. Our findings echoed those of Kontovourki (2012) who found that the level assigned to children often became internalised, limiting what they thought they could do. Equally, Morgan et al. (2008) found that early reading failure co-varied with lack of motivation and student 'avoidance of reading' (p.387).

Implications

Rather than looking at what a child cannot do, framing literacy from a social and cultural perspective challenges educators to consider what is happening outside of the child to create or exacerbate reading difficulties. Focusing on education in the USA Gutiérrez, Morales, and Martinez (2009) argued:

> From this perspective, attention shifts to how the social organization of American classrooms first arranges for children to look like failures and then attributes their lack of success to racial, gender, language, or community membership. (223)

This perspective tests the idea of best practices for children with literacy difficulties. Smagorinsky argued that 'best practices' cannot be applied universally without attention to 'contexts, cultures, and worldviews' (299). This is a useful reminder. It draws attention to the need to think about the pupil in the round and the opportunities the curriculum offers those who appear to struggle the most to remedy their difficulties. However, in and of itself such advice may not be enough. For those that work directly with children with literacy difficulties it provides little specific guidance on instruction or assessment. Given that we know that certain cognitive factors are known to both predict and underlie difficulties can we afford to focus less on them?

An interactive perspective

An interactive perspective of reading difficulties is one that acknowledges that reading difficulties emanate from a range of different interacting factors – cognitive, social, and instructional – all of which may influence the outcomes of the learning process (Wilkinson and Anderson 1995). While some factors may be easier to ameliorate than others, all need to be accounted for.

Ruddell and Unrau (2013) have developed a socio-cognitive model that exemplifies this perspective which they call 'reading as a motivated meaning-construction process' (1015). Within their model of reading the negotiation of meaning is dependent on multiple factors including but not limited to the reader and his or her use or employment of cognitive conditions and executive functions but also taking into account the interaction between these factors, the text, and the teacher within an instructional context. Without looking at these range of interacting factors, as McNaughton, Phillips, and MacDonald (2003) stated, one can be misled to think that 'a dose of instruction in a component is guaranteed immunity against low-progress' (705). Rather, from this perspective, as Foorman (2007) summarised achievement is a product of the interaction between the child and instruction.

A recent study that clearly demonstrates that gains in reading could be explained by instructional practices was a study on scaffolding by Rodgers et al. (2016) in the context of Reading Recovery (RR), an early literacy intervention that has clearly established positive effects on early literacy achievement (see D'Agostino and Harmey 2016). In this study, my co-authors and I examined the differences between the language used during instructional interactions between RR teachers and struggling readers. We found that teachers of children who achieved higher outcomes in the intervention were more likely to be able to prompt children to use information (meaning, structure, or visual information) that they neglected. In sum, we found that variation in outcomes was related to teaching.

Instruction and teacher professional development matters. Egert, Fukkink, and Eckhardt (2018), in a recent meta-analysis examining links between professional development and child outcomes, found that there was a medium effect related to the effect of teacher in-service training on child outcomes at classroom level but a small effect at child level in terms of outcomes like language, literacy, and cognition. Markussen-Brown et al. (2017) conducted a best-evidence review of the effects of language and literacy-focused professional development (PD) on both educators and children. They had mixed results and found that while PD had the potential to improve language and literacy that effects were related to intensity and duration.

Implications

This perspective demands an exploration of reading difficulties in the instructional context that they occur in and thus, shifts priority from focusing solely on either cognitive factors or context to the interaction between the both in an instructional context. Access to a teacher, therefore, with sound knowledge of the reading process is an essential factor in both the prevention and intervention of reading difficulties.

While the extent to which quality teaching impacts literacy development is unclear it is clear that content knowledge and access to intense sustained PD is essential. Reid and Weiser (2009) asserted that it is not enough for teachers to understand about the components of reading like phonics and comprehension – they must also know how these components interact and develop over time towards skilled reading and that 'knowledge of content and pedagogy must be melded with engaging, vibrant materials and meaningful, instructional interactions (p.477).

Perspectives influence policy and practice: the case of beginning texts

In the three sections above, I contrasted views of reading difficulties which place the 'locus' of the difficulty inside the child, outside the child or as an interaction between both. In this section, I exemplify how these perspectives in practice influence practice by examining the case of beginning reading texts. Many research syntheses have demonstrated the necessity to orchestrate reading connected text (c.f. Foorman et al. 2016). A key tenet of quality early literacy instruction is the provision of high-quality texts as beginning reading material. At a basic level, these texts provide the opportunity to practice the cognitive act of reading but also create opportunities for social and cultural engagement with story.

The premise of most types of beginning reading books is the control of vocabulary within the books although how vocabulary is controlled differs according to the metric used and the theory of reading that informs the approach (Price-Mohr and Price 2020). One type of beginning reading book is a decodable text. Mesmer (2000) defined decodable text as one that has 'a proportion of words with phonically regular relationships between letters and sounds' (122) and only matches what readers have been taught. These types of texts are theoretically influenced by perspectives that attend to the cognitive skills that need to be developed while reading; namely decoding.

Authentic texts or whole language texts, in contrast adhere to natural language patterns and there is no control of vocabulary or text features to simplify the text for the beginning reader. As Goodman and Goodman (1981) stated in advocating for them, these reading books should have all the features of real language. Such books privilege a perspective in which meaning is privileged over cognitive skills. Other types of books like banded or levelled books contain text features which control a range of factors but also try to adhere to general principles in terms of features of print (e.g. line placement), content, syntactical structures, number of decodable words, and length (Mesmer, Cunningham, and Hiebert 2012). These books therefore, reflect an approach that attends to language and decoding skills.

So which types of texts are most supportive of young readers? This is a contentious issue, which has links to theoretical orientations to reading which are beyond the scope of this article. What is clear is that the use of decodable texts alone is not empirically proven. And yet, in England, recent guidelines from OFSTED (2019) stated that it was important that 'reading books connect closely to the phonics knowledge pupils are taught when they are learning to read' (51). Indeed, in a recent document, Bold Beginnings (OFSTED 2017), a report which examined provision in reception in successful schools, the inspectorate stated that while story time was important, that children's reading should match phonic knowledge and that reading books should 'match the code' (p.21) that children had been taught.

Price-Mohr and Price (2020) suggest that numerous studies have failed to find evidence of positive effects from decodable texts. Mesmer (2000) in a review of research on decodable texts asserted that while there may be a developmental window when decodable texts may be useful there is a need for much more research on the efficacy of decodable texts which needs to focus on how much decodability is needed and when it is useful. This was reiterated by Castles *et al.* (2018) who stated that decodable texts have a limited window of usefulness but limit children's exposure to vocabulary and complex sentence structure. This fitted with a study by Frey (2012) who found that between groups of high, middle, and low achieving first grade readers that decodable texts seemed to only benefit the middle group. Jenkins et al. (2004) found no difference between groups of at-risk beginning readers who had received supplemental tutoring with more or less decodable texts. Indeed, Mohr and Price, found in a study comparing the use of low and high phonically decodable texts that there was a large effect in terms of comprehension in terms of low-phonically decodable texts. Mesmer (2010) found in a study that compared reading accuracy on decodable versus levelled texts, similar to those used in Reading Recovery (Clay 2016), levelled texts provided favourable results in terms of reading rates in terms of fluency. She concluded that levelled texts had a 'pronounced fluency advantage … due to the similarity of the language of books and the language of children (35)

Mesmer, Cunningham, and Hiebert (2012), argued that the debate needs to move beyond the false dichotomy of beginning reading focusing on word and parts (decodable texts) and 'texts as wholes' (authentic or levelled texts). Indeed, they argued that focusing on word recognition alone is short-sighted, and a confusion of 'means with ends' (252). They suggest that over simplified texts fail students long term, not least when they encounter the demands of complex texts in later school years that depend upon higher level comprehension skills. Indeed, Cheatham and Allor (2012) argued that decodability should be seen as a key feature of a text (amongst others) but not a type of text alone. This clearly is a challenge in the English education system where despite the now sustained focus on systematic synthetic phonics and use of decodable texts.

What of the social and cultural influence of and relevance of these texts? While the issues described previously relate to the utility of decodable texts for the use and employment of cognitive processes, the social and cultural relevance and effects of these beginning of texts as the reader interacts with the text is often neglected. In terms of reader identity, Kontovourki (2012) found that levelled texts began to frame reader's identities or how students framed their ability. This was echoed in the previously described case study by Kabuto and Harmey (2020) of a young reader so bound by the level he restricted his reading to what was deemed 'easy' enough for him.

Few studies have looked at how the cultural and linguistic features of text impact reading comprehension (Shepard-Carey 2019). In an exploration of the inference-making of primary multilingual student, Shepard-Carey found that ability to make inferences were highly contextual and depended on language and background knowledge. If reading is perceived as a social practice texts must also in some way reflect the life, language, and community of the child (Rushton 2007).

Buescher, Lightner, and Kelly (2016) argued that children develop concepts about culture, race, and gender from schooling and this must include the beginning reading texts.

Taking an interactive perspectives, texts provide opportunities to rehearse the skills of decoding and comprehension monitoring. One cannot neglect, however, that reading is essentially a meaning construction activity (Ruddell and Unrau 2013) and that texts can also act to constrain the development they are intended to support. In addition, from a social and cultural perspective, development as reader requires development of identity as reader and to see themselves reflected back in that which they read (Bishop 1990)

Conclusion

Rather than engaging in 'wars' over the best ways to deal with reading difficulties perhaps a merging of different perspectives is warranted. A more holistic perspective would demand attention to the cognitive factors involved in skilled reading with great attention to the interactions between teacher and student and an acknowledgement that instructional practices cannot be applied without attention to social and cultural contexts.

Two examples of a holistic perspective put into practice are the Three Knowledge Domains literacy assessment tool proposed by Ellis and Smith (2017) and the Biographic Literacy Profile 2.0 (Kabuto and Harmey 2020). Ellis and Smith's tool was used by student teachers working in a literacy clinic. The tool, a Venn diagram of three knowledge domains, was used to draw teachers attention to three domains of reading during assessment; the reader's cognitive knowledge and skills, his or her personal-social identity as a reader, and the cultural and social capital the reader brought to the task. Kabuto and Harmey (2020) proposed the Biographic Literacy Profile 2.0 as a tool for teachers to document a learner's skills and knowledge as well as their histories and identities as readers based on their work with a reluctant reader. In this tool, we provided questions as prompts to guide teachers to document observable behaviours of inferred cognitive problem-solving during the act of reading and writing. We proposed, however, that any such assessment must first start with a biography of the child as a learner that must be constantly re-evaluated as children move through different instructional contexts. Positioning the teacher as a biographer who documents a child's history of literacy learning (including but not limited to their likes and dislikes) permits a more nuanced co-construction of instruction with the student. Both tools fits with Unrau and Alvermann's (2013) description of work which may stimulate more 'creative resolutions, stir new insights, and spawn new understandings to explain' (85) how to deal with reading difficulties.

Learning to read, for most, is as complex cognitive process that when orchestrated with ease is used to enter social and cultural worlds through literacies. Difficulties in literacy development can occur for a range of reasons, it's incumbent on teachers to consider the multiple aspects that may cause or exacerbate reading difficulties.

Disclosure statement

No potential conflict of interest was reported by the author(s).

ORCID

Sinéad Harmey http://orcid.org/0000-0003-2846-5064

References

Alexander, P., and E. Fox. 2013. "'A Historical Perspective on Reading Research and Practice, Redux'." In *Theoretical Models and Processes of Reading*, edited by D. E. Alvermann, N. Unrau, and R. B. Ruddell, 636–657. Newark, DE: International Reading Association.

Al Otaiba, S., and D. Fuchs. 2002. "Characteristics of Children who are Unresponsive to Early Literacy Intervention: A Review of the Literature." *Remedial and Special Education* 23: 300–316. doi:10.1177/07419325020230050501.

Alvermann, D. 2001. "'Reading Adolescents' Reading Identities: Looking Back to See Ahead'." *Journal of Adolescent and Adult Literacy* 44 (8): 676–690.

Bishop, R. S. 1990. "'Mirrors, Windows, and Sliding Glass Doors'." *Perspectives: Choosing and Using Books for the Classroom* 6: ix–xi.

Boyes, M. E., S. Leitao, M. Claessen, N. A. Badcock, and M. Nayton. 2016. "'Why are Reading Difficulties Associated with Mental Health Problems?" ' *Dyslexia* 22 (3): 263–266. doi:10.1002/dys.1531.

Brooks, G. 2016. "What Works for Pupils with Literacy Difficulties?" Dyslexia-SPLD Trust. https://www.helenarkell.org.uk/documents/files/What-works-for-children-and-young-people-with-literacy-difficulties-5th-edition.pdf.

Buescher, E., S. C. Lightner, and R. H. Kelly. 2016. "Diversity of Authors and Illustrators in First Grade Core Reading Series." *Multicultural Education* 23: 31–37.

Cain, K. 2010. *Reading Difficulties and Development*. Cornwall: British Psychological Society and Blackwell Publishing.

Cain, K., and J. Oakhill. 2006. "Profiles of Children with Specific Reading Comprehension Difficulties." *British Journal of Educational Psychology* 76: 683–696. doi:10.1348/000709905X67610.

Castles, A., K. Rastle, and K. Nation. 2018. "Ending the Reading Wars: Reading Acquisition From Novice to Expert." *Psychological Science in the Public Interest* 19 (1): 5–51. doi:10.1177/1529100618772271.

Cazden, C. 1988. *Classroom Discourse: The Language of Teaching and Learning*. Portsmouth, NH: Heinemann.

Cheatham, J. P., and J. H. Allor. 2012. "The Influence of Decodability in Early Reading Text on Reading Achievement: A Review of the Evidence." *Reading and Writing* 25: 2223–2246. doi:10.1007/s11145-011-9355-2.

Clay, M. M. 2001. *Change Over Time in Children's Literacy Development*. Portsmouth, NH: Heinemann.

Clay, M. M. 2016. *Literacy Lessons Designed for Individuals*. Portsmouth, NH: Heinemann.

Coltheart, M. 2005. "Modeling reading: The dual route approach." In *The Science of Reading: A Handbook*, edited by M. J. Snowling and C. Hulme, 6–23. Malden, MA: Blackwell Publishers.

D'Agostino, J. V., and S. J. Harmey. 2016. "An International Meta-Analysis of Reading Recovery." *Journal of Education for Students Placed at Risk (JESPAR)* 21 (1): 29–46. doi:10.1080/10824669.2015.1112746.

Doyle, M. A. 2013. "'Marie M. Clay's Theoretical Perspective: A Literacy Processing Theory'." In *Theoretical Models and Processes of Reading*, 6th ed., edited by D. E. Alvermann, N. Unrau, and R. B. Ruddell, 636–656. Newark, DE: International Reading Association.

Duff, F. J., and P. J. Clarke. 2011. "'Practitioner Review: Reading Disorders: What are the Effective Interventions and how Should They be Implemented and Evaluated?" ' *Journal of Child Psychology and Psychiatry, and Allied Disciplines* 52 (1): 3–12. doi:10.1111/j.1469-7610.2010.02310.x.

Dyson, A. H. 1993. "A Sociocultural Perspective on Symbolic Development in Primary Grade Classrooms." *New Directions for Child and Adolescent Development* 61: 25–39. doi:10.1002/cd.23219936104.

Education Endowment Foundation. 2017. *Improving Literacy in Key Stage 1*. London: Education Endowment Foundation.

Egert, F., R. G. Fukkink, and A. G. Eckhardt. 2018. "Impact of in-Service Professional Development Programs for Early Childhood Teachers on Quality Ratings and Child Outcomes: A Meta-Analysis." *Review of Educational Research* 88 (3): 401–433. doi:10.3102/0034654317751918.

Ehri, L. C. 2005. "Development of Sight Word Reading: Phases and Findings." In *Blackwell Handbooks of Developmental Psychology. The Science of Reading: A Handbook*, edited by M. J. Snowling and C. Hulme, 135–154. Blackwell Publishingdoi:10.1002/9780470757642.ch8.

Ellis, S., and V. Smith. 2017. "Assessment, Teacher Education and the Emergence of Teacher Expertise." *Literacy* 51 (2): 84–93.

Every Child a Chance Trust. 2009. *The Long-Term Cost of Literacy Difficulties*. https://readingrecovery.org/wp-content/uploads/2016/12/long_term_costs_of_literacy_difficulties_2nd_edition_2009.

Foorman, B. 2007. "Primary Prevention in Classroom Reading Instruction." *Teaching Exceptional Children* 39: 24–30. doi:10.1177/004005990703900504.

Foorman, B., N. Beyler, K. Borradaile, M. Coyne, C. A. Denton, J. Dimino, J. Furgeson, et al. 2016. *Foundational Skills to Support Reading for Understanding in Kindergarten Through 3rd Grade (NCEE 2016-4008)*. Washington, DC: National Center for Education Evaluation and Regional Assistance (NCEE), Institute of Education Sciences, U.S. Department of Education. NCEE website: http://whatworks.ed.gov.

Freebody, P., and A. Luke. 1990. "Literacies Programs: Debates and Demands in Cultural Context." *Prospect: An Australian Journal of TESOL* 5: 7–16.

Frey, R. C. (2012). "Rethinking the Role of Decodable Texts." *Electonic Thesis*. https://escholarship.org/uc/item/3824429q

Goldstein, D. 2020, February 15. "An old and contested solution to boost reading scores." *The New York Times*. https://www.nytimes.com/2020/02/15/us/reading-phonics.html.

Goodman, K., and Y. Goodman. 1981. *A Whole-Language, Comprehension-Centred Reading Program*. Tucson, Arizona: Arizona University.

Gough, P. B., and W. Tunmer. 1986. "Decoding, Reading, and Reading Disability." *Remedial and Special Education* 7: 6–10. doi:10.1177/074193258600700104.

Gutiérrez, K. D., P. Z. Morales, and D. C. Martinez. 2009. "Re-mediating Literacy: Culture, Difference, and Learning for Students From Nondominant Communities." *Review of Research in Education* 33 (1): 212–245. doi:10.3102/0091732X08328267.

Hall, L. A. 2012. "'The Role of Reading Identities and Reading Abilities in Students' Discussions About Texts and Comprehension Strategies'." *Journal of Literacy Research* 44: 239–272. doi:10.1177/1086296X12445370.

Hanford, E. 2018, October 26. "Why are we Still Teaching Reading the Wrong Way?" *The New York Times*. https://www.nytimes.com/2018/10/26/opinion/sunday/phonics-teaching-reading-wrong-way.html.

Heath, S. B. 1982. "What no bed Time Story Means: Narrative Skills at Home and at School." *Language in Society* 11: 49–76. doi:10.1017/S0047404500009039.

Hoover, W. A., and P. B. Gough. 1990. "The Simple View of Reading." *Reading and Writing: an Interdisciplinary Journal* 2 (2): 27–60. doi:10.1007/BF00401799.

Hulme, C., M.J. Snowling, G. West, and M. Melby-Lervåg. 2020. "'Children's Language Skills Can Be Improved: Lessons From Psychological Science for Educational Policy'." *Current Directions in Psychological Science*. doi:10.1177/0963721420923684.

International Dyslexia Association. 2016. "IDA Urges ILA to Review and Clarify Key Points in Dyslexia Research Advisory." http://dyslexiaida.org/ida-urges-ila-to-review-and-clarify-key-points-in-dyslexia -research-advisory/.

International Literacy Association. 2016a. *Dyslexia [Research Advisory*]. Newark, DE: Author.

International Literacy Association. 2016b. *Dyslexia [Research Advisory Addendum*]. Newark, DE: Author.

Jenkins, J. R., J. A. Peyton, E. A. Sanders, and P. F. Vadasy. 2004. "Effects of Reading Decodable Texts in Supplemental First-Grade Tutoring." *Scientific Studies of Reading* 8: 53–85. doi:10.1207/s1532799xssr0801_4.

Kabuto, B., and S. Harmey. 2020. "'The Biographic Literacy Profile: Version 2.0'." In *Reclaiming Manifestations of Literacies: Cultivating a Discourse of Meaning Making*. NY, edited by R. Meyer and K. Whitmore-Barten, 64–75. New York: Routledge.

Kintsch, W. 2013. "'Revisiting the Construction-Integrastion Model of Text Comprehsion'." In *Theoretical Models and Processes of Reading*, 6th ed., edited by D. E. Alvermann, N. Unrau, and R. B. Ruddell, 807–839. Newark, DE: International Reading Association.

Kontovourki, S. 2012. "Reading Leveled Books in Assessment-Saturated Classrooms: A Close Examination of Unmarked Processes of Assessment." *Reading Research Quarterly* 47: 153–171. doi:10.1002/RRQ.014.

Kress, G. 2003. *Literacy in the new Media age*. London: Routledge.

Lee, C. D. 2006. "'"Every Good-bye Ain't Gone": Analyzing the Cultural Underpinnings of Classroom Talk'." *International Journal of Qualitative Studies in Education* 19 (3): 305–327. doi:10.1080/09518390600696729.

Lee, I. 2013. "Becoming a Writing Teacher: Using "Identity" as an Analytic Lens to Understand EFL Writing Teachers' Development." *Journal of Second Language Writing* 22 (3): 330–345.

Markussen-Brown, J., C. Carsten, S. B. Piasta, D. Bleses, A. Højen, and L. M. Justice. 2017. "The Effects of Language- and Literacy-Focused Professional Development on Early Educators and Children: A Best-Evidence Meta-Analysis." *Early Childhood Research Quarterly* 38: 97–115. doi:10.1016/j.ecresq.2016.07.002.

Mathes, P. G., and C. A. Denton. 2002. "The Prevention and Identification of Reading Disability." *Seminars in Paediatric Neurology* 9: 185–191.

McNaughton, S., G. Phillips, and S. MacDonald. 2003. "Profiling Teaching and Learning Needs in Beginning Literacy Instruction: The Case of Children in "low Decile" Schools in New Zealand." *Journal of Literacy Research* 35: 703–770.

Mesmer, H. A. 2000. "Decodable Text: A Review of What we Know." *Reading Research and Instruction* 40 (2): 121–141. doi:10.1080/19388070109558338.

Mesmer, H. A. E. 2010. "Textual Scaffolds for Developing Fluency in Beginning Readers: Accuracy and Reading Rate in Qualitatively Leveled and Decodable Text." *Literacy Research and Instruction* 49: 20–39. doi:10.1080/19388070802613450.

Mesmer, H. A., J. Cunningham, and E. F. Hiebert. 2012. "Toward a Theoretical Model of Text Complexity for the Early Grades: Learning From the Past, Anticipating the Future." *Reading Research Quarterly* 47: 235–258. doi:10.1002/rrq.019.

Morgan, P., D. Fuchs, D. L. Compton, D. S. Cordray, and L. S. Fuchs. 2008. "'Does Reading Failure Decrease Children's Reading Motivation'." *Journal of Learning Disabilities* 41: 387–404. doi:10.1177/0022219408321112.

Murphy, K., K. Farquharson, and Language and Reading Research Consortium (LARRC). 2016. ""Investigating Profiles of Lexical Quality in Preschool and Their Contribution to First Grade Reading." *Reading and Writing* 29 (9): 1745–1770. doi:10.1007/s11145-016-9651-y.

National Institute for Literacy. (2008). *Developing Early Literacy: Report of the National Early Literacy Panel*. Jessup, MD: National Institute for Literacy.

National Institute of Child Health and Development (2000) *Report of the National Reading Panel: Teaching Children to Read: An Evidence Based Assessment of the Scientific Research Literature on Reading and its Implications for Reading Instruction: Reports of the subgroups*. Rockville, MD,: NICHD Clearinghouse.

Oakhill, J., K. Cain, and C. Elbro. 2014. *Understanding and Teaching Reading Comprehension: A Handbook*. New York: The Routledge.

OFSTED. 2019. *School Inspection Handbook*. https://assets.publishing.service.gov.uk/government/uploads/system/uploads/attachment_data/file/843108/School_inspection_handbook_-_section_5.pdf.

OFSTED (Office for Standards in Education, Children's Services and Skills). 2017. *Bold Beginnings: The Reception Curriculum in a Sample of Good and Outstanding Schools.* Mancherster. https://assets.publishing.service.gov.uk/government/uploads/system/uploads/attachment_data/file/663560/28933_Ofsted_-_Early_Years_Curriculum_Report_-_Accessible.pdf.

Perfetti, C. A., N. Landi, and J. Oakhill. 2005. "The Acquisition of Reading Comprehension Skill." In *Blackwell Handbooks of Developmental Psychology. The Science of Reading: A Handbook*, edited by M. J. Snowling and C. Hulme, 227–247. Malden, MA: Blackwell Publishing.

Price-Mohr, R., and C. Price. 2020. "A Comparison of Children Aged 4–5 Years Learning to Read Through Instructional Texts Containing Either a High or a low Proportion of Phonically-Decodable Words." *Early Childhood Education Journal* 48 (1): 1–9. doi:10.1007/s10643-019-00970-4.

Reid, L. G., and B. Weiser. 2009. "Teacher Knowledge, Instructional Expertise, and the Development of Reading Proficiency." *Journal of Learning Disabilities* 42: 475–480. doi:10.1177/0022219409338741.

Rodgers, E., J. V. D'Agostino, S. Harmey, R. H. Kelly, and K. S. Brownfield. 2016. "Exploring the Nature of Effective Scaffolding." *Reading Research Quarterly* 51 (3): 345–360. doi:10.1002/rrq.142.

Rose, J. 2006. *Independent Review of the Teaching of Early Reading*. Nottingham: DfES Publications.

Roser, M., and E. Ortiz-Ospina. 2016. *Literacy*. (Published online at OurWorldInData.org). https://ourworldindata.org/literacy.

Rowe, D. W. 1994. *Preschoolers as Authors: Literacy Learning in the Social World of the Classroom*. Cresskill, NJ: Hampton Press.

Ruddell, R. B., and N. J. Unrau. 2013. "Reading as a Motivated Meaning-Construction Process: The Reader, the Text and the Teacher." In *Theoretical Models and Processes of Reading*, 6th ed, edited by D. E. Alvermann, N. Unrau, and R. B. Ruddell, 1015–1068. Newark, DE: International Reading Association.

Rumelhart, D. E. 2013. "'Toward an Interactive Model of Reading'." In *Theoretical Models and Processes of Reading*, 6th ed, edited by D. E. Alvermann, N. Unrau, and R. B. Ruddell, 636–656. Newark, DE: International Reading Association.

Rushton, K. 2007. "'The Significance of Text in the Teaching of Reading in the Early Years'." In *Future Directions in Literacy: International Conversations Conference 2007*, edited by Alyson Simpson, 256–268. Sydney: University of Sydney Press.

Shepard-Carey, L. 2019. "The Inference-Making of Elementary Emergent Multilinguals: Access and Opportunities for Learning." *Journal of Early Childhood Literacy*. doi:10.1177/1468798419870597.

Snowling, M. J., and Hulme, C. (2012). 'Interventions for Children's Language and Literacy Difficulties'. *International Journal of Language and Communication Disorders*, 47: 27–34. doi:10.1111/j.1460-6984.2011.00081.x

Stahl, S. A., and B. A. Murray. 1994. "Defining Phonological Awareness and its Relationship to Early Reading." *Journal of Educational Psychology* 86: 221–234. doi:10.1037/0022-0663.86.2.221.

Stanovich, K. E. 1986. "Matthew Effects in Reading: Some Consequences of Individual Differences in the Acquisition of Literacy." *Reading Research Quarterly* 21 (4): 360–407. doi:10.1598/RRQ.21.4.1.

Storch, S., and G. Whitehurst. 2002. "Oral Language and Code-Related Precursors to Reading: Evidence From a Longitudinal Structural Model." *Developmental Psychology* 38: 934–947. doi:10.1037/0012-1649.38.6.934.

Suggate, S. P. 2016. "A Meta-Analysis of the Long-Term Effects of Phonemic Awareness, Phonics, Fluency, and Reading Comprehension Interventions." *Journal of Learning Disabilities* 49 (1): 77–96. doi:10.1177/0022219414528540.

Sullivan, A., and M. Brown. 2013. "Social Inequalities in Cognitive Scores at Age 16: The Role of Reading. (CLS Working Papers 13/10). Centre for Longitudinal Studies, Institute of Education, University College London: London, UK.

Torgerson, C., G. Brooks, L. Gascoine, and S. Higgins. 2019. "Phonics: Reading Policy and the Evidence of Effectiveness From a Systematic 'Tertiary' Review." *Research Papers in Education* 34: 208–238.

Unrau, N. J., and D. E. Alvermann. 2013. "Literacies and Their Investigation Through Theories and Models." In *Theoretical Models and Processes of Reading*, 6th ed, edited by D. E. Alvermann, N. Unrau, and R. B. Ruddell, 47–90. Newark, DE: International Reading Association.

Vellutino, F. R., J. M. Fletcher, M. J. Snowling, and D. M. Scanlon. 2004. "'Specific Reading Disability (Dyslexia): What Have we Learned in the Past Four Decades?" ' *Journal of Child Psychology and Psychiatry* 45 (1): 2–40. doi:10.1177/00222194060390020401.

Wilkinson, I. A. G., and R. Anderson. 1995. "Sociocognitive Processes in Guided Silent Reading: A Microanalysis of Small-Group Lessons." *Reading Research Quarterly* 30: 710–740. doi:10.2307/748195.

Reading children's literature

Victoria de Rijke

ABSTRACT
This article covers the contribution reading and stories (children's literature) have made to reading, its study, its material world, and the implications for teaching and learning to read -particularly with picturebooks – at the heart of that practice. It first explores the category of children's literature as a possible 'lie', but also its special contributions: animal story or fable as a 'creativity and criticality genre' par excellence, attracting artists and writers of extraordinary talent, frequently breaking boundaries, and unashamedly taking partisan positions on matters of identity formation and socio-political justice. Distinctive experiments in crosswriting and originality are cited, and the material poetics, or 'thingness' of books, from the constructivist tradition onwards, as one of children's literature's leading innovations. The article then engages with the role children's literature has played in the 'reading wars', including teaching strategies and governmental policies for learning to read; the controversies and competitive tensions inherent in the metrics and mechanisms of reading 'for the test' or for pleasure. After decades of reader-response theory emphasising the active roles of the reader and the text, the piece concludes with a plea to re-describe reading for new, screen-based, visual literacies offering linear, radial, spatial forms of reading, or reader-as-player.

Introduction

For many artists and authors of children's books such as Maurice Sendak (2011), 'we have created an arbitrary division between adult and children's books that does not exist,' making children's literature effectively 'a lie.' C.S. Lewis felt writers should simply choose children's literature as the best art form for 'something you have to say', and Russell Hoban argued that 'books in nameless categories are needed – books for children and adults together, books that can stand in the middle of an existential nowhere and find reference points.' Hence the recommendation 'AGES: ALL' inside the dustjacket of Jon Scieszka's and Lane Smith's picturebook *The Stinky Cheeseman and Other Fairly Stupid Tales* (1992).

We might agree at least that 'before there could be children's books, there had to be children' (Rowe Townsend 1990, 3 in Rudd 2010). But could it be the other way round? Mitzi Myers (1992) exposed our habitual, cultural conditioning of a liberal, humanist conception of the child as 'not a transhistorical universal body of truth about childhood', but instead a 'tissue of assumptions, preferences and perspectives.' From the C14th story of The Pied Piper of Hamelin to those of the C21st, 'all histories of children's literature have their agendas' (Rudd 2010, 6). Children's literature development may be directly linked to the rise of the middle class, 'hung' on threads of 'impossibility' (Rose 1984), given it is adults who produce, publish and criticise it, may carry a certain narrative, dual or open address (Wall 1990) or unique cultural expressions of 'childness' (Holindale 1997). The study of children's literature is necessarily 'messy and complex' because of the 'constructed and constructive definitions of the child' (Rudd in Hunt 2004, 24) and its unequal power relations. Ultimately, all constructs of childness offer contradictory templates for what the child or children's literature might be, from imagined, Romantic innocence to more knowing or dystopian futures. Children or children's literature: it's all madey-uppy.

So, what counts as children's literature? Just as with all literature, every possible genre of fiction and non-fiction, poetry, comics, graphic novels, picturebooks, pop-up books and online forms: talking or audiobooks, ebooks, digital augmented reality books, even wider cultural definitions including cartoon, animation, film, video, and so on. As Margaret Mackey pointed out some time ago (Mackey 2004), the book now sits in a world of competing texts: audio, online, game, TV, film and product proliferation, with attendant creeping copyright issues such as Disney buying, remodelling and owning Winnie The Pooh as a trademark, but Mackey insists that reading and stories still lie at the heart of it all.

Children's literature scholars have struggled hard over decades to establish a field of study in its own right, feeling it ranked second to literary studies: the poor, or younger relation. By now, many countries can name a Children's Literature Canon with its high art/low art insiders and outsiders. If for critic Fred Inglis, '*Tom's Midnight Garden* or *Puck of Pook's Hill* are wonderful books whoever you are, and that judgment stands whether or not your child can make head or tail of them' (Inglis 1981, 7), children's literature is simply aimed at readers, some of whom may be children. Yet there are differences in cultural capital, in that not having read Shakespeare is different to not having read Sendak. Peter Hunt's dry summary is that 'in the Adult world of Canons, the book judges you; in the world of children, you judge the book' (Hunt 2017, 18). But perhaps the proletarian accessibility of children's literature comes close to Trotsky's longed-for Revolution in 1924: 'Literature and Art tuned to a different key' (Trotsky 1991, 259).

For example, the picturebook *Farmer Duck* (1995) promotes solidarity amongst (animal) workers against an oppressor (farmer), as a playful pastiche. Voted best British illustrated book of 1991 & Smarties prize-winner, it has warmth of style and gentle humour often found in picturebooks for the young reader. Yet *Farmer Duck* is a metalepsis: the trope of a trope, the metonymic substitution of a work already figurative (author Martin Waddell calls it '*Animal Farm* for 5-year olds'). As such, it is an example of children's literature's special contribution of animal story or fable as a 'creativity and criticality genre' par excellence, 'condensing' complex socio-political matters 'to the point of epigram' and, like 'old wine in new bottles,' retaining its original power yet still able to surprise (de Rijke 2014). The book is rich in reader experience, from Waddell's onomatopoeic, suspenseful text: 'They stole down the hall / they creaked up the stairs,' to Helen Oxenbury's quintessentially English farming landscape watercolour artwork, including metaphoric front and end papers providing mood, before and after the revolution. It also carries that final irony of George Orwell's *1984* that in remarkably little time, the oppressed become the oppressor. Duck is pictured last directing the harvest from the haycock's top, wing on hip. Will Duck be the next despot? (Figure 1).

Though the picturebook certainly operates at least 'two semiotic systems simultaneously: the visual and the textual' (Reynolds 2007), David Lewis concluded his study with a plea that 'we ... pay far more attention to the ways in which readers perceive them' (2001, 129) than the kinds of analysis semiotics provides. Perhaps the picturebook – a genre developed out of children's literature – is the most unique overall contribution to the literary field: attracting artists and writers of extraordinary talent, and frequently 'breaking boundaries'(Beckett 2013). Children's literature has contributed many of its own distinctive experiments in 'innovation, crosswriting and originality' (Kümmerling-Meibauer 2017), pushing the boundaries of avant-garde artwork and book design (de Rijke 2018), and unashamedly taking partisan positions on matters of identity formation and socio-political justice.

Crosswriting, innovation and originality

The best works of children's literature open up reading itself and its unlimited, free forms. As one example, the writer Russell Hoban is read by children and adults across America and Britain, and,

Figure 1. Helen Oxenbury's end papers to the picturebook *Farmer Duck* (Walker Books 1995). Words by Martin Waddell.

given the literary influence his works have undoubtedly had over five decades (not least his first and last novels *The Mouse and His Child* 1967 and *Soonchild* 2012), it is astonishing that so little has been written about his children's literature. Hoban described *The Mouse and His Child* as 'a world-picture that was an attempt to see the thingness of things in a narrow compass, a microcosm. It was published as a children's book, and for the most part, reviewed as such' (Hoban 1971:13). Scholarly works over decades have continued to focus on this classic work of existentialism to the exclusion of other significant and unique works such as *The Marzipan Pig* (1986). A pig made of marzipan falls behind the sofa and no one notices. He becomes increasingly stale with neglect. 'I am growing hard,' he said, 'And bitter. What a waste of me.' A mouse eats the pig, then falls in love with a clock which stops. The mouse too is eaten, by an owl, who then falls hopelessly for a lit up taximeter on the London streets. Is this fiction or the Butterfly Effect of chaos theory? A series of absurdist reflections on the interruption and continuation of life and love, *The Marzipan Pig*'s approach to misdirected desire and loss reads like a concrete poem, or Gertrude Stein for six-year olds. Fabulous. Hoban can certainly turn a phrase. His ear for word power in dialogue, metaphor and epigram encourage reading and re-reading certain lines and learning them by heart. Gillian McMahon-Hill, attending a writing workshop Hoban gave in 1974, described Hoban's 'careful, realized detail' which she recognized- as a teacher of English Literature- was 'at the root of Blake's belief in the minute particulars, Keats' negative capability, and Hopkins' theory of inscape and instress.' McMahon-Hill defines Hoban's essence better than any critic on Hoban I know, because she wrestles so intimately with his 'shorthand' techniques of

> ... wry brevity and clearly defined, witty perception ... His language is essentially to be read aloud: his timing is perfect; his rhythms are meticulous; no word is wasted, no idea over-expressed. It is these attributes which have made the texts for his children's books so distinctive and memorable. (McMahon-Hill 1976, 45–46)

The best writers can often attract the best illustrators: Quentin Blake's drawing for *The Marzipan Pig* has a smudgy, charcoal-like style, suiting the darker tone of the story. Equally, Alexis Deacon's terrifying red-wash scenes of hospital operations for *Jim's Lion* (2003) and pencil drawn shamanistic animals for *Soonchild* (2012) work in powerful counterpoint with the mythic strengths of the text. Hoban has written the gamut: counting books, easy readers, picturebooks, poetry, novels and essays; over seventy books for children in total. Yet his genius is still a kind of close-kept secret.

In fact and fiction, much children's literature defies or crosses generational interest: innovations in the integration of word and image from William Blake's visionary *Songs of Innocence and Experience* (1789) engraved on steel, to Edward Lear's drawings with his *Book of Nonsense* (1846) have led in modernity to fiction crosswriting, inspiring hugely successful multi-age media franchises, as with Tolkein's *Lord of the Rings* or Suzanne Collins' *The Hunger Games*. Original forms such as the verse novel, from Sharon Creech's *Love That Dog* (2001) to Kwame Alexander's *Rebound* (2018), are growing in popularity and influence, and comics have particular mastery in children's literature: from Europe's *Dandy* and *The Beano, Tin Tin* or *Astérix* to Japanese Manga and Dōjinshi. Raymond Briggs' comic-strip picturebooks from *Fungus The Bogeyman* (1977) to *Time for Lights Out* (2019) cover high art, snot, old age and death, Shaun Tan's wordless graphic novel *The Arrival* (2006) the huge complexities of race and migrancy and Brian Selznick's mixed-mode *The Invention of Hugo Cabret* (2007) continually extend subject-matter originality and innovations in form.

These experimental forms often make a deliberate feature of disjunctions, such M.T. Anderson's dystopian cyberpunk novel *Feed* (2002) or unreliable text and image, such as his *Landscape With Invisible Hand* (2017) picturing life for a visual artist in a future without landscape. Anne Fine's bold coda to *The Tulip Touch* (1996), written in response to the infamous Bulger murder (1993), leaves moral responsibility hanging dangerously open. Chris von Allsburg's picturebook without plot, *The Mysteries of Harris Burdick* (1984), apparently created by someone who has disappeared, features strange images accompanied by a title and a single line of text, encouraging readers to create their own stories. (Tellingly, Disney and C20th Fox acquired film rights to two Von Allburg picturebooks in 2019.) Children's literature has always inspired other media and aimed high: in non-fiction, Antonio Frasconi's *See and Say/Guarda e Parla/Regarde et Parle/Mira y Habla* (1955) series taught simultaneous learning in 4 languages to early readers, and the digital augmented reality book *iExplore: The Brain* (2017) allows a reader to witness science in action by placing a tablet or smartphone near the visual trigger on the page to see which part of your brain is triggered by the activity of reading!

The material poetics of books

Ironically, the digital revolution may have led many of us to notice more about the materiality of the book; or 'the book-as-object' (Chambers 1993, 174). Yet children's literature has never lost its preoccupation with the 'thingness' of a book from the start of the avant-garde. A number of poets, artists and writers in Russia under Stalin retreated into children's literature as a less monitored space where they could experiment visually and playfully. It was still a risky business, and many did not survive exile or labour camps. The poet Samuil Marshak, (who created 40 works of children's literature with Vladimir Lebedev drawing on folk traditions radically blended with cubist form and typography experiments) wrote to nonsense poet Kornei Chukovsky 'We both could have perished; the children saved us' (in Rothenstein and Budashevskaya 2013). Chukovsky's own absurdist verse and El Lissitzky's *A Supremacist Tale of Two Squares in Six Constructions* (1922) are daring precursors to 'uneducational' or 'unreadable', wordless books such as Bruno Munri's *Libro Illeggibile* (1949) made entirely of folds and cuts of coloured paper; all of which inspired my first collaborative picturebook as RebVik (Figure 2).

These radical design classics inspired later masterpieces of pop-up paper engineering such as David A Carter's *One Red Dot* (2005), Jonathan Miller and David Pelham's *The Facts of Life* (1984) boasting the only pop-up penis in publication, or Christiane Dorion's *How The World Works* (2010), where hurricanes and the water cycle spring to life off the page, and children read three-dimensionally, interactively, allowing cross-curricular study across Science, History, Geography, all at once. With such a pedigree in design innovation, children's literature often leads the field in experiments with the book's material form such as paratext innovations in Tony Ross's creative typography (for Walliams' *Demon Dentist* 2015), or Shaun Tan's end papers (eg: for *Cicada* 201).

Partisan positioning to address matters of identity and political justice

'Stories do not help us to live better; they help us understand living better. (Benton and Fox 1985, 15). Nikki Gamble's (2019) categories of 'character play' are useful:

- character against self (Max's projected rage producing monsters in Maurice Sendak's *Where The Wild Things Are 1963)*
- character against character (Frog continuing to love Duck despite Pig's prejudice in Max Velthuijs' *Frog in Love 1989*)

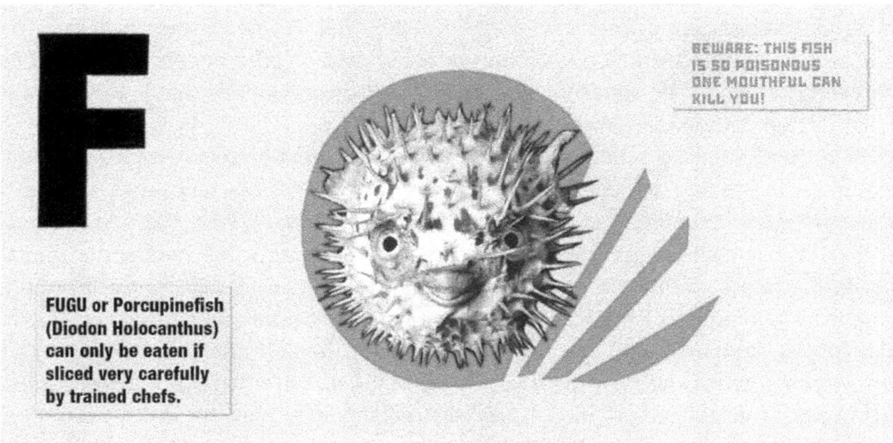

Figure 2. Constructivist inspired picturebook *The A-Z of Dangerous Food*, (Tate 2012)©Victoria de Rijke and Rebecca Sinker as RebViK.

- character against society (an urban homeless boy in Gregory Rogers *Way Home* 2003)
- character against norms (Bailey, the transboy who 'feels like a girl' in Marcus Ewert's *10,000 Dresses* 2008)

Whoever/whatever depicted, these are quests for subjective agency. Naturally enough, children's literature reflects societal changing gender concerns, waves of feminism and queer theory, such as carnivalizing cross-dressing to destabilise the binary concepts man/woman or gay/straight in Jessica Love's picturebook *Julian is a Mermaid* (2018) or Merey's graphic novel *a + e 4ever* (2012). Here, reading takes a role in identity-formation, exploring questions of affect, subjectivity and identity rights, validating gay parenting in Justin Richardson and Peter Parnell's tale of male penguins rearing a chick, *And Tango Makes Three* (2005) or understanding of HIV and AIDS in Maurice Gleitzman's novel *Two Weeks With the Queen* (1990). The texts encourage empathetic viewpoints, and, by using the literary devices of parody, metafiction and intertextuality, represent 'queer' subjectivities as dialogically constructed by a variety of social, political and emotional discourses.

Studies on reading for empowerment also suggest oppositional viewpoints, such as technology versus nature, in Jeannie Baker's *Window* (1991) and *Belonging* (2004), or migrant versus native in Armin Greder's *The Island* (2007), multiple social class viewpoint in Anthony Browne's *Voices in the Park* (1996), multiple character in Jon Scieszka and Lane Smith's *The True Story of the 3 Little Pigs* (1989), unreliable narrator in Lemony Snicket's metafictive *A Series of Unfortunate Events* with its interruptive asides: 'well-read people are less likely to be evil', 'never trust anyone who has not brought a book with them', or Mark Haddon's autistic narrator of *The Curious Incident of the Dog in the Night Time* (2003); all demand transactions with texts as a means of self-cultivation and self-development way beyond functional literacy, and for any reading age.

Learning to read and children's literature

Parallel to the 'reading wars' of the US, there has been much political and educational controversy over how to teach reading in the UK (broadly, holistic language experience versus reading or phonics schemes) from the 1950s to the present. The politics of reading over the past thirty years in particular, has become something of a scapegoat for neoliberal policy reforms, increasingly focusing the teaching of reading to standardised national tests and school Ofsted inspections for market comparisons. However, after fifteen years of raising the 'expected standard' for reading, the Ofsted Report *Reading for Pleasure and Purpose* (2004) noted that whilst reading was taught effectively, even competent readers were not being encouraged to read for pleasure. Relatively large scale reviews have taken place to explore and demonstrate the role of reading for pleasure (Clark and Rumbold 2006; National Endowment for the Arts 2007; DfE 2012). In the UK, local libraries are closing and school libraries dwindling as schools prioritise reading scheme sets and subject textbooks rather than works of children's literature, despite Ofsted's own evidence that library membership is positively co-related with reading frequency.

Competitive tension in the school budget has emerged with recent insistence on the need for schools to invest in reading scheme books that support the SSP teaching, that, for the past two decades, the DfE have promoted as the route to learning to read, with the first national test at age 6. In the UK, if a child is not decoding words by the age of 5, teachers and parents start to worry. If schools choose to buy into commercial schemes, it involves thousands of pounds' worth of investment in training and resourcing. How teaching reading balances the respective roles and merits of schemes, textbooks and 'real books' has been a fiercely contested debate for the past forty years. Arguments for the best materials being real children's literature in the context of the negative impact of (classified, ranked, labelled) reading schemes on motivation (Smith and Goodman 2008; Solity and Vousden 2009) frequently relate to the use of reading schemes in isolation, and the latest recommendations urge blending real literature with reading scheme and textbooks.

As with schemes, debates have raged for decades around popular writers such as David Walliams, Roald Dahl or Enid Blyton – all of whose literature for children has been criticised for perpetuating race, gender and class stereotypes, thus making them 'unsuitable' for child readers. Walliams acknowledges his debt both to working as a comedian and Dahl's exaggerated grotesque that he relished as a child reader. In a similar spirit, Dahl resigned from the 1988 conservative working group for the English National Curriculum on the grounds that Enid Blyton was not on their list of suggested reading. He knew her books got children reading, as his and Walliams' books do. The attractions for children of such un-PC literature remain very real: limited vocabulary or narrative structure and exaggerating characterisation might risk stereotype, but also allow for easier reading; children appreciate authors' playful humour in breaking social taboos (jokes about farts, against authority, etc.) and – as part of some authors' celebrity reach- children can enjoy a world of supplementary websites, games, TV and film spin-offs; all of which support the reader in feeling successful in the act of reading, forming author affiliations and feeling part of a community of readers.

Children's literature and reading tests

Matthew Arnold, inspecting elementary schools in 1867, reported: 'I find in them, in general, if I compare them with their former selves, a deadness, a slackness, and a discouragement which are not the signs and accompaniments of progress.' This he attributes to the school legislation of 1862. Again, in 1869, he writes: 'The circle of the children's reading has thus been narrowed and impoverished all the year for the sake of a result at the end of it, and the result is an illusion.' Are we –150 years on- building on and repeating worst practice? Children's authors such as Michael Rosen and Philip Pullman have been lobbying for years to 'give children books, not SATs,' arguing that tests limit teaching, ruin poetry, deny interpretation and reading for pleasure. As the late Grande Dame of reading, Margaret Meek repeatedly warned of the negative effects of: 'Reading and literacy … crammed with the vocabulary of military metaphors 'strategies' and 'word attack skills' (Meek in Kimberley, Meek, and Miller 1992, 231). This metrics culture, measuring children's reading in three reductive bands: 'working towards,' 'at,' or 'exceeding' 'expected' national levels is all-too-often interpreted as 'low, middle and top' groups, sets or streams. The label 'low ability reader' evokes Allan Ahlberg's poem 'I am a Slow Reader' (1983) which visually enacts the painfully slow syllabification of words in the decoding process. The poem is a powerful reminder of the negative effect of labelling on motivation for reading, ending with the words 'I/ hate – it' (Figure 3).

Following numerous reading tests, teachers, schools, districts, regions and countries are then ranked worst to best in literacy, without reminding ourselves that advantage gaps are overwhelmingly the reason (Waldfogel and Washbrook 2010; Cooper and Stewart 2013). Despite the research evidence that disadvantage affects reading more than anything else (Higgins, Katsipataki, and Coleman 2014; Save the Children 2014) and reading campaigns arguing that 'reading can be a way to escape poverty'(*Read On. Get On*. 2014) it all fails to influence government policy, as libraries close and budgets are cut. What do we even test when we test reading? It's like trying to explain or test thinking. We could say the very discourse is impoverished.

Reading aloud

> To learn to read a book … a young reader has to become both the teller (picking up the authors view and voice) and the told (the recipient of the story, the interpreter). This symbolic interaction is learned early. It is rarely, if ever, taught, except in so far as an adult stands in for the author by giving the text a 'voice' when reading to the child. (Margaret Meek 1970. How Texts Teach What Readers Learn)

It is purported that three dynamics are among the most powerful predictors of reading frequency for children aged 6–17 years: how often children are read books aloud; children's reading enjoyment; and knowledge of reading level (Wigfield and Guthrie 1997). Cooper's (2009) study of whether 'reading strategy intervention that targets children's literature unwittingly interferes with the

Slow Reader

I – am – in – the – slow
read – ers – group – my – broth
er – is – in – the – foot
ball – team – my – sis – ter
is – a – ser – ver – my
lit – tle – broth – er – was
a – wise – man – in – the
in – fants – christ – mas – play
I – am – in – the – slow
read – ers – group – that – is
all – I – am – in – I
hate – it.

Figure 3. 'Slow Reader' from *Please Mrs Butler* by Allan Ahlberg (Puffin, 2013). Illustration Janet Ahlberg. Copyright © Allan Ahlberg, 1984.

development of a reading life' raised the value of the 'untaught story' -stories read aloud purely for the story's sake- in a climate already over-prioritising decoding, comprehension and levelling. Research suggests that reading aloud regularly gives children a 'head start in life,' leading to higher reading, maths and cognitive skills (Kalb and van Ours 2014).

Though the National Curriculum for English encourages reading widely across a range of genre including 'other cultures and traditions', the UK Literacy Association (UKLA) study of Primary teachers found an over-dependence on a worryingly narrow range of books and low levels of expertise in reading or using children's literature creatively and proactively. This research into Teachers as Readers (TaRs) by Cremin et al. (2014) emphasised the 'affective impact of reading to 'reassure, to entertain, to bond, to inform or explain, to arouse curiosity, to inspire' (Trelease 2013). Ledger and Merga's (2018) Australian study acknowledged growing 'aliteracy' among the young and found that children themselves wanted to be read to, at home and at school, long after reading acquisition. The UK Egmont Report (2019) concluded: does the curriculum make reading a skill to learn, not something to do for fun? Does increased time on screens mean less time for reading and other activities? Is there a lack of awareness that we need to read to children beyond the point at which the child can read independently?

Reader response theory

Louise Rosenblatt's *Literature as Exploration* (1938) is often cited as the first presentation of reader-response theory, but she differs from her successors -and radically from current policy and testing arrangements- in emphasising both the reader and the text. Her 'transactional' theory of literature examines the reciprocal nature of the literary experience and explains why meaning is neither 'in' the text nor 'in' the reader. Each reading is 'a particular event involving a particular reader and a particular text under particular circumstances'. Emphasising the subjectivity of transactions between reader and text, placed on a continuum from 'aesthetic' (reading for pleasure) to 'efferent' (reading for meaning), since Rosenblatt, the use and study of literature has often prioritised the 'author's intentions' -supposing them to have produced the work with an 'implied reader' in mind (Iser 1978). For many, memories of studying literature are bound up with sensing the teacher holds 'one, true meaning' of a text, effectively deskilling pupils to feel stupid when they do not share or find the same meaning. The idea of the 'implied reader' is an important one for children's literature, acknowledged John Stephens (1992), yet he is critical of the text-oriented focus, as opposed to the socialisation or ideological aspect. Children's literature is particularly prey to this, as a genre aimed at young readers whose approach to literature is (wrongly) assumed to be a kind of benign, passive consumption rather than rigorous analysis, but it is also a genre produced and promoted by publicists, parents, teachers and academics, whose interests may well be economic, didactic, test-led or theory-driven. Peter Hunt's notion of childist criticism (1991) suggesting that adult critics should read, think and write like children has been critiqued as 'appealing but impossible' (Rudd 2010), so where does that leave the reader?

Reading response in school

Larry Sipes & Caroline McGuire argued that all reading responses create opportunities for 'powerful teachable moments' for learning to 'read the world as well as the word' (2006, 6).

The National Curriculum requires 'positive attitude' for reading, and teachers developing discussion, prediction and inference skills, but, compared to the research field's creative models, there is an overriding emphasis on seeing reading as 'retrieving information. Effective readers can read the lines (literal), between the lines (inference), and beyond the lines (interpretation and evaluation), which Barrett's taxonomy of comprehension takes further, including appreciation (such as emotional response or affect identification). Reader response theory, combined with Vygotskian scaffolding, suggests the guided intervention of an 'enabling adult' (Chambers 1993) will support interpretations of text. This may not allow much 'emotional space' or account for children's prior, 'experiential knowledge' (Stephens 1992) that Iser argued 'builds bridges' to help make sense of text, given, 'whenever the reader bridges the gaps, communication begins' (Gamble 2019). The success of guided reading depends entirely on high-quality interactions between teacher and pupils, knowing when and how to intervene, prompt, question and so on. In reality it is a movable feast, from teachers who may not even have read the text themselves making children read entire books aloud in painfully repetitive rotation, to well-judged supported reading, lively comprehension and response discussions (Brooks 2007; Cremin et al. 2008). Its success depends on whether teachers read themselves, as Cremin et al's research has demonstrated (2014). Charitable foundations for promoting children's literature such as CLPE (The Centre for Literacy in Primary Education) can extend teacher's skills with courses such as *The Power of Reading*.

Visual reading

As reading is a visual skill, do those who teach reading need visual literacy? The invention of the first National Curriculum in 1989 could- and should- have included visual literacy skills

Figure 4. Satoshi Kitamura's synaesthesiac speech bubbles from *In The Attic* by Hiawyn Oram and Satoshi Kitamura, text © copyright Hiawyn Oram and illustrations © copyright Satoshi Kitamura, originally published by Andersen Press Ltd in 1984.

(Hunt 2017) and should have thus recognised the deep potential of the illustration or picture-book as Mervyn Peake did for masterpieces such as *Captain Slaughterboard Drops Anchor* (1939) describing them as 'revelations to stir the imagination' (de Rijke and Hollands 2008, 242). This requires the nuanced skills of reading visual motifs and metaphoric tropes, until, as the child and tiger speech-bubble-as-picture suggests in Satoshi Kitamura's *In The Attic* (1984), we are making sense (without print) and still 'dreaming as we read' (de Rijke and Hollands 2004, 158) (Figure 4).

We are now in an era demanding transliteracies: the ability to read, write and interact across a range of platforms, tools and media from signing and orality through handwriting, print, TV, radio and film, to digital social networks is transforming reading. For example, radial eye movements that whip across a screen for computerised browsing or surfing will enhance our skimming, scanning and surface reading skills, our eye for moments of detail rather than linear narrative. Due to speed screen reading, the relative slowness of print reading may feel an unrewarding, frustrating exercise to many. Yet we still talk about what children *watch* rather than read.

A book can stabilise ideas. It can also pry things loose. In John Burningham's *Grandpa,* (1984) every page before this shows the little girl and her Grandfather doing cosy, familiar things together. But he is old and cannot last forever. The genius of the last page is an empty armchair. There is nothing to read in the linear. Radial reading gives her the lack of him and how to face it- his old comfortable green chair, her hard school chair, her bare feet, her thoughtful pose. But spatial reading gives us – the reader- plenty of empty white space to think about what may have happened. Left the room? Gone away? Hospital? Dead? (Figure 5)

Though much children's literature may be didactic, consoling, or, worst of all, 'cute,' taboo topics such as death have attracted works of such staggering fearlessness as Edward Gorey's *A-Z of Children's Deaths* (1963), Michael Rosen's *Sad Book* (2004), Wolf Erlbruch's *Duck, Death and the Tulip* (2007), or Oscar K's *The Children's Undertaker* (2008).

Figure 5. John Burningham's absent presence in *Grandpa* (Red Fox 1984).

Reader as player

In Daniil Kharms' picturebook *Igra [Play]* (1930), children run around their town imagining themselves as a car, barge, plane and a cow ... until they actually meet a cow. Which is real?

In an essay called 'The Deeper Game', linguistic anthropologist Shirley Brice-Heath has claimed:

> It is in the nature of all play, and most markedly within literacy supports in play, that the linguistic, visual and gestural congruencies, along with the all-important uses of imagination and embodiment, take place in meaningful ways. No strategy of a book illustrator is without purpose, and authors of works for children know that their greatest strength is the ambiguities of language and pictures, allowing imaginations to take their readers to a host of possible interpretations. Children outstrip most adults in their powers to fantasise, parody and riddle in wild and unpredictable directions. It is precisely their engagement in play that fuels the imaginations of the young and that allow them to embody roles they will take on in the future they are learning to project for themselves. [Shirley Brice-Heath. *The Deeper Game* 2009]

Though there is a perpetual journey in children's books, Nick Tucker (1981) critiques psychological models of reading that take the form of 'hunt the symbol', seeing reading as internalised play, in parallel to child psychologist D.W. Winnicott's imaginative third area, 'a sort of mental playground in which makers and readers of stories can operate in relative freedom and security.'(Creber 1990, 56) Winnicott's 'transitional object'- the space of play as transitional space between the child's imagination and the real world outside the child- suggests that object play can be an early bridge between self and other, allowing for open, creative interpretation. Michael Benton and Geoff Fox' use Tolkien's notion of 'Secondary Worlds,' where 'the trick is to shut out one world to enter another'. The secondary world of reading 'lies in an area of play activity between the reader's inner reality and the outer reality of the words on the page' (Benton and Fox 1985, p. 4–5). For Margaret Meek, 'the reader has to know the rules of the game' the book is playing (Meek 1988) and Victor Nell's (1988) research on 'ludic reading' sees 'pleasurable reading as a form of play,' taking readers 'out of themselves;' crucial for visual attention skills and affective control of reader's worlds. The

Book Trust survey of the C21st 'new literacy landscape' (2016) with its diverse platforms for reading in mobile and tablet technologies or gaming, for example, found a need for greater confidence in parents, educators and readers as to how to continue the positive emotional shared engagement of reading aloud together, how to read ebooks (which have multimedia features and different demands), how to avoid passive, inappropriate use or 'addiction', and how best to complement print and online reading. Interestingly, no-one in the survey seems to have viewed online reading as actual play, but, rather, as *alternatives* to (outdoor or toy) play.

CODA: reading beyond literacy

> Change is our earliest teacher, our constant companion, our dearest enemy, our most fickle friend. ... Change is motion and light and fear. Change is the standard and the thing it measures. ... Change is the what and the why of reading. [Frank Jennings *This is Reading* 1965]

Reading is changing: Alan Liu's *Transliteracies Project* (2008) viewed online reading as both individual but also new forms of social, collective reading; 'reading as gathering'. Not so much posthumanist as prehumanist, perhaps. Hunter-gatherers; reader gatherers. Lui's 'Big Bang' theory of online reading argues that new reading interfaces will result in an evolution of the nature of reading, interpreting and performing, where reading overlaps with the actions of modelling, gaming, role-playing, adapting, rendering and simulating. Yet, as early as 1992, Margaret Meek urged us to reconsider, or 'redescribe [reading] so that the teaching and learning of it does not remain a privileged activity for those who have access to texts and technologies' (in Kimberley, Meek, and Miller 1992, 226). As privileged, schooled literates, we, the educationalists, are the gatekeepers, she argues. 'Our eye has to be on the future, but we know that education has a strongly conservative effect.' (Meek 2002, 202).

Neurologically, we know that reading gave our brains 'extraordinary connectivity' (Wolf 2008) as it snaps neurons to attention, yet precisely how all the brain's 'shadow activity' works in relation to reading and cognition, we are still far from fully understanding. If children's literature, like any literature, is 'an exploration of writing, of the problems of articulating a world', with the reader attempting to 'capture its force' (Culler 1975), this power, as Meek long argued, is the defense against being victimised by the reductive power of 'functional literacy'. Children's reading competences far outstrip any descriptions of them. When reading with children, 'we see them doing things that our final expectations- an idea that there's nothing more to know about reading- have almost blinded us to. They open our eyes again' (Meek in Kimberley, Meek, and Miller 1992, 233).

Reading in relation to children's literature can be collective, personal or secret. In his autobiography *Words*, Jean Paul Sartre (1963) recalls pretending to be able to read, giving himself 'private lessons' and Meek argues readers who share preferences are 'members of networks ... like spies', or, as with readers gathered round a comic or picturebook, a sociable collective, shared by readers of widely differing abilities at once. A good reader might be one with a growing tolerance of ambiguity and uncertainty ... knowing 'texts reveal what we think we have successfully concealed even from ourselves' (Meek 1988, 35). After all, 'meanings are for the reader to find, not the storyteller (or teacher!) to impose' (Philip Pullman 2001). A good reader shows reading agency: selecting or deselecting their own reading, sharing or stopping, enthusing or critiquing; changing all the time.

READING IS: seeing (knowing) empathising, identifying with, sharing secrets or conspiring with, feeling, escaping; giving voice to taboo, trauma, longing, daring, dreaming of how things might be; not being alone; companionship, collaboration, part of the local, global collective; considering agency and what to do with it; playing, adapting, changing.

READING IS NOT: to be confused with literacy, entirely cognitive, alphabetic, phonic or comprehension-based; being tested, measured, graded, grouped, fixed or failed.

READERS NEED TO: be read aloud to (by parents, teachers, audio books, games, apps); enjoy reading as a transitional space between imagination and the real world, play around with spaces/languages/phases/genres for both comfortable and challenging reading, mess about with the materiality of books (see the role of scribbling on them, writing in the margins, cutting them up for collage,

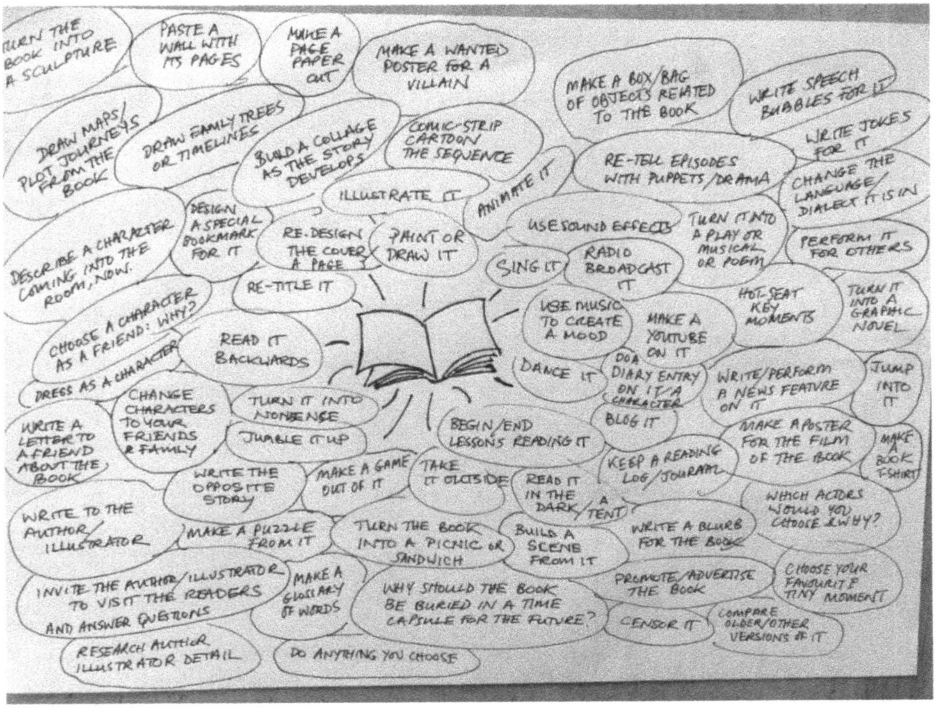

Figure 6. Things *to do with a book.* [Adapted from Benton & Fox by VdR and teacher trainees as an exercise for anyone who reads with children].

playing mis-reading and misinterpretation games), 'expand notions of reading to include the visual and re-using, refusing the text' (Hunt 2017), know that any reading is first written by real people with their own values and feelings, then interpreted by real readers with their values and feelings too, recognise change and agency/citizenship through reading (letters of complaint, blogs, tweets, posters, banners, marches), invent their own titles, lines, images, pages, books, blurbs, reviews, genres, and transform their reading into related, meaningful *acts* (Figure 6).

Disclosure statement

No potential conflict of interest was reported by the author(s).

References

Beckett, S. 2013. *Crossover Picturebooks: A Genre for all Ages*. London: Routledge.

Benton, M., and G. Fox. 1985. *Teaching Literature: Nine to Fourteen*. Oxford University Press.

Brice-Heath, S. 2009. "The Deeper Game: Intuition, Imagination and Embodiment." In *Acts of Reading: Teachers, Text and Childhood*, edited by M. Styles, and E. Arizpe, 43–58. Stoke-on-Trent: Trentham Books.

Brooks, G. W. 2007. "'Teachers as Readers and Writers and as Teachers of Reading and Writing." *Journal of Educational Research* 100 (3): 177–191.

Chambers, A. 1993. *Tell me: Children, Reading, and Talk*. Stroud: Thimble Press.

Clark, C., and K. Rumbold. 2006. *Reading for Pleasure: A Research Overview*. London: National Literacy Trust.

Cooper, P. M. 2009. "Children's Literature: Innovation and Integration." *Language Arts* 86 (3): 178–187.

Cooper, K., and K. Stewart. 2013. *Does Money Affect Children's Outcome? A Systematic Review*. York: Joseph Rowntree Foundation.

Cremin, T., E. Bearne, M. Mottram, and P. Goodwin. 2008. "Primary Teachers as Readers." *English in Education* 42 (1): 8–23.

Cremin, T., M. Mottram, F. Collins, S. Powell, and K. Safford. 2014. *Building Communities of Engaged Readers: Reading for Pleasure*. London: Routledge.

Culler, J. 1975. *Structuralist Poetics*. London: Routledge & Kegan Paul.
Department for Education. 2012. *Research Evidence on Reading for Pleasure, Education Standards Research Team*. London: UK Government.
de Rijke, V. 2014. "'Creaturely Life': Biopolitical Intensity in Selected Children's Fables." In *Politics and Ideology in Children's Literature*, edited by M. Keys and A. McGillicuddy, 45–57. Dublin: Four Courts Press.
de Rijke, V. 2018. "War-torn: A Juxtaposition of Signifiers, or Radical Collage in Children's Literature." *Journal of Literary Education* December (1).
de Rijke, V., and H. Hollands. 2004. "Crocodiles and Naked Pigs: Motifs and Motives in Max Velthuijs's Picturebooks." In *Studies in Children's Literature. 1500–2000*, edited by C. Celia Keenan and M. S. Thompson, 155–162. Dublin: Four Courts Press.
de Rijke, V., and H. Hollands. 2008. "The Thing That is Not There: Mervyn Peake's *Captain Slaughterboard Drops Anchor*." In *Children's Literature Annual no. 2. The Story and the Self. Children's Literature: Psychoanalytic Perspectives*. Vol. 2., edited by J. Plastow Jenny Plastow, 236–249. Hatfield: University of Hertfordshire.
Gamble, N. 2019. *Exploring Children's Literature: Reading for Knowledge, Understanding and Pleasure*. London: Sage.
Higgins, S., M. Katsipataki, and R. Coleman. 2014. *Reading at the Transition: Interim Evidence Brief*. London: Education Endowment Foundation.
Hoban, R. 1971. "Thoughts on a Shirtless Cyclist, Robin Hood, Johann Sebastian Bach and One or Two Other Things." *Children's Literature in Education* 4 (1): 5–23.
Holindale, P. 1997. *Signs of Childness in Children's Books*. Stroud: Thimble Press.
Hunt, P. 2004. *International Companion Encyclopaedia of Children's Literature*. London: Routledge.
Hunt, P. 2017. "Prelude to B." In *Canon Constitution and Canon Change in Children's Literature*, edited by B. Kimmerling-Meibauer and A. Müller, 6–9. London: Routledge.
Inglis, F. 1981. *The Promise of Happiness. Value and Meaning in Children's Fiction*. Cambridge: Cambridge University Press.
Iser, W. 1978. *The act of Reading*. London: Routledge and Kegan Paul.
Kalb, G., and J. van Ours. 2014. "Reading to Young Children: a Head-Start in Life." *Economic Education Review* 40: 1–24.
Kimberley, K., M. Meek, and J. Miller (Eds.). 1992. *New Readings: Contributions to an Understanding of Literacy*. London: A & C Black.
Ledger, S., and M. K. Merga. 2018. "'Reading Aloud: Children's Attitudes Toward Being Read to at Home and at School." *Australian Journal of Teacher Education* 43 (3): 124–139.
Lewis, D. 2001. *Reading Contemporary Picturebooks: Picturing Text*. London: Routledge.
Mackey, M. 2004. "Reading Outside the Book." *Explorations in Children's Literature* 14 (2): 18–27.
McMahon-Hill, G. 1976. "A Narrow Pavement Says "Walk Alone": The Books of Russell Hoban." *Children's Literature in Education* 7: 41–55.
Meek, M. 1988. *How Texts Teach What Readers Learn*, 18. London: Thimble Press.
Meek, M. 2002. *Where Texts and Children Meet*, edited by E. Bearne and V. Watson. London: Routledge.
Myers, M. 1992. "'Little Girls Lost: Rewriting Romantic Childhood, Righting Gender and Genre'." In *Teaching Children's Literature: Issues, Pedagogy, Resources*, edited by G. E. Sadler, 115–178. New York: MLA.
National Endowment for the Arts. 2007. *To Read or Not to Read: A Question of National Consequence*, Washington. No. 47. https://www.arts.gov/sites/default/files/ToRead.pdf.
Nell, V. 1988. "The Psychology of Reading for Pleasure: Needs and Gratifications." *Reading Research Quarterly* 23 (1), Winter: 6–50.
Office for Standards in Education. 2004. *Reading for Pleasure and Purpose*. London: Ofsted.
Pullman, P. 2001. "Royal Society of Literature Lecture 6 Dec." In *Daemon Voices: Essays on Storytelling*. London: David Fickling Books.
Read On. Get On. 2014. *How Reading Can Help Children Escape Poverty*. Launch Report. Save The Children. file:///Users/victoria10local/Downloads/Read_On_Get_On_launch_report_2014.pdf.
Reynolds, K. 2007. *Radical Children's Literature: Future Visions and Aesthetic Transformations in Juvenile Fiction*. London: Palgrave MacMillan.
Rose, J. 1984. *The Case of Peter Pan, or, the Impossibility of Children's Fiction*. Basingstoke: MacMillan.
Rosenblatt, L. M. 1938. *Literature as Exploration*. 5th ed. New York: Modern Language Association.
Rothenstein, J., and O. Budashevskaya, eds. 2013. *Inside The Rainbow: Russian Children's Literature 1920-1935: Beautiful Books, Terrible Times*. London: Redstone Press.
Rudd, D. 2010. *The Routledge Companion to Children's Literature*. London: Routledge.
Sartre, J.-P. 1963. *Words*. London: Penguin.
Sendak, M. 2011. *Tate Shots*. https://vimeo.com/35895317.
Sipes, L. R., and C. E. McGuire. 2006. "Young Children's Resistance to Stories." *The Reading Teacher* 60 (1): 6–13.
Smith, F., and K. S. Goodman. 2008. "On the Psycholinguistic Method of Teaching Reading, Revisited." *Language Arts* 86 (1): 61–65.
Solity, J., and J. Vousden. 2009. "Real Books vs Reading Schemes: A New Perspective From Instructional Psychology." *Educational Psychology* 29 (4): 469–511.
Stephens, J. 1992. *Language and Ideology in Children's Fiction*. Harlow: Longman.

Trelease, J. 2013. *The Read-Aloud Handbook*. UK: Penguin. www.trelease-on-reading.com.
Trotsky, L. 1991. *Literature and Revolution*. London: Red Words.
Tucker, N. 1981. *The Child and the Book: A Psychological and Literary Exploration*. Cambridge: Cambridge University Press.
Waldfogel, J., and E. Washbrook. 2010. *Low Income and Early Cognitive Development in the UK*. London: Sutton Trust.
Wall, B. 1990. *The Narrator's Voice: The Dilemma of Children's Fiction*. Basingstoke: MacMillan.
Wigfield, A., and J. T. Guthrie. 1997. "Relations of Children's Motivation for Reading to the Amount and Breadth of Their Reading." *Journal of Educational Psychology* 89 (3): 420–432.
Wolf, M. 2008. *Proust and the Squid: The Story and Science of the Reading Brain*. London: Icon Books.

Appendix. List of children's books referred to in the article

Ahlberg, A. 1983. *Please Mrs Butler*. Harmondsworth: Penguin.
Alexander, K. 2018. *Rebound*. London: Andersen Press.
Anderson, M.T. 2002. *Feed*. Massachusetts: Candlewick Press.
Anderson, M.T. 2017. *Landscape With Invisible Hand*. Massachusetts: Candlewick Press.
Baker, J. 1991. *Window*. London: Walker Books.
Baker, J. 2004. *Belonging*. London: Walker Books.
Blake, W. 2017. *Songs of Innocence and Experience*. Value Classic Reprints.
Briggs, R. 1977. *Fungus The Bogeyman*. London: Hamish Hamilton.
Briggs, R. 2019. *Time for Lights Out*. Jonathon Cape.
Browne, A. 1996. *Voices in the Park*. London: Corgi.
Burningham, J. 1984. *Grandpa*. Harmondsworth: Penguin.
Carter, D. A. 2005. *One Red Dot*. New York: Simon and Schuster.
Challoner, J. 2017. *iExplore: The Brain*. Carlton Books Ltd.
Chukovsky, K. and Gambrell, J. 1996. *Telephone*. New York: NorthSouth.
Collins, S. 2011. *The Hunger Games*. New York: Scholastic.
Creech, S. 2008. *Love That Dog*. Iowa: Turtleback Books.
Dorion, C. and Young, B. 2010. *How The World Works*. London: Templar Publishing.
Erlbruch, W. 2007. *Duck, Death and the Tulip*. Wellington: Gecko Press.
Ewert, M. 2009. *10,000 Dresses*. New York: Seven Stories Press.
Fine, A. 1996. *The Tulip Touch*. London: Puffin.
Frasconi, A. 1955. *See and Say/Guarda e Parla/Regarde et Parle/Mira y Habla*. New York: Dover Press.
Gleitzman, M. 1990. *Two Weeks With the Queen*. London: Penguin.
Gorey, E. 1963. *The Gashlycrumb Tinies, or An A-Z of Children's Deaths*. London: Bloomsbury.
Greder, A. 2007. *The Island*. New South Wales: Allen & Unwin.
Haddon, M. 2004. *The Curious Incident of the Dog in the Night Time*. London: Vintage.
Hoban, R. 1967. *The Mouse and His Child*. New York: Harper & Row.
Hoban, R. 1986. *The Marzipan Pig. New York:* Farrar Straus Giroux.
Hoban, R. 2003. *Jim's Lion*. London: Walker Books.
Hoban, R. 2012. *Soonchild*. Massachusetts: Candlewick Press.
K, O. 2008. Børnenes Bedemand *[Children's Undertaker]* Copenhagen: Gyldendal.
Kharms, D. 1930. *Igra [Play*]. Leningrad: Gosizdat.
Kipling, R. 1906. *Puck of Pook's Hill*. London: Macmillan.
Oram, H. and Kitamura, S. 1984. *In The Attic*. New York: Henry Holt & Company.
Lear, E. *The Complete Nonsense of Edward Lear*. London: Faber & Faber.
Lissitzky, E. 1922. *A Supremacist Tale of Two Squares in Six Constructions*.
Love, J. 2018. *Julian is a Mermaid*. London: Walker Books.
Merey, L. 2012. *a+e 4ever: a graphic novel*. New Jersey: Lethe Press.
Miller, J. and Pelham, D. 1984. *The Facts of Life*. New York: Viking.
Munari, B. 1949. *Libro Illeggibile*. New York: The Museum of Modern Art.
Peake, M. 1939. *Captain Slaughterboard Drops Anchor*. London: Eyre & Spotiswoode.
Pearce, P. 1958. *Tom's Midnight Garden*. Oxford University Press.
ReBViK 2010. *The A-Z of Dangerous Food*. London: Tate.
Richardson, J. and Parnell, P. 2005. *And Tango Makes Three*. New York: Simon Spotlight Entertainment.
Hathorn, L. and Rogers, G. 2003. *Way Home*. London: Andersen Press.
Rosen, M. and Blake, Q. 2004. *The Sad Book*. London: Walker Books.
Sartre, J-P. 1963. *Words*. London: Penguin Classics.
Scieszka, J. and Smith, L. 1989. *The True Story of the 3 Little Pigs*. London: Puffin.

Scieszka, J. and Smith, L. 1992. *The Stinky Cheeseman and Other Fairly Stupid Tales*. London: Puffin.
Selznick, B. 2007. *The Invention of Hugo Cabret*. New York: Scholastic.
Sendak, M. 1963. *Where The Wild Things Are*. New York: Harper & Row.
Snicket, L. and Helquist, B. 2006. *A Series of Unfortunate Events*. London: Egmont.
Tan, S. 2006. *The Arrival*. London: Hodder Children's Books.
Tan, S. 2018. *Cicada*. London: Hodder Children's Books.
Tan, S. and Crew, G. 1999. *Memorial*. Vancouver: Simply Read Books.
Tolkein, J.R. 1968. *Lord of the Rings*. London: Allen & Unwin.
Velthuijs, M. 1989. *Frog in Love*. London: Andersen Press.
von Allsburg, C. 1984. *The Mysteries of Harris Burdick*. London: Andersen Press.
Waddell, M. and Oxenbury, H. 1995. *Farmer Duck*. Massachusetts: Candlewick Press.

The reader, the text, the poem: the influence and challenge of Louise Rosenblatt

Anthony Wilson

ABSTRACT
This paper is a re-examination of Louise Rosenblatt's seminal work of reader-response theory, The Reader, The Text, The Poem. I argue that poems are essentially social in nature and that they open up a space in which conversation and interpretation can take place. With Rosenblatt I argue that until a reader engages with a poem, bringing to it a combination of her interest and experience, the text will lie dormant. I go on to argue that this implies a model of pedagogy and discourse about poetry which is currently inimical to the high stakes testing arrangements in the current context in England and the Anglophone world. Via the work of John Dewey, especially his notion of art as experience, I analyse the cultural and critical frameworks which influenced Rosenblatt innovations both directly and indirectly. This includes the tradition of the New Criticism, with its emphasis on empiricism and an assumed reader. For practitioners seeking a model of reader-response and classroom practice that promotes more than pre-prescribed comprehension questions, I offer examples of practice which prefigure the role of talk in aiding the reader's aesthetic and transactional interpretations of poems.

Hey people, come back here! These poems aren't going to appreciate themselves!
(Bart Simpson)

Introduction

To illustrate the argument I shall make in this paper, I offer a short, rhyming poem by the late U.S. poet Shel Silverstein (Wilson and Hughes 1998, 32):

Not Me

The Slithergadee has crawled out of the sea.
He may catch all the others, but he
   won't catch me.
No you won't catch me, old slithergadee,
you may catch all the others, but you wo-

I have lost count of the number of times I have read this out loud, with children and adults alike. Whatever the age group of my listeners, the reaction tends to be very similar. There is a short silence of expectation in which listeners wonder if they need to complete the word which appears to have gone missing at the poem's end. This is followed by a murmur, which burgeons slowly into laughter. Beneath this there is a lowing noise, somewhere between a groan and a sigh of relief. Eventually someone says: 'He got eaten!' (they always say 'he').

> 'How do you know?' I say.
> 'Because the poem says.'
> 'But it doesn't say.'
> 'Yes, well, it makes you think that's what's coming because it just stops.'
> 'But how do you know if it doesn't say?'
> 'Because it's there.'
> 'But it's not there. It just stops, halfway through the word 'won't'.' I even show them, to prove it.
> 'But you still know.'
> 'How?'
> 'Because it's made you think about it with the rhyme and everything'. (adapted from Wilson, Lifesaving Poems: Shel Silverstein's 'Not Me', August 24, 2013)

I also use the poem in the context of teacher education, partly because it is apparently undemanding, and funny, and I know it will entertain those in the room who have already professed a dislike of poetry, largely on account of what they are quick to tell me about the way they were taught it in school. But I also use it to persuade them that even a poem as overtly non-serious as 'Not Me' enacts before us one of the most profound lessons that reading poetry has to teach us, namely, that a poem does not need to present us with all the available 'facts' for us to know the whole story. Children as young as six can understand this, sometimes even five. But the conversation doesn't stop there.

> 'Does anyone know what a Slithergadee is?' I ask.
> 'It's a monster.'
> 'How do you know? The poem doesn't say.'
> 'Because it's slimy. And it crawls. And it lives in the sea. And it eats people.'
> Others are joining in. 'And it's got big teeth.'
> 'How do you know it's slimy? It doesn't say.'
> 'You just do. You can work it out.'
> 'But it doesn't mention teeth.'
> 'They're really sharp as well.'
> 'How do you know?'
> 'From the pictures in your mind.'
> 'Where do they come from?'
> 'The words.'
> 'Even the ones that aren't there? Draw me what you can see'. (adapted from Wilson 2013)

I have yet to encounter a student (of any age) who was not able to do so. I have not set this exchange up as such, nor do I use the phrase until we have explored all the possibilities that learners have offered me, but this is what 'poetry comprehension' can look like. I owe a debt for this approach to Rosen's notion of poetry-as-conversation (1998), Boroditskya and Rosen (2015), as well as Fox and Merrick (1981), Benton and Fox (1985), Benton (1986), Benton et al. (1988), and Rosen (1997), all of whom draw their own debt, explicitly or otherwise, to Louise Rosenblatt's seminal work of reader-response theory, *The Reader, The Text, The Poem* ([1978] 1994). What each of these thinkers acknowledges, illustrated by the responses of the children I have quoted from, is that until a reader engages with a poem, igniting it with a combination of her interest and experience, the text will lie dormant. A poem is only a living thing once it has been encountered and brought to life by a reader's re-making of it through interpretation. This paper argues that such processes of interpretation are a vital and necessary part of young readers' experience of the written word in school, and that to reduce them to prescribed and narrow sets of questions which privilege linear models of explanation is to diminish poetry's power and deplete its potentiality.

I have written elsewhere (Wilson 2004; 2014a, 2015a, 2015b) about the particular forces which have forged my hybrid identity as a writer and teacher. As I hope the above exchange from classroom dialogue illustrates, I position myself as a poet (Wilson 1996, 2002, 2006, 2012, 2015, 2019), poetry educator (Wilson and Hughes 1998; Dymoke, Lambirth, and Wilson 2013; Dymoke et al. 2014) and researcher of poetry practice in classrooms (Wilson 2009; 2010; 2013; Wilson and Myhill 2012; Myhill and Wilson 2013; Wilson and Dymoke 2017), who is always seeking to promote the poem, however private its content or mode of address, as essentially social, a space in which conversation both takes place and enacts it in the fact of its being. Within each of these overlapping identities, I draw on the work of Rosen (1998), who positioned his own identity as poet and poet-educator identity around a belief in the primacy of 'memorable speech' (Auden and Garrett 1935, 105), in that poets and poems are always in dialogue with other social actors, be they poems and writers, or a given or imagined form, political situation, relationship, experience or emotion. As Robert Pinsky has argued, poets need 'not so much an audience as to feel a need to answer' (1988, 85), even if they know that no answer will be forthcoming to their particular cry. I was trained as a teacher in the era when Donald Graves's workshop model had many followers (1983), and to this debt I also add one of gratitude to poet, publisher and writing tutor Sansom (1994). As a beginner poet I was mentored, without ever meeting, by the work of Casterton (1986) and Natalie Goldberg (1986, 1991) who insisted from a feminist perspective that to write was to 'answer' the forces of history, class and geography that would otherwise silence one. It is with this hybrid identity that I come to the work of Rosenblatt, again in a spirit of gratitude.

Rosenblatt's achievement

To understand Rosenblatt's contribution, one is reminded of Vygotsky's injunction (1978) to remember that we are all influenced by the intellectual life (88) of those around us. In the case of Rosenblatt, the 'precipitating' influences' (Beard 2000, 422) upon her work were the dominant school of New Criticism of Richards (1929) and subsequent followers (Empson 1930; Leavis 1932; Brooks 1947), which prefigured the authority of the author and his (sic) intentions. Rosenblatt was also influenced by the work of Richards (1929), not least his work on the arts as a transformative experience for both practitioner and viewer (Pike 2003). Her achievement was to reject the predominant Lockean philosophy of her time, which prefigured the empiricist belief in the primacy of the created text having a fixed meaning. As we shall discuss later, this is a model of literary analysis which still predominates in the high stakes testing arrangements of learners in England (DfE 2014).

Further, she insisted that a poem is an event in time, not the record of one ([1978] 1994, 12). To illustrate, she presents Wallace Stevens's poem 'The House Was Quiet and the World Was Calm' Stevens [1954] 2006) as a working model of the 'coming-together', [the] compenetration of a reader and a text' (Rosenblatt [1978] 1994, 12), in which the former

> brings to the text [her] past experience and present personality. Under the magnetism of the ordered symbols of the text [she] marshals [her] resources and crystallizes out from the stuff of memory, thought, and feeling a new order, a new experience, which [she] sees as the poem. This becomes part of the ongoing stream of [her] life experience, to be reflected on from any angle important to [her] as a human being. (Rosenblatt [1978] 1994, 12)

The declarative and hypnotically repetitive sentences of Stevens's poem reprise this argument as an aesthetic experience, interweaving with one another to create the impression of a reader alone with a text seeking 'perfection of thought':

> The house was quiet and the world was calm.
> The reader became the book; and summer night
> Was like the conscious being of the book.
> The house was quiet and the world was calm.
> The words were spoken as if there was no book,
> Except that the reader leaned above the page,
> Wanted to lean, wanted much most to be
> The scholar to whom his book is true, to whom
> The summer night is like a perfection of thought.
> The house was quiet because it had to be.

> The quiet was part of the meaning, part of the mind:
> The access of perfection to the page.
> And the world was calm. The truth in a calm world,
> In which there is no other meaning, itself
> Is calm, itself is summer and night, itself
> Is the reader leaning late and reading there.

As certain, as the poem sounds, it is also playfully aware of how far a tone of certainty can achieve a suggestion of dreamlike encounter and co-construction of knowledge. We read that 'the house *was* quiet and the world *was* calm' (my italics); that 'the reader *became* the book'; that the house was quiet *because it had to be*' and that 'the quiet *was part of the meaning*'. These apparently artless statements climax across the poem's final four lines, in one extraordinary sentence, which would lead us to believe that 'the truth in a calm world' 'itself/ Is calm', 'in which there is *no other meaning*'. And yet there are gaps between the confident tone of certainty set up by the poem's assertions and the similes at its heart. The reader might have become her book, but the summer night is only '*like* the conscious being of the book'. The scholar wants to lean, wants 'much most to be/ The scholar to whom his book is true': it is as though consciousness of wanting so much from the reading experience creates an awareness that any summer night can only ever be '*like* a perfection of thought'. There is a book and there is a scholar. But the poem would also want us to believe that it was '*as if* there was no book'. Thus, the poem simultaneously undercuts and outstrips its own certainties, by creating the possibility of saying things it does not appear to mean. Without these gaps, there is no co-construction of meaning between the reader and text in the poem, and no poetry for readers of the poem.

Rosenblatt adopts various metaphors to explain the transactional process between reader and poem: the poem as play script; as musical score, the poet setting down 'notations' (Rosenblatt [1978] 1994, 13) for the reader; and as electric circuit with different working components which change, and therefore the poem with it, and are dependent upon the reader's experience and the time and place in which they encounter the poem. In this sense, poems become machines which teach their reader how they are to be read, leading to the injunction among poetry teachers that each poem is only as 'good' as its reader (Sansom 1994).

Poetry in a neoliberal context

The current context of assessment and formal reporting in English primary education is not one that is favourable to the teaching of poetry. In part, this is for historical reasons. At least as far back as the Bullock Report (DES 1975) and arguably further (see the surveys of Benton 1986 and Wade and Sidaway 1990), before the establishment of the National Curriculum (DES 1990) in England and Wales and formal procedures of testing and league tables which underpin the current high stakes context (Sainsbury 2009), Benton felt confident in naming poetry teaching the 'Cinderella' of the English curriculum (1978, 114). Similarly, and with greater research evidence to support their claims, Ofsted's now-distant survey of poetry pedagogy (2007) in English schools bemoaned a lack of depth in teachers' subject knowledge, concomitant with, and, one could argue, a lack of confidence, based upon ideas received from their own schooling. Again, this was not new news: Yarlott and Harpin (1970, 1971), Benton (1986) and HMI (DES 1987) describe a similar picture in surveys from a different era. At the same time, one also notices the effects of years of neoliberal policy in education across the U.K. and Anglophone world as a whole (Wright 2012; Connell 2013; Lipman 2013; Slater 2015;), characterised by high stakes reporting, centralisation of education policy, a narrowing of the curriculum and an almost permanent, taken-for-granted 'discourse of derision' (Ball 1990, 73) towards teachers. When Rosenblatt prefaced *The Reader, The Text, The Poem* by noting that her methodology for selecting from great works of philosophy, psychology and literary theory was guided by 'a sense of the human being in a reciprocal relationship with the natural and social environment' (Rosenblatt, [1978] 1994, xiv) she could have been summarising all that was aspirational about recent government policy in England, with its emphasis on 'discursive [...] high quality oral work' (DfEE 1998, 8), the emphasis on the integration of speaking, listening, reading and writing (DfEE/QCA 1999, 50) and the current emphasis on 'a strong command of the spoken [...] word' (DfE 2013, 3). I also argue, however, that the movement of poetry's status from 'Cinderella' (Benton 1978) to 'mixed' (Wilson 2009) is a mirror of what has happened within language arts education in England as a whole and is entirely in keeping with neoliberal education policy reforms. After drama, possibly the least notionally utilitarian domain of knowledge and practice in the primary and secondary English education, poetry has now been colonised by a testing regime which seeks to measure that which is measurable, not that which is always of value.

I argue that evidence of this can be seen in the way that successive U.K. governments of all parties have deliberately engaged in a bifurcated discourse (Alexander 2004; Brehony 2005; Hartley 2006) in the domain of education policy as it relates to the language arts (Alexander 2010). To take a recent example, within the last decade this has seen reforms to education which included a 'phonics partnership grant programme' (DfE 2015, 5), funding for a programme supporting the setting up of book clubs for pupils in KS2, and a request for 'all schools to arrange library membership for all their Year 3 pupils' (4, 5, 21). This intervention also included the promotion of learning poetry by heart and an extension of the national competition for poetry recitation of the same name (2, 6, 23). The headline-grabbing push for library membership and learning of poems by heart masks the deeper reality of the same government cutting state funding for libraries by up to £30% under the aegis of austerity (Busby 2019; Flood 2019; UNISON 2019), and that book loans to children fell between 32%–56% in some parts of England in the same period (Harris 2017). As with so many education policy announcements during and since the New Labour era (Alexander 2004; Brehony 2005; Hartley 2006; Galton 2007), the key policy identifier regarding reading pedagogy, an injection of £23.7 m for 14,000 selected schools to buy government-approved phonics resources (DfE 2015, 9), has remained long after the softer-edged wrappings of promises for library membership and learning poetry by heart have vanished from the headlines.

In this way, I argue that the bifurcated discourse, noted by Rosen (2018a), of recent governments in relation to reading policy in England has co-opted and rebranded poetry as a 'heritage product' from the past, conjuring folkloric (and, no doubt for some, comforting) images in the popular media of Victorian rote learning methods, with obedient children sitting in rows and chanting classic verse chosen by their teachers. Indeed, drawing on the definition of colonisation used by Pirbhai-Illich et al. (2017), I would go further and argue that, as with grammar (Cameron 1995; Myhill 2009) poetry has been colonised by successive Conservative-led U.K. governments because of what it symbolises in the popular imagination, in which 'the poet' (Rosen 2015, 2018b) colludes with the examiner as an all-knowing authority figure who determines the meanings of poems, guiding learners towards fixed answers from which there can be no deviation, even though perfectly reasonable alternatives are available. Thus, as Rosen (2015, 2018b) has shown, poems are atomised in Year 6 National Tests (DfE 2014) to narrow the space of 'conversation' (Rosen 1998; Boroditskya and Rosen 2015) that poems so naturally afford. I argue that a wider conversation about poetry, who is publishing and reading it, is long overdue in the U.K. Notwithstanding the popularity in U.K. classrooms of single-author collections and anthologies, by, among others, John Agard and Grace Nichols (1994, 1998, 2011), Agard (2005), James Berry (1984, 1991, 2002), Valerie Bloom (2004, 2008, 2009), Jackie Kay (1994, 1996, 2007), Grace Nichols (1990, 2006) and Benjamin Zephaniah (1994, 1996), and the anti-racist and pro-justice work that these and other authors have consistently promoted, the Black Writers' Guild (2020) have called on British publishers to address the 'the deep-rooted racial inequalities in the major corporate publishing companies'. Recent calls to decolonise the history curriculum (see Goodfellow 2019; and Moncrieffe et al. 2019) are no less relevant in the case of poetry.

I argue that the co-operative and dialogic model of learning promoted by Barnes, Britton, and Torbe (1986), Cazden (2001) and Alexander (2008, 2010), reimagined in the poetry-specific context by, among others, Rosen (1997, 1998), Benton (1986), Benton et al. (1988) and Dymoke et al.

(2014) is under threat from recent orders (DfE 2013). This is evidenced by, and symptomatic of, the neoliberal 'grip of market logic' (Connell 2013, 102) as the essential model for education, with its concomitant emphasis on performativity (Ball 2003; Craft and Jeffrey 2008; Burnard and White 2008; Troman 2008; Connell 2013; Munday 2014; Keddie 2016), across all sectors of education in the Anglophone world. As Wyse and Opfer (2010) and more recently Soler (2016) have demonstrated, in the subject domain of reading, especially early reading, so-called reading wars have been used by policy makers to foster a climate of distrust in expert research (Soler 2016) and which promote reductionist models of what reading is, based on evidence that is questionable (Wyse and Styles 2007; Wyse and Goswami 2008; Ellis and Moss 2014; Clark 2018a, 2018b). Far from parents, schools and learners being offered choice of curricula and pedagogical approach, neoliberal education policy, as iterated by successive U.K. governments, has consistently centralised policy and constricted classroom implementation, characterised by over-reliance on prescribed teaching materials promoted by vested interests (Mansell 2012) and the disregarding of practitioners' and researchers' judgements and findings (Soler 2016). Soler is especially scathing about this, not least because markets have been seen so palpably to have failed in the recent societal and economic crises sparked by the financial crash of 2008. What she says is worth quoting in full:

> The current emphasis on depoliticization, individualism, and financialization is central to the way the reading wars have been enacted and situated in public debates and professional discourses. We can see the impact of these foundational ideals—embodied within neoliberalism—in the increasing deprofessionalization and commodification of early-literacy teaching and programmes. Further, an international domination of neoliberal-based literacy policies and curricula can potentially accentuate what Lather (2012) calls the "quantitative reductionism" that follows the "metric mania" that neoliberalism promotes. (Soler 2016, 431)

As Lather (2012) has put it, under the aegis of neoliberalism 'we have seen the abuses of the use of scientific authority in the interests of the state' (1023).

Rosenblatt's contribution

Rosenblatt ([1978] 1994) shows how she drew on the ideas of Dewey (1934 and [[1896] 1963), Dewey and Bentley (1949) and Bentley (1954) to frame her theory of 'transactional' reading (16 and ff.). This presupposes that, far from viewing an organism (the reader) and its environment (the text) as 'separate, self-contained, and already defined entities' (17), acting or interacting on one another, like two billiard balls colliding (17), the transaction between them is mutual. Rejecting a model of reading in which 'the reader interprets the text' and/or 'the text produces a response in the reader' (16), Rosenblatt is unequivocal: 'the relationship between reader and text is not linear'. Instead, borrowing from Bentley (1954, 285) reading is an 'event' (16), a word she uses throughout *The Reader, The Text, The Poem* to emphasise that reading is a situational activity occurring in different times and spaces. Further, Rosenblatt, again via Dewey, goes on to stress that this process of mutual and non-linear transaction is active. During the reading event, each element (reader/text) is 'conditioned by' and conditions the other (17) in 'continuing activity' (Dewey [[1896] 1963, 255). In this way Rosenblatt, via Dewey and Bentley, rejects a dualistic model of reading. This interplay of different kinds of thinking at different times and places, what Benton (1986) has called a 'continuous shuttling' (63), is also what takes place between Rosenblatt's other key contribution (Rosenblatt [1978] 1994), namely her defining of efferent and aesthetic reading (23–24). As I have argued, this model of reading is far from that which is proposed by curricular orders and testing arrangements in the current context.

Rosenblatt's distinction (Rosenblatt [1978] 1994) between efferent and aesthetic reading is a pivotal insight into the different motivations readers have for reading as well as the different processes at work when they do so. She defines efferent reading (22) as the 'residue of information' (25) that remains '*after*' the reading is finished (23, author's italics), whether that is contained in the form of an action to take, a solution to a problem, or new information which is absorbed (23). This presupposes the reader arriving to the moment of reading with agency and being an active participant in the process of locating, understanding and retrieval of salient information. As Dewey says, '[A text] *becomes* the stimulus in virtue of what the organism is already preoccupied with' ([[1896] 1963, 255) (author's italics). During aesthetic reading, on the other hand, while also presupposing the reader as having agency in the reading process, *'the reader's attention is centered directly on what [she] is living through during [her] relationship with that particular text' (25,* author's italics). Rosenblatt expands this idea with two sentences which are tellingly conditional ('If a literary work of art is to ensue ... '; 'Only if the reader turns [her] attention inward ... ', 28) but nevertheless argue for the primacy of intent that a reader brings to the moment of encountering a poem. Crucially, this argues that a poem will only happen if the reader's attention is focused as much upon the poem-as-object as it is upon the 'transaction' (28) that occurs between them, or to use a phrase of Coleridge quoted by Rosenblatt, upon *'the pleasurable activity of mind excited by the attractions of the journey itself'* (1907, 6) (author's italics).

There is much congruence here with a metaphor used by Iser (1978) which is also couched in conditional terms. In his explication of reader-response theory, via a passage of Laurence Sterne's *Tristram Shandy*, Iser writes about 'the game of the imagination' (1978, 108) which allow the reader to bring their 'own faculties into play' (108). It is only at this point, he argues, that the reader becomes 'productive' (108). This cannot be achieved, he argues, 'if the text sets out to be anything more than a set of governing rules' (108). This again has echoes of Dewey ([[1896] 1963). As in Dewey, he replaces the notion of the 'subject-object relationship' (1978, 109) with the idea of a 'moving viewpoint which travels along *inside* that which it has to apprehend' (109) (author's italics). This also contains shades of a metaphor employed by Nobel-laureate Heaney (1988), which is itself reminiscent of Coleridge. Heaney frames the reading (and writing) of poetry as '[holding] attention for a space [...] a focus where our power to concentrate is concentrated back on ourselves' (108). As noted by Wilson (2008), could it be that Seamus Heaney's description of what occurs between the reader and writer of a poem is also a description of fully realised pedagogy, as a site of dialogic reflexivity?

The influence of Rosenblatt on post-war practitioners

Benton (1993) has given a full account of reader-response and transactional theories (Rosenblatt [1978] 1994; Iser 1978) and their influence upon modern classrooms and pedagogy. His premise is that during the 1940s and 1960s, under the influence of American New Criticism (Richards 1929; Empson 1930), 'the reader was hidden from view' in literary studies (1993, 9), a situation which was to change from the 1960s with its emphasis on education. According to Benton this 'direct relationship with pedagogy' (1993, 12) is a key principle underpinning Rosenblatt and Iser's work, not least in the way that they engaged with 'real and implied readers' (11) as opposed to the assumed reader found in New Criticism. Benton ascribes to these theorists a 'sea-change' (1993, 12) in the 'culture of the classroom' (11) which is at the same time the 'evolutionary successor to Leavisite liberal humanism' (12). A second founding premise of this work is that 'the text cannot be said to have a meaningful existence outside the relationship between itself and its readers' (11–12). It is this 'transfer of power' (12) which is the real marker of impact upon teachers and their classrooms.

Although Rosenblatt's work is singular and seminal in itself, with varying degrees of direct acknowledgement it was also a key influence on the work of scholars who argued for poetry's uniqueness and primacy during the late post-war period and bridged the space between theory and practice (Benton et al. 1988; Benton and Fox 1985; Benton 1986), before the arrival of the first National Curriculum in England (DES 1990). Also shadowing these important texts is the work of James Britton (1986; 1982a; 1982b) and Wade (1981): the former for re-asserting that reading poetry is an experience (1982a, 12), and, via the work of Brooks (1947), an event in its own right (1982b, 27); the latter for analysing pupils' classroom talk when discussing poems. Again, with varying degrees of direct acknowledgement, it could also be argued that Britton and his colleagues' work (Barnes, Britton, and Torbe 1986) on the unchaperoned classroom talk of pupils was also an important influence on Benton (1986) and Benton et al. (1988) whose analyses of pupils discussing poems without a teacher being present to guide (or hinder) them remain both an inspiration and a challenge to this day.

Aesthetic and transactional reading in practice

For practitioners wanting to locate positive examples of the benefits of aesthetic and transactional reading of poetry by pupils in the classroom, several instances can be found in the work of Benton (1986), Hurst (1988), and Wilson (2014a, 2014b, 2015b). To take the work of P. Benton first, it is worth pointing out that the method used for capturing pupils' talk was to record small groups of unsupervised Year 9 pupils discussing specific poems in rooms that were near to the rest of the class, but without intervention from other pupils or teachers. Discussions were not given a time limit. Benton (1986) gives a detailed account of one of these, reporting 'over 600 exchanges' and 'forty-five minutes' of talk between pupils (36) discussing Ted Hughes's 'The Warm and the Cold' (*Season Songs*, 1976; see Appendix). As he drily notes, 'even with a skilful and enlightened teacher, the group's engagement with the poem would probably have taken quite a different form' (36). I shall draw out some wider points of pedagogical implication at the end of this section, but note, for now, his intended corollary, that pupils are seldom allowed such unfettered freedom to talk in the classroom, let alone about individual poems, and in such detail.

Practitioners in search of a working model of students demonstrating talk that is accountable (Michaels, O'Connor, and Resnick 2008) to fellow students, to standards of reasoning and to knowledge (2008, 283) will find a 'word-hoard' (Heaney 1975, 20) that is as rich in questioning and hypothesis-testing as it is in personal honesty:

Nick	One thing about this poem is that it's a lot of effort to read it –
Graham	Yeah.
Tom	Yeah. Some poems.
Zoe	On your own. It's not so much effort when you're doing it all together but on your own – to get right into it like we have done –
Graham	But in class –
Tom	we wouldn't bother really looking. (Benton 1986, 34)

In these exchanges one discovers a mimetic similarity between students 'really looking' at a poem, going and getting 'right into it' (34) as they put it, and active listening. They socially construct their learning in a situated, non-linear fashion that is almost a textbook example of constructivism at work (Vygotsky 1978), relying on the scaffolding (Wood, Bruner, and Ross 1976) of the others' questions and prompts as much as their hesitations and misconceptions. The features of this talk, as analysed by P. Benton, are:

- Concentration on the meanings of single words and images combined with 'an intuitive feeling for the central concerns of the poem' (36);
- Thinking aloud, via repetition and 'savouring' of key lines and phrases, implicitly recognising that 'meaning- making may require words to be read aloud and not heard only in the head' (38);
- The 'need for clear visualisation of […] images' (39);
- 'A willingness to declare uncertainty or puzzlement' (38).

As well as moving *from* efferent *to* aesthetic reading, then, we see in this summary a consistent interplay between them, which is present throughout the entire exchange. Examples of moving from unpicking meanings of particular words to exposition of wider themes can be seen right from the outset of the discussion, as the students begin reading the poem (exchanges 1–17, 36). This is taken to a new level of depth in the following set of exchanges (47–66, 39), when the group combine to correct Nick's misconceived inference that the owl 'on the gatepost' in line 11 of stanza 2 is there because it is having 'a rest', 'asleep' 'in the middle of the afternoon' (39):

Tom	It's not the middle of the afternoon, is it?
Zoe	It makes it feel like dusk.
Nick	It's dusk.
Tom	It's dusk. Well, I mean …
Zoe	Late afternoon.
Tom	It's not the afternoon is it?
Zoe	Late afternoon.
Tom	Seven o'clock, isn't it?
Graham	Look: 'Freezing dusk has tightened/ Like a nut screwed tight.' It's clever.
Zoe	It's getting darker and darker.
Tom	Yeah, yeah! *(excitedly)*

This is a layered and complex exchange. Tom's role is not merely negative ('It's not the afternoon is it?'); he also makes a leap of the imagination in suggesting it is 'seven o'clock', a very precise notation that cannot be found in the text of the poem. Nick's recollection that the poem is describing dusk (stanza 1, line 1; stanza 2, line 1) prompts Graham, several interjections later, to clarify the timeframe of the poem's action not by explication but by rereading the stanza's opening lines ('Freezing dusk has tightened … '). This in turn prompts Zoe to see, in P. Benton's words, that 'a process is at work in the poem, that it is not static' (39). As Benton notes: 'Graham, caught almost unawares by the poem's 'cleverness', reads on without prompting' (39) the opening four lines of the poem's next stanza. P. Benton also remarks that this kind of sophisticated 'leapfrogging of listening and speaking' (Britton 1986, 120) recalls Rosenblatt's drawing upon Coleridge's famous lines about the 'attractions of the journey itself' (1907, 6) outweighing both the reader's 'curiosity' and their desire to arrive at a 'solution' (Rosenblatt [1978] 1994, 28).

The pedagogical implication of this is that students need plenty of time if they are to engage with poems at an aesthetic level, not least efferently. Poems do not yield the layers of their meaning, sonically, lexically, figuratively and formally, combining and setting off connections and provocations, some of which are 'useful' and others less so, unless pupils are given time to explore and experience, to make meaning for themselves without the pressure of believing that there is a secret 'correct' answer to which they will be ushered in due course, either for or against their better judgement.

Valuing students' talk about poems

Another example of recording (and displaying) children's voices as they discuss poems is given by Wilson (2014b). This tells the story of a support teacher who would withdraw small groups of pupils, whose language needs were complex and at risk of being overlooked in the large classes to which they belonged, to read and discuss poems. Influenced by Chambers (2011), she based her pedagogy in trying to do as little talking as possible, opening her lessons with the question 'Tell me … '. As pupils grew in confidence and fluency, news of these support groups began to circulate among staff and pupils alike. With the pupils' permission, the teacher recorded, transcribed and displayed their conversation about Frank Collymore's poem 'The Spider' (Agard and Nichols 1994; see Appendix):

> The effect was electrifying. Children crowded round the display board, jostling to see their names in print next to the poem. Calling their friends to come and see their work, they swapped high-fives, laughing to recall what they had said in the lesson, thrilled to see their own names. Watching them, the teacher thought she discerned a new language being spoken, one she had not heard in the school before […] Each day for a week that corridor was never empty. (Wilson 2014b, 207; 2015b, 66)

The implications for pedagogy which flow from this example, much as those from Benton (1986) and Benton et al. (1988) which precede it, is much less to do with technology (recording and transcribing) and much more to do with intrinsically and explicitly valuing pupils' classroom talk. This is a fundamental pedagogical belief which expects pupils to have experiences, knowledge and views that are influenced by their lives *outside* of the classroom (Martin 2008; Catling and Martin 2011; Little and Chesworth 2017) and celebrates these *inside* the classroom. It opposes the folkloric view of pupil-as-empty-vessel (Bruner 1996, 49; Rodriguez 2012) who waits to be filled with teacher-knowledge. In poetic terms it promotes poetry as a site of conversation (Rosen 1997, 1998), from pupil to pupil as well as teacher to pupil, and between pupils and poems. As Rosen has pointed out, poetry's 'scavenging' capacity to pay 'close attention to feelings, ideas, unfamiliar ways of looking at the world, suggestiveness, open-ended questioning and ludic approaches to language' (Boroditskya and Rosen 2015, 73, 69), is under threat from the prescribed model of 'comprehension', and thus of pedagogy, exemplified in recent orders (DfE 2013) and exemplifications (see Rosen 2015, 2018b, on DfE 2014) because it 'eliminates the child's point of view from the permitted range of responses' to poems (Boroditskya and Rosen 2015, 69).

We end with another example of classroom discourse which exemplifies the advantages of prefiguring pupil's genuine responses to poems in a safe and dialogic environment. The following is a critical incident from the field notes of Wilson's PhD study (2004) into the poetry writing of KS2 pupils. He describes a lesson from the beginning of his study, when he was still getting to know his participants, in which he read to them 'The Tyger' by William Blake (see Appendix). Again, it is worth quoting in full:

> After reading 'The Tyger' to the class I chose to ask what pictures went through their minds as I was reading the poem. After a few slightly predictable answers about forests and tigers one boy put up his hand and said this: 'I think it is about a big forest and a little forest. The little forest is trapped inside the big forest and is struggling to escape from it. It is a real struggle. Eventually the little forest breaks free and makes its way to edge of the big forest. It looks out. What it can see on the other side is the First World War.' There was a silence. Nobody knew what to say next. I thanked the boy for his comment and said that I found it interesting. Then I did something I had not done consciously in my teaching before. Instead of saying what I wanted to say, which was to debate with the boy's interpretation of the poem, or read another poem perhaps, I asked the class if the boy's answer had made anyone else think about the poem differently. All their hands went up. (Wilson 2014b, 2015, 63)

First, it is important to recognise the bravery and commitment of this pupil's comment. At the time I was not well-known to the class; we were still in the early stages of getting to know one another, a phase often characterised by answers to questions which seek to please the teacher rather than ones, like this, which provoke more questions and which refuse to fall out of the conversation Bakhtin (1986, 168). The pedagogical implication of this incident is not that the pupil's interpretation was inaccurate (how could we expect it to be otherwise after only one hearing of the poem?), but that we can see in it the potential for a discussion about the poem's sense of menace and danger, the fear of entrapment, the question of what constitutes 'nature', and how that same nature, red in tooth and claw, can be seen to be created 'good'. As teachers we make countless choices on a moment-by-moment basis: we live with the inherent tension of all classroom interaction that to include one response is to exclude another; to validate one pupil's perspective is to (unconsciously or otherwise) question another's. As Wilson goes on to say, allowing personal responses that may not include a so-called 'right answer' into our poetry pedagogy is 'disruptive and risky: disruptive because it foregrounds poetry's essence as a democratic and subjective art-form; and risky because it requires enough confidence not to take control and dominate the discussion, both in terms of subject and pedagogical knowledge. In this way, poetry can help us enjoy the paradox of 'losing' power in order to gain new kinds of knowledge' (2015, 63). In moments such as these, we begin to see the truth of Heaney's metaphor of poems as 'thresholds' 'constantly approached and [...] departed from' (1988, 107–108). This implied message of such a pedagogy bears out the rhetorical claim of Fox and Merrick (1981) and Benton and Fox (1985), namely, that poems are to be experienced by students before they are analysed.

Conclusion

Teachers' uncertainty about teaching poetry remains persistent on many levels and has existed for many years (see Yarlott and Harpin 1970, 1971; Benton 1986, 9–33; DES 1987; Wade and Sidaway

1990; and, more recently, Ofsted 2007). In the collusive context of current testing arrangements, the threat of poetry pedagogy as a 'sterile game' (Benton 1986, 35) or domineered by the 'one-way traffic' (DES 1975, 9.21) of teacher talk, characterised by teachers seeking 'confirmation of their own interpretation rather than encouraging [...] pupils' personal search for meaning' (Benton 1986, 35) is never far away. To read Hurst, a poetry enthusiast, reflecting on his own teaching as 'guilt-ridden' and full of 'unease and doubt' (1988, 157) is to encounter again a deep sense of the unfulfilled gap between the promise of poetry and the reality of many classrooms. Rosenblatt (Rosenblatt [1978] 1994, 3), shows us that debates as to the value of poetry in society and education are not new. The main effort of her project, as vital now as it was in her very different context, was to challenge the role of the reader as 'invisible eavesdropper' (2) and to move her to 'the center of the stage' (4). Rosenblatt argued that this privileges neither 'extreme subjectivism' (4) on the one hand, which positions the reader as a 'tabula rasa' 'receiving the imprint of "the poem"' (4), nor a view of the text as 'empty, awaiting the content brought by the reader' (4) on the other. Even further away from the high stakes context we currently enjoy, LAG Strong insisted that 'A child's misconceptions may be of much greater value [...] than the explanation which destroys it' (Strong 1946, 1). Unless policy makers learn to trust the value of this dictum by encouraging pedagogy that risks explicit valuing of pupils' aesthetic interpretations of poems, we face a greater risk of losing poetry's potentiality in the culture at large. I argue that Rosenblatt's placing the reader at the centre of 'the limelight' (Rosenblatt [1978] 1994, 5) is of more urgent concern to us as educators than ever before.

Acknowledgement

I am deeply grateful for the comments of Roger Beard and Victoria de Rijke on my first draft of this article.]

Disclosure statement

No potential conflict of interest was reported by the author(s).

ORCID

Anthony Wilson http://orcid.org/0000-0003-3268-1886

References

Agard, J. 2005. *Half-Caste and Other Poems*. London: Hodder.

Agard, J., and G. Nichols. 1994. *A Caribbean Dozen: Poems From Caribbean Poets*. London: Walker Books.

Agard, J., and G. Nichols. 1998. *No Hickory, no Dickory, no Dock: A Collection of Caribbean Nursery Rhymes*. London: Puffin.

Agard, J., and G. Nichols. 2011. *Under the Moon & Over the sea: A Collection of Poetry From the Caribbean*. London: Walker Books.

Alexander, R. 2004. "Still no Pedagogy? Principle, Pragmatism and Compliance in Primary Education." *Cambridge Journal of Education* 34 (1): 7–33.

Alexander, R. 2008. *Towards Dialogic Teaching: Rethinking Classroom Talk*. 4th ed. Dialogos: Cambridge.

Alexander, R. 2010. "Speaking but not Listening? Accountable Talk in an Unaccountable Context." *Literacy* 44 (3): 103–111.

Auden, W. H., and J. Garrett. 1935. "Introduction to *The Poet's Tongue*." In *W. H. Auden, Prose 1926-1938: Essays and Reviews and Travel Books in Prose and Verse*, edited by E. Mendelson. London: Faber and Faber.

Bakhtin, M. 1986. *Speech Genres and Other Essays*. Austin, TX: University of Texas Press.

Ball, S. J. 1990. *Politics and Policy-Making in Education: Explorations in Policy Sociology*. London: Routledge.

Ball, S. J. 2003. "The Teacher's Soul and the Terrors of Performativity." *Journal of Education Policy* 18 (2): 215–228. doi: 10.1080/0268093022000043065.

Barnes, D., J. Britton, and M. Torbe. 1986. *Language, the Learner and the School*. 3rd ed. Harmondsworth: Penguin.

Beard, R. 2000. "Research and the National Literacy Strategy." *Oxford Review of Education* 26 (3–4): 421–436. doi: 10.1080/713688544.

Bentley, A. F. 1954. "Kennetic Inquiry." In *Inquiry Into Inquiries*, edited by S. Rather, 337–354. Boston, MA: Beacon Press.

Benton, M. 1978. "Poetry for Children: A Neglected art." *Children's Literature in Education* 9 (3): 111–126.

Benton, P. 1986. *Pupil, Teacher, Poem*. London: Hodder and Stoughton.

Benton, M. 1993. "Reader Response Criticism in Children's Literature." Occasional Papers, 15, University of Southampton, Centre for Language Education, pp. 1–48.

Benton, M., and G. Fox. 1985. *Teaching Literature: Nine to Fourteen*. Oxford: Oxford University Press.

Benton, M., J. Teasey, R. Bell, and K. Hurst. 1988. *Young Readers Responding to Poems*. London: Routledge.

Berry, J. 1984. *News for Babylon*. London: Chatto and Windus.

Berry, J. 1991. *When I Dance*. London: Harcourt Children's Books.

Berry, J. 2002. *A Nest Full of Stars*. London: Macmillan Children's Books.

Black Writers' Guild. 2020. "An Open Letter to UK Publishing from the Black Writers' Guild." Accessed July 21 2020. https://www.thebookseller.com/blogs/open-letter-black-writers-guild-1206765#.

Bloom, V. 2004. *Whoop an' Shout*. London: Macmillan's Children's Books.

Bloom, V. 2008. *Let me Touch the sky: Selected Poems for Children*. London: Caboodle Books Limited.

Bloom, V. 2009. *Hot Like Fire*. London: Bloomsbury.

Boroditskya, M., and M. Rosen. 2015. "Children's Poetry and Politics: A Conversation." *Modern Poetry in Translation* 2: 67–74.

Brehony, K. J. 2005. "Primary Schooling Under New Labour: The Irresolvable Contradiction of Excellence and Enjoyment." *Oxford Review of Education* 31 (1): 29–46. doi:10.1080/0305498042000337174.

Britton, J. 1982a. "Reading and Writing Poetry." In *Prospect and Retrospect: Selected Essays of James Britton*, edited by G. M. Pradl, 9–19. Montclair, NJ: Boynton/Cook Publishers, Inc.

Britton, J. 1982b. "Poetry and Our Pattern of Culture." In *Prospect and Retrospect: Selected Essays of James Britton*, edited by G. M. Pradl, 24–31. Montclair, NJ: Boynton/Cook Publishers, Inc.

Britton, J. 1986. "Talking to Learn." In *Language, the Learner and the School* (3rd ed.), edited by D. Barnes, J. Britton, and M. Torbe, 89–130. Harmondsworth: Penguin.

Brooks, C. 1947. *The Well Wrought Urn: Studies in the Structure of Poetry*. New York, NY: Harcourt Brace.

Bruner, J. 1996. *The Culture of Education*. Cambridge, MA: Harvard University Press.

Burnard, P., and J. White. 2008. "Creativity and Performativity: Counterpoints in British and Australian Education." *British Educational Research Journal* 34 (5): 667–682. doi:10.1080/01411920802224238.

Busby, E. 2019. "Nearly 800 Public Libraries Closed Since Austerity Launched in 2010." *The Independent*. December 6. Accessed June 11 2020. https://www.independent.co.uk/news/uk/home-news/library-closure-austerity-funding-cuts-conservative-government-a9235561.html.

Cameron, D. 1995. *Verbal Hygiene*. London: Routledge.

Casterton, J. 1986. *Creative Writing: A Practical Guide*. London: Macmillan Education Ltd.

Catling, S., and F. Martin. 2011. "Contesting *Powerful Knowledge*: the Primary Geography Curriculum as an Articulation Between Academic and Children's (Ethno-) Geographies." *Curriculum Journal* 22 (3): 317–335. doi:10.1080/09585176.2011.601624.

Cazden, C. 2001. *Classroom Discourse: The Language of Teaching and Learning* (2nd ed). Portsmouth, NH: Heinemann.

Chambers, A. 2011. *Tell me: Children, Reading and Talk, with the Reading Environment: How Adults Help Children Enjoy Books*. Stroud: Thimble Press.

Clark, M. 2018a. "How Justified is it to Dominate Government Policy on Early Literacy with Synthetic Phonics and the Phonics Screening Check? Evidence, Effects and Expenditure. Part I: Recent Evidence on Effects and Expenditure." *Education Journal* 35: 18–21.

Clark, M. 2018b. "How Justified is it to Dominate Government Policy on Early Literacy with Synthetic Phonics and the Phonics Screening Check? Part II A Critique of the Evidence." *Education Journal* 352: 15–29.

Coleridge, S. T. 1907. *Biographica Literaria*, edited by J. Shawcross. London: Oxford University Press.

Collymore, F. 1994. "The Spider." In *A Caribbean Dozen: Poems from Caribbean Poets*, edited by John Agard and Grace Nichols, 88. London: Walker Books.

Connell, R. 2013. "The Neoliberal Cascade and Education: an Essay on the Market Agenda and its Consequences." *Critical Studies in Education* 54 (2): 99–112. doi:10.1080/17508487.2013.776990.

Craft, A., and B. Jeffrey. 2008. "Creativity and Performativity in Teaching and Learning: Tensions, Dilemmas, Constraints, Accommodations and Synthesis." *British Educational Research Journal* 34 (5): 577–584. doi:10.1080/01411920802223842.

Department for Education. 2013. *The National Curriculum in England: Key Stages 1 and 2 Framework Document*. London: Author.

Department for Education. 2014. *Key Stage 1 English Reading Sample Questions, Mark Schemes and Commentary for 2016 Assessments*. London: Author. Accessed June 2 2020. https://assets.publishing.service.gov.uk/government/uploads/system/uploads/attachment_data/file/328853/2014_KS1_English_reading_sample_materials.pdf.

Department for Education. 2015. *Reading: the Next Steps: Supporting Higher Standards in Schools*. London: Author.

Department for Education and Employment. 1998. *The National Literacy Strategy: Framework for Teaching*. Sudbury: Author.

Department for Education and Employment and Qualifications and Curriculum Authority. 1999. *English: The National Curriculum for England (Key Stages 1-4)*. London: The Stationery Office.

Department of Education and Science. 1975. *A Language for Life: The Report of the Bullock Committee (The Bullock Report)*. London: HMSO.

Department of Education and Science. 1987. *Teaching Poetry in the Secondary School: An HMI View*. London: HMSO.
Department of Education and Science. 1990. *English in the National Curriculum. Department of Education and Science and the Welsh Office*. London: HMSO.
Dewey, J. 1934. *Art as Experience*. New York, NY: Berkeley Publishing.
Dewey, J. ([1896] 1963). "The Reflex Arc Concept in Psychology." *Psychological Review* 3: 357–370.
Dewey, J., and A. F. Bentley. 1949. *Knowing and the Known*. Boston, MA: Beacon Press.
Dymoke, S., M. Barrs, A. Lambirth, and A. Wilson. 2014. *Making Poetry Happen: Transforming the Poetry Classroom*. London: Bloomsbury.
Dymoke, S., A. Lambirth, and A. Wilson. 2013. *Making Poetry Matter: International Research on Poetry Pedagogy*. London: Bloomsbury.
Ellis, S., and G. Moss. 2014. "Ethics, Education Policy and Research: the Phonics Question Reconsidered." *British Education Research Journal* 40 (2): 241–260. doi:10.1002/berj.3039.
Empson, W. 1930. *Seven Types of Ambiguity*. London: Chatto and Windus.
Flood, A. 2019. 'Britain has Closed Almost 800 Libraries since 2010, Figures Show'. *The Guardian*. Accessed June 11 2020. December 6. https://www.theguardian.com/books/2019/dec/06/britain-has-closed-almost-800-libraries-since-2010-figures-show.
Fox, G., and B. Merrick. 1981. "Thirty-six Things to do with a Poem." *Children's Literature in Education* 12: 50–55.
Galton, M. 2007. "New Labour and Education: An Evidence-Based Analysis." *Forum (chicago, Ill)* 49 (1 & 2): 157–177.
Goldberg, N. 1986. *Writing Down the Bones: Freeing the Writer Within*. Boston, MA: Shambhala Publications Inc.
Goldberg, N. 1991. *Wild Mind: Living the Writer's Life*. London: Rider.
Goodfellow, M. 2019. 'Put our Colonial History on the Curriculum – then we'll Understand who we Really are'. *The Guardian*. Accessed July 21 2020. December 5. https://www.theguardian.com/commentisfree/2019/dec/05/britain-colonial-history-curriculum-racism-migration?fbclid=IwAR23evKFJUDc1m6k588KRP5F8Er-6Gy2D_A2AFA0AFGndUTmUWcVggjr_bc.
Graves, D. H. 1983. *Writing: Teachers and Children at Work*. Portsmouth, NH: Heinemann.
Harris, J. 2017. 'The Tories are Savaging Libraries – and Closing the Book on Social Mobility'. *The Guardian*. December 15. Accessed June 11 2020. https://www.theguardian.com/commentisfree/2017/dec/15/tories-libraries-social-mobility-conservative.
Hartley, D. 2006. "Excellence and Enjoyment: the Logic of a "Contradiction"." *British Journal of Educational Studies* 54 (1): 3–14. doi:10.1111/j.1467-8527.2005.00331.x.
Heaney, S. 1975. *North*. London: Faber and Faber Ltd.
Heaney, S. 1988. *The Government of the Tongue: The 1986T.S. Eliot Memorial Lectures and Other Critical Writings*. London: Faber and Faber.
Hughes, T. 1976. *Season Songs*. London: Faber and Faber Ltd.
Hughes, T. 2003. *Collected Poems*. London: Faber and Faber Ltd.
Hurst, K. 1988. "Group Discussions of Poetry." In *Young Readers Responding to Poems*, edited by M. Benton, J. Teasey, R. Bell, and K. Hurst, 157–201. London: Routledge.
Iser, W. 1978. *The act of Reading: A Theory of Aesthetic Response*. London: Routledge and Kegan Paul.
Kay, J. 1994. *Two's Company*. London: Puffin.
Kay, J. 1996. *Three has Gone*. London: Puffin.
Kay, J. 2007. *Red, Cherry Red*. London: Bloomsbury.
Keddie, A. 2016. "Children of the Market: Performativity, Neoliberal Responsibilisation and the Construction of Student Identities." *Oxford Review of Education* 42 (1): 108–122. doi:10.1080/03054985.2016.1142865.
Lather, P. 2012. "The Ruins of Neo-Liberalism and the Construction of a new (Scientific) Subjectivity." *Cultural Studies of Science Education* 7: 1021–1025.
Leavis, F. R. 1932. *New Bearings in English Poetry: A Study of the Contemporary Situation*. London: Chatto and Windus.
Lipman, P. 2013. "Economic Crisis, Accountability, and the State's Coercive Assault on Public Education in the USA." *Journal of Education Policy* 28 (5): 557–573. doi:10.1080/02680939.2012.758816.
Little, S., and L. Chesworth. 2017. "Funds of Knowledge." Accessed June 9 2020. http://euliteracy.eu/wp-content/uploads/2017/07/Funds-of-Knowledge.pdf.
Mansell, W. 2012. "The New National Curriculum: Made to order?" *The Guardian*. November 12. Accessed May 11 2020. https://www.theguardian.com/education/2012/nov/12/primary-national-curriculum-review.
Martin, F. 2008. "Ethnogeography: Towards Liberatory Geography Education." *Children's Geographies* 6 (4): 437–450. doi:10.1080/14733280802338130.
Michaels, S., C. O'Connor, and L. B. Resnick. 2008. "Deliberative Discourse Idealized and Realized: Accountable Talk in the Classroom and Civic Life." *Studies in Philosophy and Education* 27: 283–297.
Moncrieffe, M., Y. Asare, R. Dunford, and H. Youssef. 2019. *Decolonising the Curriculum: Teaching and Learning About Race Equality 1*. Brighton: University of Brighton, Centre for Learning and Teaching. Accessed September 4 2019. https://cris.brighton.ac.uk/ws/portalfiles/portal/6443632/Decolonising_the_curriculum_MONCRIEFFE_32_pages_4th_July.pdf.
Munday, I. 2014. "Creativity: Performativity's Poison or its Antidote?" *Cambridge Journal of Education* 44 (3): 319–332. doi:10.1080/0305764X.2014.904274.

Myhill, D. 2009. "Becoming a Designer: Trajectories of Linguistic Development." In *The Sage Handbook of Writing Development*, edited by R. Beard, D. Myhill, J. Riley, and M. Nystrand, 402–414. London: Sage.

Myhill, D., and A. Wilson. 2013. "Playing it Safe: Teachers' Views of Creativity in Poetry Writing." *Thinking Skills and Creativity* 10: 101–111. doi:10.1016/j.tsc.2013.07.002.

Nichols, G. 1990. *Poetry Jump-up: An Anthology of Black Poetry*. London: Puffin.

Nichols, G. 2006. *Everybody got a Gift*. London: A. and C. Black Publishers Ltd.

Office for Standards in Education. 2007. *Poetry in Schools A Survey of Practice, 2006/07*. London: Ofsted.

Pike, M. A. 2003. "From Personal to Social Transaction: A Model of Aesthetic Reading in the Classroom." *The Journal of Aesthetic Education* 37 (2): 61–72. doi:10.1353/jae.2003.0018.

Pinsky, R. 1988. *Poetry and the World*. Hopewell, NJ: The Ecco Press.

Pirbhai-Illich, F., D. Osberg, F. Martin, S. Chave, M. Sabbah, and H. Griffiths. 2017. *Re-thinking the Educational Relationship: Research Report*.

Richards, I. A. 1929. *Practical Criticism: A Study of Literary Judgment*. London: Kegan Paul, Trench, Trubner.

Rodriguez, V. 2012. "The Teaching Brain and the end of the Empty Vessel." *Mind, Brain, and Education* 6 (4): 177–185.

Rosen, M. 1997. "Making Poetry Matter." In *A Year with Poetry: Teachers Write About Teaching Poetry*, edited by M. Barrs and M. Rosen. London: Centre for Language in Primary Education.

Rosen, M. 1998. *Did I Hear you Write?* Nottingham: Five Leaves Publications.

Rosen, M. 2015. 'Dear Ms Morgan: Your Guidance is a Mini-Syllabus on How to Wreck Poetry'. *The Guardian*. April 7. Accessed June 11 2020. https://www.theguardian.com/education/2015/apr/07/key-stage-1-poetry-assessment-wrecks-poems-for-children.

Rosen, M. 2018a. 'Dear Damian Hinds, What's so Difficult About Giving Every Child a Library Ticket?' *The Guardian*. October 23. Accessed June 11 2020. https://www.theguardian.com/education/2018/oct/23/what-difficult-giving-every-child-library-ticket-michael-rosen.

Rosen, M. 2018b. 'Dear Damian Hinds, please stop wrecking poetry for children'. *The Guardian*. November 27. Accessed June 11 2020. https://www.theguardian.com/education/2018/nov/27/damian-hinds-stop-wrecking-poetry-children-michael-rosen.

Rosenblatt, L. ([1978] 1994). *The Reader, the Text, the Poem: The Transactional Theory of the Literary Work*. Edwardsville, MI: Southern Illinois University Press.

Sainsbury, M. 2009. "Developing Writing in a High-Stakes Environment." In *The Sage Handbook of Writing Development*, edited by R. Beard, D. Myhill, J. Riley, and M. Nystrand, 545–560. London: Sage.

Sansom, P. 1994. *Writing Poems*. Newcastle upon Tyne: Bloodaxe Books.

Slater, G. B. 2015. "Education as Recovery: Neoliberalism, School Reform, and the Politics of Crisis." *Journal of Education Policy* 30 (1): 1–20. doi:10.1080/02680939.2014.904930.

Soler, J. 2016. "The Politics of the Teaching of Reading." *Prospects* 46: 423–433.

Stevens, W. ([1954] 2006). *Collected Poems*. London: Faber and Faber Ltd.

Strong, L. A. G. 1946. "Poetry in the School." In *The Teaching of English in Schools*, edited by V. de Sola Pinto. London: Macmillan.

Troman, G. 2008. "Primary Teacher Identity, Commitment and Career in Performative School Cultures." *British Educational Research Journal* 34 (5): 619–633. doi:10.1080/01411920802223925.

UNISON. 2019. *Shocking Picture of Austerity Cuts to Local Services is Revealed by UNISON*. December 6. Accessed June 11 2020. https://www.unison.org.uk/news/article/2019/12/shocking-picture-austerity-cuts-local-services-revealed-unison/.

Vygotsky, L. S. 1978. *Mind in Society: The Development of Higher Mental Processes*. Cambridge, MA: Harvard University Press.

Wade, B. 1981. "Assessing Pupils' Contributions in Appreciating a Poem." *British Journal of Teacher Education* 7 (1): 40–49. doi:10.1080/0260747810070105.

Wade, B., and S. Sidaway. 1990. "Poetry in the Curriculum: A Crisis of Confidence." *Educational Studies* 16 (1): 75–83.

Wilson, A. 1996. *How Far From Here is Home?* Exeter: Stride Publications.

Wilson, A. 2002. *Nowhere Better Than This*. Tonbridge: Worple Press.

Wilson, A. C. 2004. "A Study of Teaching Poetry Writing at Key Stage Two." Unpublished PhD diss., University of Exeter, Exeter.

Wilson, A. 2006. *Full Stretch: Poems 1996-2006*. Tonbridge: Worple Press.

Wilson, A. C. 2008. "*'New Directions in Poetry Pedagogy: Practice and Paradigms'*." Poster presented at Graduate school of education research Conference, University of Exeter, May.

Wilson, A. C. 2009. "Creativity and Constraint: Developing as a Writer of Poetry." In *The Sage Handbook of Writing Development*, edited by R. Beard, D. Myhill, J. Riley, and M. Nystrand, 387–401. London: Sage.

Wilson, A. C. 2010. "Teachers' Conceptualisations of the Intuitive and the Intentional in Poetry Composition." *English Teaching: Practice and Critique* 9 (3): 53–74. https://files.eric.ed.gov/fulltext/EJ912623.pdf.

Wilson, A. 2012. *Riddance*. Tonbridge: Worple Press.

Wilson, A. 2013. "A Joyous Lifeline in a Target-Driven Job: Teachers' Metaphors of Teaching Poetry Writing." *Cambridge Journal of Education* 43 (1): 69–87. doi:10.1080/0305764X.2012.749217.

Wilson, A. C. 2014a. *"Poetry and Performance."* Paper presented at NATE primary Day Conference 2014: The English curriculum – challenge and change, Bristol, June.
Wilson, A. C. 2014b. "Practical Implications: A Pedagogy of Permission." In *Making Poetry Happen: Transforming the Poetry Classroom*, edited by S. Dymoke, M. Barrs, A. Lambirth, and A. Wilson, 201–208. London: Bloomsbury.
Wilson, A. 2015a. *Lifesaving Poems*. Hexham: Bloodaxe Books Ltd.
Wilson, A. C. 2015b. "The Power of Poetry." *Anglo Files: Journal of English Teaching (The Danish Association of Teachers of English)* #175: 57–67.
Wilson, A. 2019. *The Afterlife*. Tonbridge: Worple Press.
Wilson, A. C., and S. Dymoke. 2017. "Towards a Model of Poetry Writing as a Socially Contextualised Process." *Journal of Writing Research* 9 (2): 127–150. doi: 10.17239/jowr-2017.09.02.02.
Wilson, A., and S. Hughes. 1998. *The Poetry Book for Primary Schools*. London: The Poetry Society.
Wilson, A., and D. A. Myhill. 2012. "Ways With Words: Teachers' Personal Epistemologies of the Role of Metalanguage in the Teaching of Poetry Writing." *Language and Education* 26 (6): 553–568. doi:10.1080/09500782.2012.669768.
Wood, D., J. S. Bruner, and G. Ross. 1976. "The Role of Tutoring in Problem-Solving." *Journal of Child Psychology and Psychiatry* 17 (2): 89–100.
Wright, A. 2012. "Fantasies of Empowerment: Mapping Neoliberal Discourse in the Coalition Government's Schools Policy." *Journal of Education Policy* 27 (3): 279–294. doi:10.1080/02680939.2011.607516.
Wyse, D., and U. Goswami. 2008. "Synthetic Phonics and the Teaching of Reading." *British Educational Research Journal* 34: 691–710. doi:10.1080/01411920802268912.
Wyse, D., and D. Opfer. 2010. "Globalization and the International Context for Literacy Policy Reform in England." In *The Routledge International Handbook of English, Language and Literacy Teaching*, edited by D. Wyse, R. Andrews, and J. Hoffman, 438–447. Abingdon: Taylor & Francis.
Wyse, D., and M. Styles. 2007. "Synthetic Phonics and the Teaching of Reading: the Debate Surrounding England's "Rose Report"." *Literacy* 41 (1): 35–42. doi:10.1111/j.1467-9345.2007.00455.x.
Yarlott, G., and W. S. Harpin. 1970. "1000 Responses to English Literature (1)." *Educational Research* 13 (1): 3–11. doi:10.1080/0013188700130101.
Yarlott, G., and W. S. Harpin. 1971. "1000 Responses to English Literature (2)." *Educational Research* 13 (2): 87–97. doi:10.1080/0013188710130201.
Zephaniah, B. 1994. *Talking Turkeys*. London: Puffin.
Zephaniah, B. 1996. *Funky Chickens*. London: Puffin.

Appendix

The Warm and the Cold

Freezing dusk is closing
  Like a slow trap of steel
On trees and roads and hills and all
  That can no longer feel.
But the carp is in its depth
    Like a planet in its heaven.
And the badger in its bedding
    Like a loaf in the oven.
And the butterfly in its mummy
    Like a viol in its case.
And the owl in its feathers
    Like a doll in its lace.

Freezing dusk has tightened
  Like a nut screwed tight
On the starry aeroplane
  Of the soaring night.
But the trout is in its hole
    Like a chuckle in a sleeper.
The hare strays down the highway
    Like a root going deeper.
The snail is dry in the outhouse
    Like a seed in a sunflower.
The owl is pale on the gatepost
    Like a clock on its tower.

Moonlight freezes the shaggy world
Like a mammoth of ice –
The past and the future
Are the jaws of a steel vice.
But the cod is in the tide-rip
Like a key in a purse.
The deer are on the bare-blown hill
Like smiles on a nurse.
The flies are behind the plaster
Like the lost score of a jig.
Sparrows are in the ivy-clump
Like money in a pig.

Such a frost
The flimsy moon
Has lost her wits.

A star falls.

The sweating farmers
Turn in their sleep
Like oxen on spits.

Ted Hughes, from *Season Songs* (Faber, 2003)

The Spider

I'm told that the spider
Has coiled up inside her
Enough silky material
To spin an aerial
One-way track
To the moon and back,
Whilst I
Cannot even catch a fly.

Frank Collymore, from *A Caribbean Dozen* (Walker Books, 1994)

The Tyger

Tyger Tyger, burning bright,
In the forests of the night;
What immortal hand or eye,
Could frame thy fearful symmetry?

In what distant deeps or skies.
Burnt the fire of thine eyes?
On what wings dare he aspire?
What the hand, dare seize the fire?

And what shoulder, & what art,
Could twist the sinews of thy heart?
And when thy heart began to beat,
What dread hand? & what dread feet?

What the hammer? what the chain,
In what furnace was thy brain?
What the anvil? what dread grasp,
Dare its deadly terrors clasp!

When the stars threw down their spears
And water'd heaven with their tears:
Did he smile his work to see?

Did he who made the Lamb make thee?

Tyger Tyger burning bright,
In the forests of the night:
What immortal hand or eye,
Dare frame thy fearful symmetry?

William Blake

Reading with technology: the new normal

Guy Merchant

ABSTRACT
Widespread changes in communication associated with new technologies have led to a growing interest in digital literacy. Although the concept of digital literacy suffers from a lack of agreed definition, this paper suggests that reading and writing with technology remains a key point of concern. The written word, a central feature of evolving patterns of communication, is now used in new ways and often in combination with different media as new devices and physical practices are recruited to the task of meaning making. The influence of different ways of thinking about these new communicative practices has led to the development of the diverse body of research outlined here. Tracing these strands in current research and writing about digital practice is used in order to identify how literacy has both expanded and diversified. Because it is now a significant aspect of full participation in social and cultural life, reading with technology raises important questions for education. This paper suggests that in England policy in this area is poorly articulated and argues that there is a pressing need for more focused classroom research to develop practices that support digital literacy.

Introduction

When the U.S. President, Donald Trump tweeted a message of support for the newly elected British Prime Minister, Boris Johnson, he had no need to wait for a TV broadcast or newspaper report, he knew that his words would be read by millions. They would be read on Twitter, on screens large and small, in all sorts of locations, in many parts of the world; they would be liked, re-tweeted, and commented on, and they would quickly travel across different media platforms. Aside from the political ramifications of all this, the tweet directly illustrates the power and ubiquity of digital literacy in our everyday lives, and how what it means to read and write has been modified and expanded by new technology. In what follows I explore the relationship between reading, writing and technology in the context of digital literacy, how it is understood and investigated in the literature, and the implications of this for research and practice. To provide some context to this I look at the changing appearance of the written word in the current milieu.

For many people today a large part of everyday experience is mediated by the written word. Urban environments in particular are densely lettered and notices, advertisements, directions, instructions, brand names, and graffiti appear at every turn. The level of saturation is such that it rapidly becomes normal, escaping from our conscious attention. In a similar way the communicative practices of new technology appearing on devices of various shapes and sizes are easily taken for granted. Screens, once associated with cinemas and small TV sets, are everywhere. They are a ubiquitous feature of the digital era playing a central role in everyday interpersonal communication. In fact over the last twenty years what is often referred to as digital literacy has become so fully installed in people's day to day lives that it has become the 'new normal', despite the fact that its distribution and take-up is not even or universal. It is nonetheless part of the hyper-literate textual environment of contemporary life.

In a society in which public services, commercial and financial transactions, business and entertainment are nearly all conducted online, the practices of digital communication have rapidly become a necessity for full participation. And although much has been said and written about the diversification of communication and the power of visual images in contemporary life (see Kress 2003, for example), written language continues to be of central importance in this changing environment (Merchant 2007; Burnett and Merchant 2020). Written words, whether produced by hand, by print or on screen are a dominant force in contemporary life. The study of reading, and also the study of writing, which in the end prove so difficult to disentangle, are key to our understanding of this context as they take on new forms and raise new issues for researchers and educators.

The changing nature of reading and writing practices can be looked at from a wide range of different perspectives and this is reflected in the literature. Unsurprisingly, the rapid advance of new communications technology and the millennial spread of the internet has led to an explosion of scholarly work on the topic; work that often generates more questions than answers, leading to surprisingly few conclusions that might inform literacy policy or practice (Burnett et al. 2014). Even the term digital literacy is contested. Originally coined by Gilster (1997, 1) to describe the ability 'to understand and use information in multiple formats from a wide range of sources when it is presented via computers', digital literacy has since been pressed into service to describe just about everything from keyboard skills to the restructuring and distribution of knowledge and information. In a useful conceptual piece Nichols and Stornaiuolo (2019) review the changing uses of the term, pointing out its inadequacies and ambiguities, and providing a refreshed model to account for contemporary concerns, such as those associated with surveillance, control, and profit. Important as these issues undoubtedly are – and certainly they should be included in any informed discussion of the topic – I want to avoid the temptation to define or fix digital literacy. Instead I approach digital literacy as a fuzzy concept, something that means different things to different people, an idea that is open and amenable to discussion – a weak description of the multiple ways in which a relatively new technology is entangled with a complex traffic of material, economic, social and political forces. But despite this fuzziness, if there is one thing that is at the heart of discussions about digital literacy it is the technology itself, and I use this as a stepping off point.

Reading and writing with technology

If written language is a central feature of our rapidly changing hyper-literate textual environment it is certainly worth reconsidering the fundamental and longstanding relationship between the written word and the ways in which it can be produced, distributed and read. From this perspective, it is important to recognise that technology and the written word are related in two distinct yet interdependent ways.

Firstly, writing is itself a technology. Writing is a technology in the sense that it is a human invention serving a range of practical purposes. In essence the written word enables meaning to enjoy a degree of independence from time and space. Writing is a way of recording, relaying and regulating communication, and it allows us to read in a particular time and place what has been written in another. As such written language has proved to be a particularly powerful technology and a means of enacting influence, control, and exclusion as well as emancipation, enrichment, and enjoyment (Snaza 2019). Even a cursory look at digital literacy bears this out – from targeted advertising on social media, based on algorithms that track what we read, to the organisation of mass protest through the use of mobile technology. The written word is a powerful technology now, as it has been through most of its history.

Secondly, technology is necessary for any kind of text production. Making something that can be read always involves some kind of technological apparatus. The long history of the written word is punctuated by innovations in technology and the creative adaptation of a wide range of materials and tools (Harris 2001). This includes the preparation of relatively smooth flat surfaces (clay, bark, vellum, papyrus) and a variety of tools and techniques for making marks on them (stylus impressions, brushes or pens loaded with ink, paint and so on). The geographical spread of these and other innovations in text production immediately dispels any conceit about the distinctiveness of Western civilisation. A full history of writing would need to include early markings on clay pots found in mainland China, Phoenician ledgers, birch-bark texts from Northern Pakistan, and the invention of moveable type in Korea. And, of course, such a history would extend from early experiments with computer-based communication to our current use of mobile technologies to exchange email, text messages and all the rest.

In short then, what we call digital literacy can be seen as an attempt to describe the latest phase in the evolution of literacy. The nature of the changes involved and their implications for research and practice in literacy education is a central concern of this paper. Whilst it is often suggested that we have experienced an epochal shift, entered into a new era, or lived through a digital revolution, it is also worth noting that those same old symbols, rendered here in Times New Roman, from Stanley Morrison's original 1932 typeface design, share much in common with much older versions of the alphabet – and that the decoding skills necessary to make sense of words, sentences and paragraphs as they appear on screen are still of fundamental importance, persisting in the face of many other changes. Despite all the ways in which communication is altering, and all the debates about what literacy now is, or indeed could be, there is something fundamental about this act of reading. Learning how to read, a core concern of education, is still of crucial importance even though students' everyday experiences of literacy, the texts they encounter, and their ways of accessing them may have changed quite fundamentally. It remains important even though the writing system itself is changing with an ever-expanding stock of words, common usages, abbreviations, emojis and gifs. It is worth keeping this in mind whilst also acknowledging that new technologies 'facilitate expanded communicative repertoires and multiple forms of participation, collaboration and civic engagement' (Mills and Stornaiuolo 2018, 1). This expansion and diversification of communication is a key characteristic of our current milieu, and it is one in which screens play a key role.

Thinking about the differences between page and screen has attracted a fair amount of attention from scholars working in the field. Initial work attempted to underline the overall significance of screen-based communication for educational practice (Snyder 1998 is an early example of this). More recent work has responded to a moral panic about the amount of time spent in front of screens (Squire and Steinkuehler 2017; Livingstone and Franklin 2018). Sitting alongside this is research that seeks to compare different kinds of reading. In this domain there have been a number of investigations of young children's experience of reading e-books and print texts (e.g. Moody, Justice, and Cabell 2010). Short of making recommendations to e-book and app designers these studies have generally found little difference in how children learn from reading a page as opposed to a screen (Reich, Yau, and Warschauer 2016). However, a systematic review of experimental research did find small benefits in paper reading when considering reading performance and metacognition (Clinton 2019). The specific uptake of portable devices, including iPads and other tablet computers has also attracted attention, and in the light of their popularity with educators, researchers have looked at how they can be used in reading and writing activity in the classroom (Burnett et al. 2017).

Seen together these studies suggest that although making meaning from written script is still a key skill in reading on screen, many related behaviours, such as those concerned with narration and navigation, the technical skills of working on screen and accessing apps involve distinct and sometimes device-specific knowledge. Drawing on the pioneering work of Clay (1975) who identified the concepts of print required for book reading, there is a strong case to be made for thinking about the equivalent 'concepts of screen' (Merchant 2005; Wohlwend 2015; Kervin and Mantei 2016), those fundamental understandings that are necessary in order to access and navigate onscreen texts.

Identifying these is not exactly a straightforward task. If we consider the relatively short history of computers, the user interfaces that proscribe the physical actions that we must take to make things happen on screen have themselves diversified, and continue to do so. Twenty years ago we might have been talking about clicking and scrolling with a mouse, and although these actions still apply, touchscreen technology has ushered in a whole gestural vocabulary that currently includes tapping, pinching and swiping – gestures that young children need to master in order to read a touchscreen tablet (Merchant 2015). Just as reading always requires some sort of technological apparatus so it also involves particular kinds of bodily engagement and enables or constrains certain kinds of physical movement.

Other developments in technology begin to gnaw away at some more fundamental assumptions about reading and writing. This is evident in the increased sophistication of voice recognition software, text-to-speech and speech-to-text applications which invite us to reconsider what it might mean to write and read. It is now perfectly feasible to claim that you have 'read' ('listened to?') a book without ever having laid eyes upon it or held it in your hands – and then, perhaps, to write a review of it without recourse to pen, paper or keyboard. Until relatively recently this would have been unthinkable. Of course listening to what is read aloud is very different from the visual experience of reading, and the same goes for dictating writing – but the point is that both practices are now easily available and regularly used. To this extent, at least, literacy has changed radically. Clearly for some, such as the visually impaired, this is a great gain, but more generally it raises significant questions in how we might think about and research digital literacy, what sort of literacies we value, and what reading we should promote in educational contexts. In what follows I address these questions, beginning first by overviewing some of the more influential ideas that have informed research and scholarship in this area.

Influential perspectives in the study of digital literacy

Although the term digital literacy has been widely used in a range of different contexts its specific application to the study of reading and writing has been dominated by research with a sociocultural emphasis. This could be because the rise of computer-mediated communication is so closely interwoven with widespread changes in society. A rather poetic commentary from Michel Serres captures the spirit of this:

> In brief, Western humanity abruptly moved, during the 1960s, from means and forces of production to communication networks: the beginning of our century made the victory of the global internet and mobile phones complete. Hermes, the god of intermediaries and translators, the Angels bearing messages and their incalculable number took the place of Prometheus, the old solitary hero of fire. (Serres 2019, 17)

Here, Serres is alluding to the shift from a form of social organisation and lifestyle firmly rooted in industrial production to the more fluid structures associated with a post-industrial economy. Taking a sociological point of view, Wellman has characterised this as a move from local or neighbourhood affiliations to what he calls 'networked individualism' in which social ties are simultaneously both distributed and technologically mediated (Rainie and Wellman 2012).

However important this may be, another reason for the dominance of sociocultural perspectives in the study of digital literacy relates less to this broad context and more to the local disciplinary influence of two significant bodies of scholarship. Firstly, social constructivism, associated with the work of Vygotsky (1980) and Bruner (1986), which places its emphasis on social context, and has had a marked impact on recent educational thought and secondly, sociolinguistics, which underscores the role of social and cultural forces on language use and has exerted a strong formative influence in the study of literacy (Heath 1983; Street 1984). Ways of thinking about digital literacy from a sociocultural perspective, informed by such thinking, have a number of different (and sometimes overlapping) concerns. Below I identify three influential strands in the field.

1. Literacy studies

Street's ideas (1984) were instrumental in defining a field of study, now generally referred to as literacy studies, which favoured situated descriptions of communicative practices and research with a distinctly anthropological orientation. In this developing tradition, the prime focus was on reading and writing as social action, and it centred on literacy events embedded in specific contexts, conceptualised as local instantiations of more generalised literacy practices (Barton and Hamilton 1998; Street 2003). In the study of digital literacy, examples of this sort of work include Barton and Lee's (2013) study of photo-sharing, Gillen's (2014) work on the virtual world at the hub of the Schome Park programme and my own focus on young children reading story apps (Merchant 2015). However, the influence of literacy studies has been far reaching and constitutes a large and diverse body of work that would be challenging to summarise in such a short article. Taken together though, studies in this strand have served to illuminate the breadth and diversity of digital literacy practices that span a wide range of age groups, populations and languages.

2. New literacies

The emergence of a distinct field of inquiry into 'new literacies' mostly attaches to the pioneering work of Lankshear and Knobel (2003). With a more explicit focus on the digital, Lankshear and Knobel launched an inquiry into new and emerging practices, and particularly those that involved the use of new technology – practices that often challenged traditional ways of thinking about literacy, and notably how it was defined within the context of compulsory schooling. Drawing on the work of internet scholars and digital activists the third edition of *New Literacies* (Lankshear and Knobel 2011) clarifies their interest in both the newness of post-typographic texts (which they refer to as the 'new *technical* stuff', p. 55) and the newness of a mindset that valorises interactivity, participation and collaboration (they call this the 'new *ethos* stuff', p. 55). New literacies has been important in charting the development of a whole range of digital literacies from virtual world play (Thomas 2001) and videogaming (Gee 2003), to blogging (Davies and Merchant 2009), fanfiction (Black 2008), memes (Knobel and Lankshear 2007), and machinima (Marsh 2015). In some ways this identification of new trends and practices has now been taken up by media scholars, and can be traced through the work of Jenkins (e.g. Jenkins, Ford, and Green 2018), Ito (e.g. Ito et al. 2009), and others.

3. Multimodality

Drawing inspiration from the pioneering work of Halliday (1978), a social semiotic approach has also proved fruitful as a way of understanding screen-based communication. Kress's thinking on multimodality is key to this. Not only does multimodality offer a different perspective on literacy, it also highlights how we might read text on screens (Kress 2003 Kress 2010). Furthermore, emphasising the role of the visual and auditory dimensions of communication has direct relevance to how we might read something like a WhatsApp post or a Facebook page in which the visual layout, the use of still and moving image, and sound are an integral part of the experience. Meaning is at least partly made by the way in which these different modes interact (Jewitt 2006). It is also useful to consider the significance of what have been called reading pathways – where attention rests, what is read and looked at, and in which order, and indeed what is ignored. Close observation combined with multimodal analysis has been helpful in this respect (Simpson, Walsh, and Rowsell 2013; Kervin and Mantei 2016). Although it would be a mistake to assume that print text is always read in a linear fashion there are certainly more degrees of freedom in screen-based digital texts, and this may allow for more variety in the reading pathways taken, leading to the idea that such texts are often read in a non-linear fashion (Walsh 2006). Multimodality has frequently been used to describe digital texts, but there is also interest in using its descriptive vocabulary to analyse the interactions that happen around texts. For instance, in an empirical study of young children's interactions with touchscreen tablets Daniels (2016) looked at their speech, gaze and movement as they read on screen using a form of multimodal coding. These findings speak to the increased mobility and interactivity associated with reading the digital.

To summarise then, *literacy studies* is driven by an interest in specific social practices and contexts; *new literacies* with the key changes precipitated by the spread of new technologies; and *multimodality* with the characteristics and defining features of texts and their interactional setting. Although it is helpful to separate out these three strands of socioculturally informed research and scholarship, in many empirical studies of digital literacy they are closely woven together. For example, a recent study of literacy in an early years science classroom uses a literacy studies perspective to investigate an instance of new literacies and uses a multimodal approach to analyse the data (Britsch 2019). The combination of these themes is a strength of the paper.

However generative of empirical investigation sociocultural perspectives may have been, they certainly do not hold a monopoly on knowledge and understanding. Recently, some scholars have argued that a sociocultural analysis offers an inadequate or limited description of reading in the digital age. They have drawn on and developed a range of alternative perspectives. As an example of this, the next section looks at the growing interest in materiality, before giving an overview of what has come to be referred to as the socio-material orientation in the study of digital literacy.

Departures – towards a sociomaterial orientation

In her important study of reading hypertext fiction, Mangen (2008) underlined the need for a more detailed examination of the relationship between embodiment and reading on screen. She highlighted the significance of manual dexterity and haptic perception in reading and the pressing need for an account of reading processes that were 'attentive to the affective affordances of different materialities and their relation to the physiology of bodily reception of meaning' (Mangen 2008, 405). This call for more attention to embodiment signalled a return to considering the materiality of reading technology. As we have seen, the recent surge of interest in mobile technologies has brought materiality as well as embodiment and movement to the fore once again.

At the same time though, literacy scholars have begun to test the limits of sociocultural perspectives (Kuby 2017). Drawing on ideas from new materialism (e.g. Fox and Aldred 2017), post-humanism (e.g. Braidotti 2013), and material semiotics (e.g. Law and Moll 2002) researchers have critiqued the anthropocentric and logocentric focus of sociocultural perspectives (Snaza 2019). They have raised the concern that by privileging human rationality and sociality, questions of affect, bodily experience, and its complex inter-relation with the material (more-than-human) world are neglected. We can find examples of this sort of emphasis in the literacy research of Leander and Boldt (2013), Theil (2015), and Hackett and Sommerville (2017). Not all of this has concerned itself with reading on screens but the connections are easy enough to make.

My own research with Cathy Burnett and others has worked with these ideas in a variety of contexts, all of which involve children using new technology in one way or another (Burnett and Merchant 2018a). A sociomaterial orientation to the topic of reading on screen proves to be useful in highlighting a number of relevant issues. A full treatment of these can be found elsewhere (Burnett and Merchant 2020). Here I give a sense of this work by highlighting three of the more important themes:

Material agency – sometimes referred to as 'thing-power' (Bennett 2010), material agency underlines the close connection between humans and non-humans by drawing attention to how materials act on us. This is particularly noticeable when we consider everyday artefacts or technologies. Sometimes this can be as simple as the way that the Peppa Pig theme tune invites a child to engage with a story app (Burnett, Merchant, and Neumann 2019a). Clearly, the technologies of literacy, in both the senses referred to above, act on us in ways that can be defined and observed. But new technologies, apart from simply interesting us (or not) are designed to attract our attention. Portable devices that vibrate, chime, or simply display alerts are an aspect of what is sometimes referred to as push technology. Content is pushed to the individual user. It is personalised, and in doing this it contributes to the variety of ways in which screens invite us to read them. At the same time, as we are increasingly aware, these screens 'read' us too, logging our activity, often with the aim of further personalising the content we subsequently receive. If noting this modifies how we might think about reading, the simple fact that machines regularly read each other spreads the activity of reading right across the human/non-human domain.

Textual instability – watching young children playing and working in a context in which tablet computers are freely available offers plenty of interesting insights (Burnett, Merchant, and Neumann 2019a; 2019b). For instance, we noted in this sort of setting that tablets were used for all sorts of purposes, to sit on, to skate on and to pile wooden bricks on. Often they were ignored, fading into the general background of bookcases, plastic trays, toy dinosaurs and all the rest. And then at other times they would be brought into play, as cameras for taking selfies, for the games they might display, or for the story apps we had loaded onto them. At these times they become a text, a text to read or flip through or, as sometimes happened, a text that only had a relatively brief appearance before a small finger pressed the home button, a battery died, or a child simply wandered off. In short, as multifunctional devices computers can become all sorts of things, but they only become texts when the appropriate sociomaterial arrangements line up.

Affective encounters – it has long been accepted that we can be inspired or angered, enchanted or intrigued by what we read. Whether it's Donald Trump's Twitter feed (as in the beginning of this paper), a Murakami novel, or an email from a friend, the reader's response nearly always has an affective dimension to it. But recent thinking on affect extends this idea beyond the realms of individual response and uses it to account for 'the ways in which people and things come together and generate, perhaps by chance, something that interrupts a situation, and by doing so brings something new into play' (Burnett and Merchant 2018b, 64). In our work on affective encounters, we use examples of reading digital media to illustrate how a particular mood may be unexpectedly and spontaneously generated through social material relations. Following work that has theorised and investigated 'affective atmosphere' (Anderson 2014; Ehret, Boegel, and Manuel-Nekouei 2018) we have shown how affect or mood emerges out of human/non-human encounters that include digital devices in different ways.

This brief exploration of the sociomaterial view of literacy helps to illustrate the diversity of approaches and responses that can inform the study of digital practice, and some of the newer directions of research in the field. However, it is interesting to note that in this line of inquiry specific technologies participate in events but never define them or become a focus. This is partly because such technologies are now more common place, and in this sense unremarkable, but also because researchers may wish to counter a monolithic discourse of 'the digital' – a discourse which often inflates its transformative potential at the expense of a more reflective and analytical look at what lies behind particular applications, in terms of their design, programming, algorithms and all the rest (see Burnett and Merchant 2020). Complementing this sort of analysis, is a growing sensitivity to the ways in which reading technologies are now big business and how corporate interest is entering children's literacy lives, at home, school and the spaces in between in new ways and on a much larger scale than ever before (Paakari, Rautio, and Valsmo 2019).

Digital reading and its implications for research and practice

Whilst it has not been possible in this relatively short piece to give a complete overview of all the relevant research on digital literacy, the sociocultural and sociomaterial approaches I have focused on generate powerful insights into the current state of literacy. But there is also a substantial amount of work in the cognitive sciences that could be brought to bear on the topic. Partly because of my own research interests, and a belief in the importance of looking at digital literacy in context, I have remained with the research I am familiar with, and that which seems to me to have the most relevance to educational contexts. In this final section, I turn to the implications of this work for research and practice in digital literacy, with an emphasis on the topic of reading.

Digital literacy has become a significant aspect of full participation in society. Reading from screens, is a dominant mode of communication here in the UK, and elsewhere too. Nonetheless, other ways of reading and writing have not been displaced. Many people still prefer the print form, enjoy reading and collecting books, and choose pen and paper instead of a keyboard. In fact there is little evidence to support the idea of a decline in the popularity of those well-established reading technologies that have enjoyed a long history. Nor is there evidence to suggest any decline in the use of literacy. In fact Brandt (2015) provides clear evidence that we write more than we have ever done before; and since there is no point in writing without readership, the clear implication is that we read more as well.

It would seem then that the key message is that reading and writing have expanded and diversified in the early years of the twenty-first century – a state of affairs that I have referred to here as hyper-literacy. People's reading practices and habits are changed as a result. For instance, it has been suggested that whilst we may read more, we may not read in such a sustained way as we once did (Liu 2005). However, such changes are almost impossible to quantify. A more pragmatic approach would recognise that digital literacy is now an integral part of contemporary life, a key component of becoming literate and that its accomplishment is largely, but not exclusively, dependent on reading the written word.

Research and scholarship, as traced through this paper, has a key role to play in shaping what we know about the changing reading environment, and about the specific experiences and practices that texture the lives of children and young people. Such work is increasingly concerned with digital text, whether, for example, the focus is on very young children, their digital play and early encounters with alphabet apps (Merchant 2014), or on older children's reading and writing in the service of other activity, such as in the development of film scripts (Parry, Taylor, and Haerizadeh-Yazdi 2017). Clearly research in the sociocultural tradition, as well as in emerging paradigms, has much to offer in this respect.

But new reading technologies also raise specific pedagogical questions. For example, as we have seen, beginning readers need a repertoire of 'concepts of screen' in the first instance, and educators need to know how these can be nurtured and developed. It is also important to know about different kinds of resources for reading. Work on the efficacy of particular story apps in supporting early literacy is useful because this impacts on both classroom activity and the advice that educators might offer to parents (Sari, Takacs, and Bus 2019). It is equally important to know more about reading comprehension in a digital environment, and how this may be supported in the classroom (see for example, Kiili et al. 2018).

On a broader front, educators need to ensure that children have equal access to technology and to know how to build their confidence in using it. This includes striking a balance between an authentic online experience and developing a sensitivity to risk. Although there is plenty of literature, practical guidance and critique on internet safety aimed at children and young people (Haddon and Livingstone 2017), recent trends suggest that this is becoming an ever more complex area. Measures to protect children from exposure to inappropriate material remain important, but there are other concerns too. Fake news, untrustworthy websites, and the circulation of extremist propaganda suggest the need for a new kind of critical reading (Luke et al. 2018). Furthermore, the increasing concern over surveillance and aggressive consumerism, signalled at several points in this paper, raise further issues for this sort of reading. At the time of writing this is terrain that has yet to be fully explored in classroom contexts.

The rise of digital reading and writing in hyper-literate contexts underscores the need for coherent curriculum provision in the school system. In Burnett et al. (2014), the authors looked at educational responses in a range of different jurisdictions, and there are some useful examples to draw on here. Currently, in the UK at least, the policy is poorly articulated and curriculum guidance on digital reading is hard to locate. Aspirational statements about how digital technology will transform society and help to grow the economy are abundant, but how parents and teachers might support the kinds of critical digital reading that are so necessary to participation remains an open question. If digital literacy is the new normal, then some broad agreement on the kinds of practices we value and wish to support in the classroom is well overdue.

Disclosure statement

No potential conflict of interest was reported by the author(s).

References

Anderson, B. 2014. *Encountering Affect: Capacities, Apparatuses, Conditions.* London: Routledge.

Barton, D., and M. Hamilton. 1998. *Local Literacies: Reading and Writing in One Community.* London: Routledge.

Barton, D., and C. Lee. 2013. *Language Online: Investigating Digital Texts and Practices.* London: Routledge.

Bennett, J. 2010. *Vibrant Matter: A Political Ecology of Things.* London: Duke University Press.

Black, R. 2008. *Adolescents and Online Fan Fiction.* New York: Peter Lang.

Braidotti, R. 2013. *The Posthuman.* Cambridge: Polity Press.

Brandt, D. 2015. *The Rise of Writing: Redefining Mass Literacy.* Cambridge: Cambridge University Press.

Britsch, S. 2019. "Exploring Science Visually: Science and Photography with Pre-Kindergarten Children." *Journal of Early Childhood Literacy* 19 (1): 55–81.

Bruner, J. 1986. *Actual Minds, Possible Worlds.* London: Harvard University Press.

Burnett, C., J. Davies, G. Merchant, and J. Rowsell. 2014. *New Literacies Around the Globe: Policy and Pedagogy.* London: Routledge.

Burnett, C., and G. Merchant. 2018a. *New Media in the Classroom: Rethinking Primary Literacy.* London: Sage.

Burnett, C., and G. Merchant. 2018b. "Affective Encounters: Enchantment and the Possibility of Reading for Pleasure." *Literacy* 52 (2): 62–69.

Burnett, C., and G. Merchant. 2020. *Undoing the Digital: Sociomaterialism and Literacy Education.* London: Routledge.

Burnett, C., G. Merchant, and M. Neumann. 2019a. "The Appearance of Literacy in New Communicative Practices: Interrogating the Politics of Noticing." *Cambridge Journal of Education* 50 (2): 67–183.

Burnett, C., G. Merchant, and M. M. Neumann. 2019b. "Closing the Gap? Overcoming Limitations in Sociomaterial Accounts of Early Literacy." *Journal of Early Childhood Literacy* 20 (1): 111–133.

Burnett, C., G. Merchant, A. Simpson, and M. Walsh. 2017. *The Case of the IPad: Mobile Literacies in Education.* Singapore: Springer.

Clay, M. 1975. *What Did I Write?* London: Heinemann Educational.

Clinton, V. 2019. "Reading from Paper Compared to Screens: A Systematic Review and Meta-Analysis." *Journal of Research in Reading* 42 (2): 288–325.

Daniels, K. 2016. "Young Children in an Education Context: Apps, Cultural Agency and Expanding Communicative Repertoires." In *Apps, Technology and Young Learners: International Evidence for Teaching*, edited by N. Kucirkova and G. Falloon, 280–292. London: Routledge.

Davies, J., and G. Merchant. 2009. *Web 2.0 for Schools: Learning and Social Participation.* New York: Peter Lang.

Ehret, C., J. Boegel, and R. Manuel-Nekouei. 2018. "The Role of Affect in Adolescents' Online Literacies: Participatory Pressures in BookTube Culture." *Journal of Adolescent and Adult Literacy* 62 (2): 151–161.

Fox, N., and P. Aldred. 2017. *Sociology and the New Materialism: Theory, Research, Action.* London: Sage.

Gee, J. 2003. *What Videogames Have to Teach Us about Learning and Literacy.* London: Palgrave Macmillan.

Gillen, J. 2014. *Digital Literacies.* London: Routledge.

Gilster, P. 1997. *Digital Literacy.* New York: Wiley.

Hackett, A., and M. Somerville. 2017. "Posthuman Literacies: Young Children Moving in Time, Place and More-Than-Human Worlds." *Journal of Early Childhood Literacy* 17 (3): 374–391.

Haddon, L., and S. Livingstone. 2017. "Risks, Opportunities, and Risky Opportunities: How Children Make Sense of the Online Environment." In *Cognitive Development in Digital Contexts*, edited by F. Blumberg and P. Brooks, 275–302. London: Academic Press.

Halliday, M. 1978. *Language as Social Semiotic: The Social Interpretation of Language and Meaning.* London: Edward Arnold.

Harris, R. 2001. *Rethinking Writing.* London: Continuum.

Heath, S. 1983. *Ways with Words: Language, Life and Work in Communities and Classrooms.* Cambridge: Cambridge University Press.

Ito, M., S. Baumer, M. Bittanti, D. Boyd, R. Cody, B. Herr-Stephenson, and H. Horst. 2009. *Hanging Out, Messing Around, and Geeking Out: Kids Living and Learning with New Media.* Cambridge: MIT Press.

Jenkins, H., S. Ford, and J. Green. 2018. *Spreadable Media: Creating Value and Meaning in a Networked Culture*. New York: New York University Press.
Jewitt, C. 2006. *Technology, Literacy, Learning: A Multimodal Approach*. London: Routledge.
Kervin, L., and J. Mantei. 2016. "Assessing Emergent Readers' Knowledge about Online Reading." *The Reading Teacher* 69 (6): 647–651.
Kiili, C., D. Leu, J. Utriainen, J. Coiro, L. Kanniainen, A. Tolvanen, K. Lohvansuu, and P. H. Leppänen. 2018. "Reading to Learn from Online Information: Modeling the Factor Structure." *Journal of Literacy Research* 50 (3): 304–334.
Knobel, M., and C. Lankshear. 2007. "Online Memes, Affinities, and Cultural Production." In *A New Literacies Sampler*, edited by M. Knobel and C. Lankshear, 199–227. New York: Peter Lang.
Kress, G. 2003. *Literacy in the New Media Age*. London: Routledge.
Kress, G. 2010. *Multimodality: A Social Semiotic Approach to Contemporary Communication*. London: Routledge.
Kuby, C. R. 2017. "Why a Paradigm Shift of 'More Than Human Ontologies' is Needed: Putting to Work Poststructural and Posthuman Theories in Writers' Studio." *International Journal of Qualitative Studies in Education* 30 (9): 877–896.
Lankshear, C., and M. Knobel. 2003. *New Literacies: Changing Knowledge and Classroom Learning*. Buckingham: Open University Press.
Lankshear, C., and M. Knobel. 2011. *New Literacies: Everyday Practices and Social Learning*. Maidenhead: Open University Press.
Law, J., and A. Moll. 2002. *Complexities: Social Studies of Knowledge Practices*. London: Dule University Press.
Leander, K., and G. Boldt. 2013. "Rereading 'a Pedagogy of Multiliteracies' Bodies, Texts, and Emergence." *Journal of Literacy Research* 45 (1): 22–46.
Liu, Z. 2005. "Reading Behavior in the Digital Environment." *Journal of Documentation* 61 (6): 700–712.
Livingstone, S., and K. Franklin. 2018. "Families with Young Children and 'Screen Time'." *Journal of Health Visiting* 6 (9): 434–439.
Luke, A., J. Sefton-Green, P. Graham, D. Kellner, and J. Ladwig. 2018. "Digital Ethics, Political Economy and the Curriculum: This Changes Everything." In *Handbook of Writing, Literacies and Education in Digital Cultures*, edited by K. Mills, A. Stornaiuolo, A. Smith, and J. Pandya, 251–262. London: Routledge.
Mangen, A. 2008. "Hypertext Fiction Reading: Haptics and Immersion." *Journal of Research in Reading* 31 (4): 404–419.
Marsh, J. 2015. "Discourses of Celebrity in the Fanvid of Machinima of Club Penguin." In *Discourse and Digital Practices: Doing Discourse Analysis in the Digital Age*, edited by R. Jones, A. Chik, and C. Hafner, 193–208. London: Routledge.
Merchant, G. 2005. "Barbie Meets Bob the Builder at the Workstation: Learning to Write on Screen." In *Popular Culture, New Media and Digital Literacy in Early Childhood*, edited by J. Marsh, 183–200. London: Routledge.
Merchant, G. 2007. "Writing the Future in the Digital Age." *Literacy* 41 (3): 118–128.
Merchant, G. 2014. "Moving with the Times: How Mobile Digital Literacies are Changing Childhood." In *Landscapes of Specific Literacies in Contemporary Society*, edited by V. Duckworth and G. Ade-Ojo, 117–130. London: Routledge.
Merchant, G. 2015. "Keep Taking the Tablets: IPads, Story Apps and Early Literacy." *Australian Journal of Language and Literacy* 38 (1): 3–11.
Mills, K., and A. Stornaiuolo. 2018. "Digital Diversity, Ideology, and the Politics of a Writing Revolution." In *Handbook of Writing, Literacies and Education in Digital Cultures*, edited by K. Mills, A. Stornaiuolo, A. Smith, and J. Pandya, 1–9. London: Routledge.
Moody, A. K., L. M. Justice, and S. Q. Cabell. 2010. "Electronic Versus Traditional Storybooks: Relative Influence on Preschool Children's Engagement and Communication." *Journal of Early Childhood Literacy* 10 (3): 294–313.
Nichols, T. P., and A. Stornaiuolo. 2019. "Assembling 'Digital Literacies': Contingent Pasts, Possible Futures." *Media and Communication* 7 (2): 14–24.
Paakari, A., P. Rautio, and V. Valsmo. 2019. "Digital Labour in School: Smartphones and Their Consequences in the Classroom." *Learning, Culture and Social Interaction* 21: 161–169.
Parry, B., L. Taylor, and N. Haerizadeh-Yazdi. 2017. "Time Travels in Literacy and Pedagogy: From Script to Screen." In *Literacy, Media, Technology: Past, Present, Future*, edited by B. Parry, C. Burnett, and G. Merchant, 147–162. London: Bloomsbury.
Rainie, L. and B. Wellman. 2012. *Networked: The New Social Operating System*. Cambridge, MA: Massachusetts Institute of Technology.
Reich, S. M., J. C. Yau, and M. Warschauer. 2016. "Tablet-Based eBooks for Young Children: What Does the Research Say?" *Journal of Developmental and Behavioral Pediatrics* 37 (7): 585–591.
Sari, B., Z. K. Takacs, and A. G. Bus. 2019. "What Are We Downloading for Our Children? Best-Selling Children's Apps in Four European Countries." *Journal of Early Childhood Literacy* 19 (4): 515–532.
Serres, M. 2019. *Hominessence*. Translated by R. Burks. London: Bloomsbury.
Simpson, A., M. Walsh, and J. Rowsell. 2013. "The Digital Reading Path: Researching Modes and Multidirectionality with IPads." *Literacy* 47 (3): 123–130.
Snaza, N. 2019. *Animated Literacies: Literature, Affect and the Politics of Humanism*. Durham: Duke University Press.
Snyder, I. 1998. "Page to Screen." In *Page to Screen: Taking Literacy into the Electronic era*, edited by I. Snyder, xx–xxxvi. London: Routledge.
Squire, K., and C. Steinkuehler. 2017. "The Problem with Screen Time." *Teachers College Record* 119 (12): 1–24.

Street, B. 1984. *Literacy in Theory and Practice*. Cambridge: Cambridge University Press.

Street, B. 2003. "What's 'New' in New Literacy Studies? Critical Approaches to Literacy in Theory and Practice." *Current Issues in Comparative Education* 5 (2): 77–91.

Theil, J. J. 2015. "Vibrant Matter: The Intra-Active Role of Objects in the Construction of Young Children's Literacies." *Literacy Research: Theory, Method and Practice* 64: 112–131.

Thomas, A. 2001. "Cyber Children: Discursive and Subjective Practices in the Palace." *disClosure: A Journal of Social Theory* 10 (13): 143–175.

Vygotsky, L. 1980. *Mind in Society: The Development of Higher Psychological Processes*. London: Harvard University Press.

Walsh, M. 2006. "The 'Textual Shift': Examining the Reading Process with Print, Visual and Multimodal Texts." *Australian Journal of Language and Literacy* 29 (1): 24.

Wohlwend, K. E. 2015. "One Screen, Many Fingers: Young Children's Collaborative Literacy Play with Digital Puppetry Apps and Touchscreen Technologies." *Theory into Practice* 54 (2): 154–162.

Exploring reading in social semiotics: theory and methods

Jeff Bezemer and Kate Cowan

ABSTRACT
The aim of this paper is to critically review how social semiotics has contributed to the study of reading and to develop an agenda for further research. We consider the theoretical and methodological resources that social semiotics has developed to account for multimodal text in the contemporary semiotic landscape, and explore how they can be used to teach critical reading skills to young people to support their participation in different social domains. We reflect on the possibilities and limitations of different analytical frameworks, highlighting barriers and possibilities for advancing social semiotic scholarship on reading and beyond. We end with a sketch of a new research agenda for social semiotics, in the light of technological change and its implications for reading.

Introduction

Social semiotics explores the systems, principles, and resources that people develop to make meaning of, in and with the world around them. It examines the mechanisms through which material formations are made to mean, that is, how people conjoin forms and formations with meanings. It recognises that material (stone, light, ink, air, muscles, etc.) can be manipulated and explored in distinctly different ways, offering distinct possibilities and limitations for meaning-making; *and* that it is possible to describe, at a more abstract level, common principles for making meaning, considering, for example, the commonalities and differences between writing on paper, drawing on an iPad, communicating on a video conferencing platform, and building with Lego blocks.

That is a big ambition. Scholars often work separately on specific types of semiotic formations, such as talking, writing, drawing, painting, photography, film, installation, performance arts, and so on. There are good reasons for scholars to divide the world up along such lines, even if these lines often reflect old notions of meaning-making and institutionalised professional boundaries. After all, it is not feasible for any single semiotician to grasp the specialist workings of all these different types of formations. Each one is embedded in a set of social semiotic practices, reflecting and constituting the social worlds of specific communities of practice and the affordances of the material resources in use. Yet increasingly expressions in the contemporary digital world defy old disciplinary boundaries, thus forcing those who aim to understand their practices – to inform teaching, for example – to radically rethink existing theoretical and methodological frameworks.

In this paper, we will be considering examples of semiotic formations that are (a) shared with, and usually made (scripted/orchestrated) for an audience; and (b) appear on a two-dimensional surface, such as books, tablets, banners, canvasses. This leads us to attend to different types of graphics – writing, image, moving image – and sounds played concomitantly, whether as speech, music, sound effects or otherwise; and the ways in which they are combined to form *multimodal text*. In so doing we significantly expand the traditional notion of text, which was focused almost entirely on writing. From a social semiotic perspective, all texts that children encounter or make themselves are worthy of detailed attention, providing a unique window onto their social worlds.

We recognise that our perspective is at odds with many school curricula, in which not all types of texts, or all aspects of text, are valued equally. In part, this is related to a view of 'reading' associated mainly with written text. For instance, in England's National Curriculum for children ages 5-11, reading is defined in terms of two 'dimensions': word reading (where phonic decoding is emphasised) and comprehension (stressing the importance of vocabulary and grammar). It states:

> The overarching aim for English in the national curriculum is to promote high standards of language and literacy by equipping pupils with a strong command of the *spoken and written word*, and to develop their love of literature through widespread reading for enjoyment. (Department for Education 2013, 3. Emphasis added)

Teachers are therefore expected to select some texts and background others, draw attention to selected features of texts, and introduce students to selected languages for explicating 'how text works'. Often these texts privilege and prioritise writing and do not reflect the diverse multimodal texts children routinely encounter and create themselves beyond the classroom.

We propose an alternative perspective, drawing on arguments for multimodal literacies which recognise and support children's capacities (Kress 1997; Cope and Kalantzis 2000; Kress 2003; Jewitt and Kress 2003). This perspective has informed policymaking in some countries. For example in Singapore, there have been concerted efforts in teacher training to support students' critical reading and design of their own multimodal texts (Lim and Tan 2018). Similarly, in Australia a broad definition of 'text' and 'reading' has been adopted, contrasting the narrow English curriculum noted above:

> Literacy involves students listening to, reading, viewing, speaking, writing and creating oral, print, visual and digital texts, and using and modifying language for different purposes in a range of contexts ... [Texts] can be written, spoken, visual, multimodal, and in print or digital/online forms. Multimodal texts combine language with other means of communication such as visual images, soundtrack or spoken words, as in film or computer presentation media. (Australian Curriculum, Assessment and Reporting Authority 2020)

However, there is still a way to go in challenging and changing established curricula and educational practice across the globe. Social semiotics can help by making explicit the principles underpinning multimodal text of all kinds, across the contemporary semiotic landscape. In so doing it offers an entirely different starting point for ongoing discussions about children's reading today, giving, for example, due recognition to the multimodality of children's books, magazines, learning materials, television, film, games and social media content produced by children themselves. It also supports the development of 'critical readers' by developing means to describe and reflect on multimodal text, which in turn supports creative and critical production of such texts. This paper reviews what those means currently look like and are capable of, and how they might be developed further.

Sign making

Our theory of reading, and of meaning-making more generally, is grounded in the notion of the sign. The sign is the basic unit of meaning-making. Eco (1976), following Peirce, defines it as 'everything that, on the grounds of a previously established social convention, can be taken as something standing for something else' (16). The model of the sign we adopt in this paper originates from Saussure (1916), and has been adapted by Kress (2010) to refer to conjunctions of meaning and a material form. *Social* semiotics is concerned with the ways in which people recognise (selections of) forms and invest them with meaning. Inscriptions, sounds, vibrations, shapes, shades and movements are all examples of forms ('signifiers') that can come to stand for something ('signifieds') to somebody. Meaning is always the product of human agency, of someone performing a semiotic act, of whatever kind.

Social semiotics draws on four basic premises about sign making. The first premise is that sign makers draw on *regularities* and *conventions* developed from social histories. Over time, some forms have come to be associated with particular meanings among a social or cultural group. The regularities are the result of social interactions. At the same time, they enable members of the group to communicate: they are generative, allowing people to guess, with some degree of plausibility, what others mean by the forms they produce. Social semiotics sets out to identify regularities that a given social network has developed over time in response to their social needs.

The second premise is that sign makers build and recognise *configurations* of and *relations* between different forms: they create semiotic formations. For example, readers of a textbook make connections between (selections of) graphic elements that are arranged on a spread: orthographic elements, diagrammatic elements, photographic elements, and so on; and their relation with e.g. someone's pointing gesture indexing one of these elements. Parties to face-to-face encounters also make connections between forms of various kinds: a co-occurring string of sounds and hand movement may be recognised as a speech-gesture-whole, carrying meaning that is greater than and different to the sum of its individual parts. Social semiotics aims to identify the principles underpinning these operations.

The third premise is that sign-making is always *particular* to a sign maker and a situation. That means that even if a social or cultural group can draw on a long history of social interaction and strongly developed shared understandings, their meaning-making is never entirely predictable. Shared understandings may have been made explicit in grammars, dictionaries, textbooks, and so on, yet these 'code books' do not account for the situated semiotic work of an individual sign maker. Sign makers use regularities in sign making as resources, rather than as prescriptions, in response to dynamic, unpredictable, emergent situations. The signs that people make, even when orienting to what appears to be the 'same' form, will vary depending on their prior professional/life experiences. Social semiotics sets out to identify how sign makers through each new semiotic act transform meaning potentials of forms, thus expanding possibilities for interpretation and expression (Kress 2010).

The fourth premise is that *semiotic effort* is gradual: the work that sign makers put into interpretation and expression varies. Their commitment is not evenly spread; some signifiers are given more attention than others. Engaging with Twitter, for example, 'reading' might mean anything from scrolling down five tweets per second to identifying tweets that might contain relevant information through a hashtag to skim-reading a text of 180 words and scrutinising a drawing. Equally, a teacher making a drawing on the interactive whiteboard will focus their efforts on those elements that they want to highlight and deem of particular relevance to the communication. Social semiotics aims to identify the principles of selection and distribution of effort. This includes a concern with the means that sign makers have at their disposal to shape the semiotic efforts of others.

Multimodal text

New technologies are having significant impact on text making and reading. Readers engage with text using different technologies (tablet, mobile phone, virtual reality headset) in different media (film, magazine, social media) and genres (short story, adventure game, instructional text) on different platforms (Instagram, YouTube, TikTok). These texts are differently configured (linear-non-linear, still-moving) and projected (two-dimensional, three-dimensional), using different 'modes' (writing, image, speech, music), thus facilitating different kinds of engagement/reading: instant and intense, intermittent and extensive, and so on.

To separate our approach to the traditional focus on decoding writing, we use the terms 'engagement', 'interpretation', 'signification' to refer to the ways in which audiences make meaning of a semiotic formation. We reserve the term 'reading' to refer to audiences making meaning of multimodal *text*. Thus, we differentiate between the general principles of engaging with semiotic formations, and that which is distinctly different about reading text, which we just defined as semiotic formations that are shared with, and usually made (scripted/orchestrated) for an audience, and that appear on a two-dimensional surface, such as books, tablets, banners, canvasses. We assume that engaging with text is different from engaging with, say, a teddy bear, or a gesture, given, for example, the different senses involved and the different possibilities for examination. These differences are only now beginning to be explored (see e.g. work on touch by Jewitt et al. 2020). In relation to this, we want to note that much of what we will say about reading in this paper applies only to readers with eyesight, which is testimony to one remarkable gap in social semiotic research.

In the past two decades or so, 'mode' has become a defining dimension of text, in social semiotics and beyond. Thus the text is now commonly broken down and described in terms of the different 'modes' in which the signs that make up the text are made. A number of definitions of mode have been proposed (Kress 2014; Bateman, Hiippala, and Wildfeuer 2017). Our working definition is that modes are conventionalised means of communicating meaning that are organised around a particular set of material resources and means of and tools for manipulating these resources. For example, writing is produced by manipulating materials (with pen and paper or keyboard and screen) to produce conventionalised marks on a surface. Marks are made to represent letters; they are arranged into formations – words – that can be arranged into bigger formations – sentences and paragraphs. In that way, signs are made through choices of, e.g. font, lexis, grammar. Each of these choices produces meaning.

The other commonly postulated mode is 'image'. While the constituent elements of drawings are unlike letters, images are also made through choices of various kinds that produce meaning. Social semiotics has produced schemes to begin to describe these choices, with Kress and van Leeuwen's 'Reading Images' (2006) being one of the most widely used. Analogous to Halliday's systemic functional analysis of language (1978), they describe some of the mechanisms that are used to shape representation ('ideational metafunction'), create author–reader relationships ('interpersonal metafunction'), and integrate signs in image ('textual metafunction'). This scheme has been applied widely to texts by and for children. For example, Mavers (2011) looked in detail at children's drawings, revealing the resourcefulness and purposiveness in texts which may usually pass unnoticed. Others have looked at picturebooks, ebooks, film and video games (see, for example, Serafini 2010; Bateman and Schmidt 2012; Burn 2013; Painter, Martin, and Unsworth 2013). Schemes have also been proposed to describe how writing and image are integrated, thus making a text that is more than the sum of its parts, with implications for the teaching of reading (see Bearne et al., 2007; Serafini 2014; O'Halloran, Tan, and Marissa 2017; Lim 2018).

Textual formations can be observed in the real world and subjected to close inspection. Claims made about text can be made plausible by sharing (scans, photographs, stills of) the text. Principles of production can be inferred from the text. For example, Gunther Kress, one of the founders of social semiotics, often presented the example of a drawing made by his then 3-year-old son (see, e.g. 2010). By offering (a scan of) the original drawing and a snippet of what the son said to the father as he presented his drawing ('this is a car') he evidenced his claim that the marks made by the boy represented circles, and that the child operated on the principle of analogy ('wheels are like circles'). Kress also shared some knowledge of the child's lifeworld; for example, what car he was used to being in (a Volkswagen Golf). Yet, on the whole, this semiotic account relies almost exclusively on the text itself; it does not detail how the drawing event unfolded through action and interaction.

To illustrate this text-analytical approach further, we present a multimodal analysis of a video posted on Tiktok, (https://www.tiktok.com/@ling.kt/video/6771839650446331142), a social media platform that is popular in China, the US and elsewhere, especially among young people. TikTok describe themselves as 'the leading destination for short-form mobile video', with a mission to 'inspire creativity and bring joy' (tiktok.com: 22 Feb 2020). The platform hosts content created by young people themselves, which, we assume, they learn to engage with through participation, without explicit teaching, as with e.g. canonical literary text of the school. At the time of this paper, the above video was watched 504,600 times, liked 112,600 times, and had received 143 comments. We draw on Burn's multimodal analytical scheme, which recognises that film is the product of a number of distinct domains of semiotic work, each involving a different set of modes, including 'embodied modes' ('dramatic action' and 'speech'), 'auditory modes' (music) and 'visual modes' (lighting and set design), as well as the modes of filming and editing. (see Figure 1).

The video is 12 seconds long and has 6 scenes of about 2 seconds each. Acoustic-style guitar music plays throughout. The video is accompanied by the description, 'Anyone can relate?', and several hashtags including '#girlfriendvsboyfriend'. We present video grabs of each scene in Figure 2. Each scene contains visual material and a short text. In the first scene, the camera moves from left to right, offering, first, a close-up of a girl, and then of a boy sitting next to her. The writing, 'This is my boyfriend', is projected onto the video from the beginning, in black font against a white backdrop. The camera work and writing positions the depicted girl as the narrator who introduces her boyfriend to the viewer. Both girl and boy being represented are interacting with the viewer: they look into the camera, and the boy tilts his head to get into the frame then raises his eyebrows. Their clothing and backdrop suggest a homely environment, their bodily expressions content and comfort.

In Scene Two the narrator takes the viewer to a different time and place by showing a photograph of the couple on a stage in a 'Hard Rock café', smiling, wearing performance outfits, holding an electric guitar, and posing for the camera. The writing reveals that 'We've been together for 7 years'. As the camera zooms in on the medium-shot photo, another text box appears, this time in white against a pink backdrop, saying, 'Throw back omg'. The writing thus frames the scene depicted in the photograph as a 'happy memory'. In Scene Three the narrator takes the viewer back to the present and homely environment by showing a close-up of a cat on its back, surrendering to padding under its chin by someone with long nails (the narrator?) and writing that 'We have a fur baby together' followed by an emoticon of a smiley face surrounded by hearts. Scene Four maintains this warm,

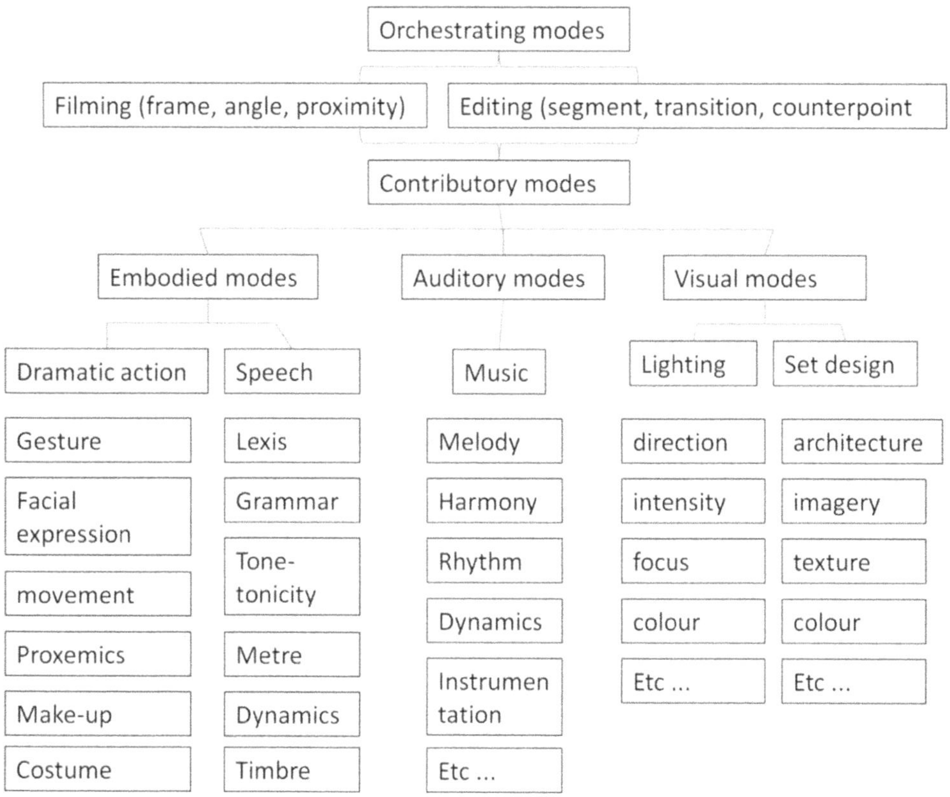

Figure 1. Burn's framework for analysing moving image (from Burn 2013).

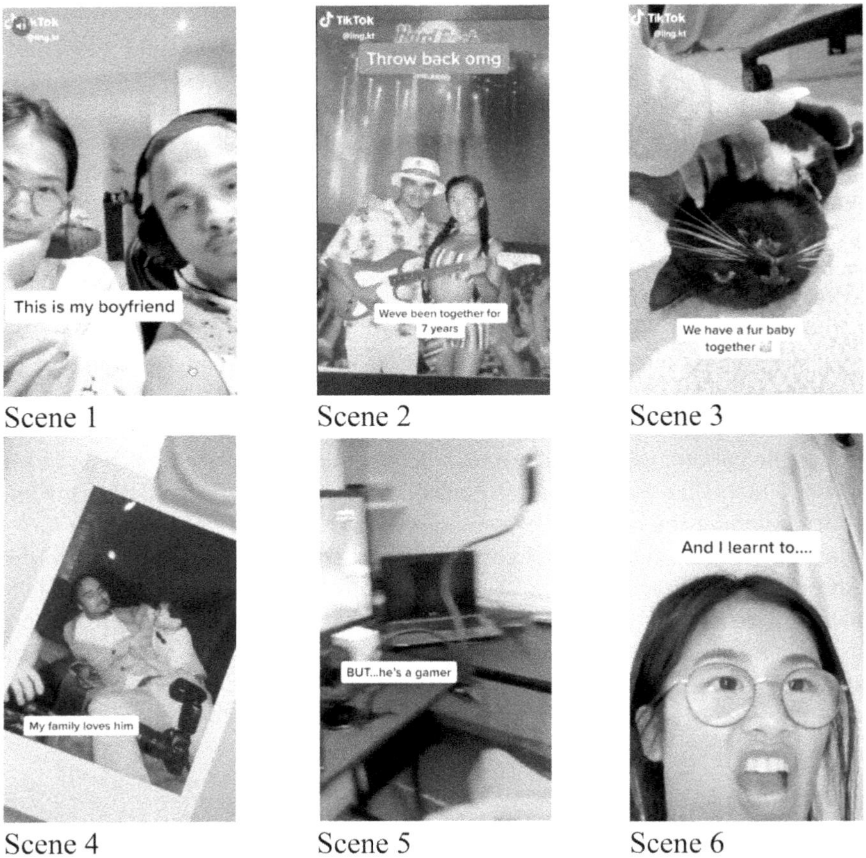

Figure 2. Screen grabs from a video posted on Tiktok.

homely atmosphere, showing a Polaroid photo of the boy lying on the floor while playing with a little boy (a nephew?), while writing that 'My family loves him'. The photo's tilt relative to the camera frame resembles a common layout of family photo albums.

Scene Five introduces a twist. The viewer is shown a room. As the camera moves from left to right, we see a clock and a computer camera, a big screen that displays animation graphics, and the arm of someone sitting in front of it (presumably the boyfriend). The writing frames this scene in contrast to the previous ones: 'BUT … he's a gamer'. Scene Six completes the story by presenting the narrator's resolution to the conundrum she has just sketched. The resolution is presented in two parts. The first part is in writing: 'And I learnt to … ' The second part appears in the music, which until then sounds an upbeat guitar accord, now plays a man singing 'shut the fuck up', in a light-hearted tone. The girl mouths along, with a strong dramatic facial expression.

Burn's scheme can serve as a checklist to consider how the video was built, i.e. how different sets of semiotic resources were used to construct a scene (the 'ideational metafunction'), establish a relationship with the audience (the 'interpersonal metafunction'), and develop a coherent narrative ('the textual metafunction'). In doing so we can give due recognition to meanings made, and to the semiotic work (skills!) that went into it. Burn's scheme helps us to draw out different domains of that work – in this case: dramatic embodied action, set design, filming, editing, music, writing – and the ways in which they interact. Looking across corpora of texts we could expand this account and look at conventionalisation, i.e. how certain forms come to be associated with meanings among particular groups of makers and readers: a recurring facial expression, phrase, dress feature, dance move, backdrop, beat, camera angle, and so on.

Our example illustrates how multimodal textual analysis draws attention to and names features of contemporary text making and reading. It makes explicit tacit semiotic knowledge that gives access to participation in communication and identity work within particular social networks. It also makes this knowledge available for learning and critical reflection, both by wannabe-participants and interested outsiders, including teachers who are looking to make connections with the canonical texts that are prescribed by the school curriculum.

Limitations of multimodal social semiotic analysis of text

While multimodality provides a useful overarching frame for theorising text making and reading, some pressing questions have yet to be settled. First, *modes* are often presumed, and ill-defined. Some signs are automatically classified as separate modes, while others are automatically clustered together. Is colour separable from image and orthography? What about graphics such as emoji's – are they 'image' or 'writing' – neither or both? Are drawing, photography and moving image all part of the mode of image, or do they constitute separate modes? Second, while multimodal analytical schemes draw attention to some resources, they also close down prematurely the process of *discovering and classifying signs* if they are simply imposed onto new text. We propose that definitions and lists of 'modes' are not taken for granted; that each time a text is considered, modes are defined anew. The aim should be to aptly categorise and name signs identified in a text, not to map all signs onto a limited list of pre-defined modes. Third, as demonstrated in our example above, in a textual analysis the question of *authorship* is hardly considered; in the above example, we simply assumed that the author of the video was the person who posted it and who was presented in it as the narrator. We did not ask, precisely what semiotic work was done by whom and how?

Nor did we ask, What was done by the presumed author, and what was done by algorithms, filters, and other digital tools (also called 'semiotic technologies' – see Djonov and Van Leeuwen 2018; Zhao, Djonov, and van Leeuwen 2014)? As possibilities for digital editing and distribution evolve, the question of semiotic agency becomes both more poignant and more difficult to address without ethnographic understanding of the process of production. There is also a risk that the more we try to tease out the semiotic work that went into the making and/or reading of a text, the less our categories resonate with actual experiences and practices of text makers and readers? What categories do the makers and readers of, say, memes, use to describe their own semiotic work? And do we get any closer to understanding and explicating their tacit knowledge by focusing on the social semiotic notion of 'mode'?

Ethnography takes the documentation of 'context' further. By observing and recording the *process and conditions of text production* and interviewing authors, claims about how text means can be substantiated. For instance, it is possible to use time-lapsed animations of a painter, or cartoonist at work, to explore how text makers organise their semiotic work. In some cases, text is made in a linear process, with different steps or stages, and different sets of choices made in each. This is shaped in part by platforms. For example, when an image is uploaded on Whatsapp, the sender is prompted to add a caption. In other cases, the process is non-linear. Often multiple 'makers' are involved, who divide up the semiotic work in certain ways. A group of young people making a meme for Tiktok might have a choreographer, a cameraperson, someone editing the video footage, choosing music, and so on. Similarly, in her ethnographic study of Filipino British youth in London, Domingo (2011) analysed hip hop music videos produced and edited by the young people in her study, closely attending to the layering of modes such as gestures, language, visual effects and sound effects, considering how these editorial decisions were used to assert social identities to their audience (see also Potter 2005, 2010).

While social semiotics has given much attention to texts and their production, it has somewhat neglected *reading*. According to Kress's theory of sign making, the principles of *authoring* and *reading* are the same: both authors and readers 'make' signs. Alluding to Barthes' seminal essay on 'the death of the author', he insists on the 'dominant role of the reader in communication', i.e. in processes of 'making and remaking meaning through the making of signs' (Kress 2010, 34). In this perspective, reading text is a process of *transformative* engagement: readers do not simply 'adopt' meanings made by the author, they transform them, appropriate them. In some cases, the 'reader' recognises conventional signs, attaching meaning to, say, a formation of lexical, graphic, or gestural forms relatively effortlessly. On other occasions, they encounter formations that prompt close examination through inspection, touch, and so on. Many factors shape the transformative engagement of the reader, not least the design of the text, the life experiences of the interpreter, the occasion for the interpretation, and the social actions of those around the interpreter.

One key question for social semiotics is how reading can be made evident. Claims about composition can be substantiated with evidence from the text, claims about reading cannot: reading leaves no traces in a text (though navigational choices of readers are tracked on digital devices). Thus in social semiotics we can develop hypotheses about, e.g. what was 'criterial' for a text *maker* about that which is signified (in Gunther Kress's example, the wheels of a car), but we face challenges developing hypotheses about what was criterial for a reader of that text. In what follows we discuss how these challenges can be addressed.

Multimodal textual sequence

One possibility is to explore texts that are produced in response to the read text, i.e. to look at a *sequence of texts*. For instance, in their study of children reading picture books, Arizpe and Styles (2016) analysed drawings children made in response to reading picture books, looking for insights into the children's reading experiences. Drawing was seen as a particularly apt method of response since the children were reading texts that were highly visual, and so offered insights not afforded by interviews. In her research into online texts, Adami studied video responses uploaded onto YouTube videos, analysing chains of semiosis in video-interaction (Adami 2009). Diamantopoulou, Insulander, and Lindstrand (2012) take this one step further by looking at more 'loosely' related texts: they looked at children's drawings to gauge their interpretations of the texts they encountered in a museum. Frederico (2018) combined observations with interviews. She observed families – preschoolers and their parents – in libraries who were given a picturebook app. She highlights the role of body in 'joint-reading events'.

We will illustrate the potential of this approach by revisiting the example from Tiktok. A selection of the 143 comments (Figure 3) shows the range of different, short, written responses that the narrator received. All reveal something about how the commentators read the text: As a 'funny' story, as a portrayal of a 'cute' couple, as a depiction an aspect of social life that the commentator identifies with ('well said', 'same with my boyfriend'), and as an invitation to give advice, e.g. about the girl's conundrum ('Play w him?') and the boy's games ('Tell him to try FIFA'), which some apparently recognised from the split second it is shown on the video.

Hahahahahaha so funny and so cute
Lol this made me laugh
Same with my Boyfriend 😟😂
I want a bf so I can play video games WITH him [rolling over the floor laughing]
He looks like Chris brown abit
I thought you was @sarahmagusara without makeup on
Play w him?
Well said
That cat ain't gonna last long
Tell him to try FIFA
Is that fortnite? Finish him if it is

Figure 3. Comments on the Tiktok video.

Multimodal performance

Another way of getting at reading through a semiotic approach is to look at how text is *read out*. An early example of this work is Woodward and Serebrin (1989); they observed how a three-year-old child and his father jointly read materials selected by the child. By video-recording these 'story reading conversations' they were able to work out how the child shapes the joint reading of the text by noticing and drawing attention to features that the parents had not attended to. While they recorded authentic reading sessions, Kachorsky et al. (2017) asked children directly about the meanings they made of the picture books given to them. Whether one observes children's responses to text that are spontaneous or solicited, the analyst must take the mediating effects of the means of communication used to give expression to interpretations into account. Attention should be given to all expressions, not just those in speech; and the limits of different means of communication should be considered. Considering children's gestures alongside their speech provides a better understanding of their reading than attending to speech alone.

Thus it is possible to explore reading by looking at larger semiotic formations that are jointly produced in response to a text. What we're considering here is how a text is acted out, performed, and embedded into a larger semiotic formation of signs in different modes. Now the process of jointly remaking text is in focus: how, for example, teacher and students negotiate what to attend to, through gaze, pointing, speech; how they attach meaning to the forms that they attend to; and how students respond to multimodal enactments of text. For example, Flewitt, Nind, and Payler (2009) draw on multimodal analysis of video recordings of read-aloud sessions facilitated by a teacher (Jackie) involving a four-year-old child (Mandy) in a school for children with special needs:

> Throughout this learning episode, all Mandy's communicative moves are interpreted by Jackie as intentional and meaningful. For example, when Jackie reads about the plans to make baby bear 'a birthday cake', Mandy stops sucking her thumb, leans towards the book to see the picture of the cake, begins to rock excitedly to and fro and vocalizes sounds as she does so. Quietly, before continuing to read, Jackie says to her 'you like that don't you?' and continues with the reading. Mandy's communicative 'turn' is cued by the story and Jackie's response validates her understanding, including it as a contribution to the group's enjoyment of the book reading. Jackie recognizes Mandy as a symbolic being, able to express precise meanings albeit in non-linguistic and non-conventional modes. (225–230)

The teacher takes the child's bodily conduct as responses to her reading, more specifically, as signs of the child's *reading* of the text.

Eye-tracking

Thirdly, semiotic analysis can be enhanced by *tracking readers' eye movements*, a technique that has been widely used in psychology, and psycholinguistics. Eye-tracking glasses record what people fixate on and how they shift fixations as they engage with a semiotic formation. The recordings show what features of the formation are noticed, for how long they are considered, and in what order. For instance, Holsanova, Rahm, and Holmqvist (2006) tracked the eye movements of people reading newspapers. Whilst such studies give insights into readers' visual attention, we note that this remains a partial trace of the reading experience. Much of the data generated from tracking technologies is measurement based (e.g. how often an element of the text is attended to, or how long for), but still does not tell us conclusively *why* such elements have been attended to; which is an area that social semiotics has proposed hypotheses about. For example, Holsanova, Rahm, and Holmqvist (2006) found that readers' engagement – as indicated by eye movements – often aligned with social semiotic accounts of the text maker's efforts to guide a reader's attention. However, their readers did not fixate on intense colours and font sizes in newspaper adverts; such items were largely ignored.

The patterns found in eye-tracking studies confirm that while there is significant variation in patterns and levels of engagement, there is always a degree of selection. Readers build an interpretation on the basis of partial engagement: they concentrate on specific areas to identify specific forms, which are taken to stand for something else (e.g. 'advert that can be ignored'). The more familiar we are with the type of text it is presumed to be an instance of, the more we rely on partial engagement. Thus we draw on (tacit) knowledge of the 'criterial' features that come to 'stand for' something else. In this way, eye tracking technologies might provide helpful supplementary data for social semiotic studies of reading.

One fundamental challenge that remains is that 'meanings expressed' may not represent 'meanings made'. Kress (2010), following Saussure, acknowledges this difference by making a distinction between 'inward' and 'outward' meaning-making. Regardless of whether we focus on text, or sequences of texts, or processes of text making and reading, the analyst, just like any other reader, always relies on observable expression. Expressions are shaped by the modes that are (made) available. In some joint reading in the early years, children may be encouraged to express their understandings of the text in bodily expressions or in drawings; in interviews, they might be encouraged to articulate their understandings in speech. Neither of these modes of expression might be felt to be apt to wholly express the reader's affective responses to text.

Resetting the research agenda for social semiotics

Social semiotics has made significant contributions to a multimodal understanding of reading. By combining close textual analysis with ethnographic and eye-tracking data it can render visible skills in text making and reading, and make explicit some of the principles of meaning-making across different domains and sites. It recognises the distinct possibilities for the expression of all means of representation and communication, and the ways signs are combined to make meaning. It has informed educational policy in a number of different countries, encouraging teachers and curriculum designers to recognise the role of image in the contemporary digital landscape and its potential for teaching and learning, although some curricula (such as England) stay more firmly wedded to 'traditional' notions of literacy and text.

We have considered visual materials produced by learners and teachers, such as drawings and social media texts. We have commented on the *rise of the visual*, in schools and beyond; and reflected on the curricular and pedagogic implications of this trend, which is likely to continue. In everyday digital communication, photographs and (live) videos are shared on a large scale through mobile technologies and social media platforms. In schools, workplaces and public spaces digital technologies will continue to replace pen and paper and create more opportunities for the digital production and dissemination of visual material. Photo- and video-editing have already become widespread, albeit often unrecognzied semiotic skills, without which participation in vast swathes of social activity is blocked. 'Infographics' and data-visualisation are pervading journalism and academia. Visual records have become a common means of documenting learning (Flewitt and Cowan 2019).

The visual is now taking another turn: it has gone *three-dimensional.* Augmented and virtual reality can now be used to add visual layers onto the real world and generate holograms. At the moment, AR glasses and VR headsets are still relatively expensive, and not yet widely used. But their potential for learning is already beginning to be noted, e.g. to support those learning to examine and manipulate complex physical objects – an engine, a human body – in vocational education, museums, and workplaces. Although specialist equipment is expensive, cameras on phones and tablets can be used to layer digital content. For example, the company Curiscope has produced a 'virtuali-tee' t-shirt printed with a QR code in the shape of a ribcage which, when scanned with a phone/tablet equipped with an accompanying app, displays digital animation showing the inner workings of the human body layered onto the t-shirt of the wearer (see https://www.curiscope.co.uk/products/virtuali-tee). Such technology opens up possibilities of visually experiencing previously unknown and inaccessible places in entirely new ways. Think, for example, how this representation differs from visual depictions in science textbooks, which already differ significantly from earlier textbooks in which image was less dominant (see Bezemer and Kress 2010). For social semiotics, these developments prompt a return to 'old' questions about the design of and engagement with multimodal learning environments. What are the affordances? What is gained and what is lost? What do the newly constituted texts draw attention to? How do they position the learner? (in the case of our example, a primary school student might find itself in a position that is closer to that of a medical professional).

Another trend is the rise in the automated *tracking* of (young) people's engagements with the world, and in the development of *algorithms* that can identify and visualise patterns in data thus collected. Multimodality has offered ample arguments against crude measurements of (reading) skills. Yet the new tracking possibilities can be used in different ways. Traditionally, a guide (a parent, say) might observe a learner, make a judgement, and articulate this judgement (in multimodal ensembles), thus providing feedback and instruction. Now, this guidance can be augmented with, or even replaced by, 'intelligent feedback systems', which measure and make explicit proxies of engagement and learning. As well as tracking what learners attend to on (touch)screens, *body motions* of all kinds (whole-body, eyes, hands, heart) can now be monitored, analysed, and translated into signs for learners.

Indeed, the capabilities of technologies for sensing, interpreting, communicating and learning are now such that they should be treated as *semiotic agents*. For social semioticians, and for everyone else interested in communication and learning, one task will be to account for and critically review the redistribution of 'semiotic work', and with it, of agency and power, among learner, teacher, technology designer, and technology. We need to explore what learning is made evident by what semiotic agent. What signs of learning can teachers and learners recognise in drawings and video recordings of embodied interaction, and how do they relate to the signs of learning that might be recognised by 'intelligent feedback systems'? And crucially, who dictates what signs ought to be recognised, and for what purposes? When does 'a culture of recognition' become 'surveillance capitalism' (Zuboff 2019)?

The question of shifts in the distribution of semiotic work reaches further still. In all domains of social life, technologies are emerging as semiotic agents that get involved in signification and communication where that was, until then, the exclusive domain of human sign makers. Technologies select and arrange the multimodal texts that children read on online media platforms. They interpret the body, outperforming the diagnostic capabilities of, e.g. the radiologist. At home, they listen and respond to our spoken questions about the world and our instructions for action. They warn drivers, and intervene, when they approach objects too fast. All of this has far reaching consequences for learning and communication, and for the education of today's children. It also has significant implications for the theory outlined in this contribution, which was focused on human agency, while ignoring contributions from, e.g. biosemiotics and post-humanist notions of communication. Reconsidering that focus in the light of ongoing technological and social change should be one, if not the, focus for future work in social semiotics.

Disclosure statement

No potential conflict of interest was reported by the author(s).

References

Adami, E. 2009. "'We/YouTube': Exploring Sign-Making in Video-Interaction." *Visual Communication* 8 (4): 379–399. doi:10.1177/1470357209343357.

Arizpe, E., and M. Styles. 2016. *Children Reading Picturebooks: Interpreting Visual Texts.* 2nd edn. London: Routledge.

Australian Curriculum, Assessment and Reporting Authority. 2020. *Australian Curriculum F-10: Literacy.* https://www.australiancurriculum.edu.au/f-10-curriculum/general-capabilities/literacy/.

Bateman, John, Tuomo Hiippala, and Janina Wildfeuer. 2017. *Multimodality: Foundations, Research and Analysis – A Problem-Oriented Introduction.* Berlin: De Gruyter Mouton.

Bateman, J. A., and K.-H. Schmidt. 2012. *Multimodal Film Analysis: How Films Mean.* London: Routledge.

Bearne, E, and United Kingdom Literacy Association, & Qualifications and Curriculum Authority. 2007. *Reading on Screen.* Leicester: United Kingdom Literacy Association.

Bezemer, J., and G. Kress. 2010. "Changing Text: A Social Semiotic Analysis of Textbooks." *Designs for Learning* 3 (1–2): 10–29. doi:10.16993/dfl.26.

Burn, A. 2013. "The Kineikonic Mode: Towards a Multimodal Approach To Moving Image Media". London: National Centre for Research Methods. *Working Paper Series*. http://eprints.ncrm.ac.uk/3085/1/KINEIKONIC_MODE.pdf.

Cope, B., M. Kalantzis, and the New London Group 2000. *Multiliteracies: Literacy Learning and the Design of Social Futures*. London: Routledge.

Department for Education. 2013. *English Programmes of Study: Key Stages 1 and 2*. London: DfE. https://assets.publishing.service.gov.uk/government/uploads/system/uploads/attachment_data/file/335186/PRIMARY_national_curriculum_-_English_220714.pdf.

Diamantopoulou, S., E. Insulander, and F. Lindstrand. 2012. "Making Meaning in Museum Exhibitions: Design, Agency and (Re-)representation." *Designs for Learning* 5 (1–2): 11–29. doi:10.2478/dfl-2014-0002.

Djonov, E., and T. Van Leeuwen. 2018. "Social Media as Semiotic Technology and Social Practice: The Case of ResearchGate's Design and its Potential to Transform Social Practice." *Social Semiotics* 28 (5): 641–664. doi:10.1080/10350330.2018.1504715.

Domingo, M. 2011. "Analyzing Layering in Textual Design: A Multimodal Approach for Examining Cultural, Linguistic, and Social Migrations in Digital Video." *International Journal of Social Research Methodology* 14 (3): 219–230. doi:10.1080/13645579.2011.563619.

Eco, U. 1976. *A Theory of Semiotics*. Bloomington: Indiana University Press.

Flewitt, R., and K. Cowan. 2019. *Valuing Young Children's Signs of Learning: Observation and Digital Documentation of Play in Early Years Classrooms*. London: The Froebel Trust.

Flewitt, R., M. Nind, and J. Payler. 2009. "If She's Left with Books She'll Just eat Them: Considering Inclusive Multimodal Literacy Practices." *Journal of Early Childhood Literacy* 9 (2): 211–233. doi:10.1177/1468798409105587.

Frederico, A. 2018. *Embodiment and Agency in Digital Reading: Preschoolers Making Meaning with Literary Apps*. Online. https://doi.org/10.17863/CAM.31007.

Halliday, M. A. K. 1978. *Language as Social Semiotic: The Social Interpretation of Language and Meaning (9th Impression)*. London: Edward Arnold.

Holsanova, J., H. Rahm, and K. Holmqvist. 2006. "Entry Points and Reading Paths on Newspaper Spreads: Comparing a Semiotic Analysis with Eye-Tracking Measurements." *Visual Communication* 5 (1), doi:10.1177/1470357206061005.

Jewitt, C., and G. Kress. 2003. *Multimodal Literacy*. New York: Peter Lang.

Jewitt, C., S. Price, K. Leder Mackley, N. Yiannoutsou, and D. Atkinson. 2020. *Interdisciplinary Insights for Digital Touch Communication*. Online. https://doi.org/10.1007/978-3-030-24564-1.

Kachorsky, D., L. Moses, F. Serafini, and M. Hoelting. 2017. "Meaning Making with Picturebooks: Young Children's Use of Semiotic Resources." *Literacy Research and Instruction* 56 (3): 231–249. doi:10.1080/19388071.2017.1304595.

Kress, G. 1997. *Before Writing: Rethinking the Paths to Literacy*. London: Routledge.

Kress, G. 2003. *Literacy in the New Media Age*. London: Routledge.

Kress, G. 2010. *Multimodality: A Social Semiotic Approach to Contemporary Communication*. London: Routledge.

Kress, G. 2014. "What is a Mode?" In *The Routledge Handbook of Multimodal Analysis*, edited by C. Jewit, 60–75. London: Routledge.

Kress, G., and T. Van Leeuwen. 2006. *Reading Images: The Grammar of Visual Design*. 2nd Ed. London: Routledge Falmer.

Lim, F. V. 2018. "Developing a Systemic Functional Approach to Teach Multimodal Literacy." *Functional Linguistics* 5 (13), doi:10.1186/s40554-018-0066-8.

Lim, F. V., and S. K. Y. Tan. 2018. "Developing Multimodal Literacy Through Teaching the Critical Viewing of Films in Singapore." *Journal of Adolescent & Adult Literacy* 62 (3): 291–300. doi:10.1002/jaal.882.

Mavers, D. 2011. *Children's Drawing and Writing: The Remarkable in the Unremarkable*. London: Routledge.

O'Halloran, K. L., S. Tan, and K. L. E. Marissa. 2017. "Multimodal Analysis for Critical Thinking." *Learning, Media and Technology* 42 (2): 147–170. doi:10.1080/17439884.2016.1101003.

Painter, C., J. R. Martin, and L. Unsworth. 2013. *Reading Visual Narratives: Image Analysis of Children's Picture Books*. Sheffield: Equinox Pub.

Potter, J. 2005. "'This Brings Back a Lot of Memories' – A Case Study in the Analysis of Digital Video Production by Young Learners." *Education, Communication & Information* 5 (1): 5–23. doi:10.1080/14636310500061052.

Potter, J. 2010. "Photoshopping/Photosharing: New Media, Digital Literacies and Curatorship." In *DIY Media: Creating, Sharing and Learning with New Technologies*, edited by M. Knobel and C. Lankshear, 103–133. New York: Peter Lang.

Saussure, F. de. 1916. *Cours de Linguistique Générale*. Paris: Payot.

Serafini, F. 2010. "Reading Multimodal Texts: Perceptual, Structural and Ideological Perspectives." *Children's Literature in Education* 41 (2): 85–104. doi:10.1007/s10583-010-9100-5.

Serafini, F. 2014. *Reading the Visual: An Introduction to Teaching Multimodal Literacy*. New York: Teachers College Press.

Woodward, Virginia A., and Wayne G Serebrin. 1989. "Reading Between the Signs: The Social Semiotics of Collaborative Story Reading." *Linguistics and Education* 1 (4): 393–414.

Zhao, S., E. Djonov, and T. van Leeuwen. 2014. "Semiotic Technology and Practice: A Multimodal Social Semiotic Approach to PowerPoint." *TextL & Talk* 34 (3): 349–375. doi:10.1515/text-2014-0005.

Zuboff, S. 2019. *The age of Surveillance Capitalism: The Fight for the Future at the new Frontier of Power*. London: Profile Books.

Index

For Product Safety Concerns and Information please contact our EU
representative GPSR@taylorandfrancis.com
Taylor & Francis Verlag GmbH, Kaufingerstraße 24, 80331 München, Germany

www.ingramcontent.com/pod-product-compliance
Ingram Content Group UK Ltd.
Pitfield, Milton Keynes, MK11 3LW, UK
UKHW052048230926
475702UK00025B/965
* 9 7 8 1 0 3 2 0 7 7 5 4 3 *